SAMS
Teach Yourself

iMovie™ and iDVD™

in 24 Hours

Todd Kelsey

SAMS 201 West 103rd St., Indianapolis, Indiana, 46290 USA

Sams Teach Yourself iMovie™ and iDVD™ in 24 Hours

Copyright © 2003 by Sams Publishing

International Standard Book Number: 0-672-32484-9

Library of Congress Catalog Card Number: 2002-115931

Printed in the United States of America

First Printing: June 2003

06 05 04 03   4 3 2 1

Trademarks

Warning and Disclaimer

Bulk Sales

Sams Publishing offers excellent discounts on this book when ordered in quantity for bulk purchases or special sales. For more information, please contact:

U.S. Corporate and Government Sales
1-800-382-3419
corpsales@pearsontechgroup.com

For sales outside of the U.S., please contact:

International Sales
+1-317-581-3793
international@pearsontechgroup.com

ACQUISITIONS EDITOR
Betsy Brown

DEVELOPMENT EDITOR
Jonathan Steever

MANAGING EDITOR
Charlotte Clapp

PROJECT EDITOR
George Nedeff

COPY EDITOR
Mike Henry

INDEXER
Heather McNeil

PROOFREADER
Jessica McCarty

TECHNICAL EDITORS
Kate Binder
Robyn Ness

TEAM COORDINATOR
Vanessa Evans

DESIGNER
Gary Adair

PRODUCTION
Kelly Maish

Contents at a Glance

Contents

About the Author

TODD KELSEY is a writer, musician and digital media professional living in the Chicago area. He is co-author of the *MacWorld DVD Studio Pro Bible*, *Flash MX Design for TV and Video*, *Make Your Own DVDs*, and an as yet unpublished novel based on the story of an American pilot who flew with the Royal Air Force during the summer of 1940 in the Battle of Britain. When he's not on the road, he teaches digital media at College of DuPage, a 30,000-student institution located in Glen Ellyn, Illinois.

As a musician, Todd has been involved in independent projects such as Neocelt (www.neocelt.net—an eclectic mix of poetry, industrial and folk music, and Irish poetry), and the Gerbil Liberation Front (www.gerbilfront.com—has made people laugh across the country), as well as a major label band called Sister Soleil that toured in the U.S. and recorded an album at Peter Gabriel's Real World Studios. As a digital media expert, Todd's interests have tended to revolve around a desire to share creative visions, and help others to share their own. Recently, his vision has evolved into the formation of a new live band based out of Chicago, and the formation of a company to support his own creative efforts and the efforts of others.

His ultimate goal is to develop and promote the philosophy of redistributive capitalism, by creating new things, developing resources, and dedicating some of those resources for charity. The purchase of this book is an example—10% of the royalties will be going to charity (see www.cftw.net).

Acknowledgments

First, I want to thank God for being a kick-ass friend. I sure hope we all see each other on the other side. Then, I want to thank my parents, for co-authoring me, and then undergoing a long and intensive editorial process. Additionally, I want to thank my brother, who I hope will become my new best friend. Dude, you are truly a hero to me. (And thanks for bringing your Mac home from college back in 1984.)

I want to thank Todd Beamer, again and again, for storming the cockpit on Flight 93. I never knew you at Wheaton ('91), just like I never knew Billy Graham ('53) or Wes Craven ('69), but I sure know you now. Shine on, brother.

Thanks to all the folks who helped with this book, especially the folks who let me subject them to videotaping, including Nancy, Alicia, Brian, Mena and the cats of Alunniland, Andrew Sole, the infamous Detholz: Ben/Carl/Jim/Jamsie, Howie of Lord Gimlet's Lair, and many others. And I really appreciate my beta testers, especially Rachel.

Couldn't have done it without Betsy Brown, Jon Steever, George Nedeff, Mike Henry, and the rest of the crew at Sams, who worked with me 'round the clock to get this out. Amazing!

Wow, to my new friend at Apple, Aimee Mackey, for restoring my faith in the company, and to Steve Jobs and Steve Wozniak for founding Apple—I hope I have the chance to meet you someday, in this life or the next. I am *so* honored to be able to write any book about Macs, which have been like good friends keeping me company for 20 years.

To Mary Cagney: What a long strange trip it's been, eh, you rascal? Thanks so much for all your help, typing, patience, and good cheerful humor. I literally couldn't have done it without you.

And finally, to Bill Gates: Thanks for sharing your billions with those in need. But dude, wouldn't you say it's about time to make the switch?

Tell Us What You Think!

As the reader of this book, *you* are our most important critic and commentator. We value your opinion and want to know what we're doing right, what we could do better, what areas you'd like to see us publish in, and any other words of wisdom you're willing to pass our way.

You can email or write me directly to let me know what you did or didn't like about this book—as well as what we can do to make our books stronger.

Please note that I cannot help you with technical problems related to the topic of this book, and that due to the high volume of mail I receive, I might not be able to reply to every message.

When you write, please be sure to include this book's title and author as well as your name and phone number or email address. I will carefully review your comments and share them with the author and editors who worked on the book.

Email: `graphics@samspublishing.com`

Mail: Mark Taber
       Associate Publisher
       Sams Publishing
       201 West 103rd Street
       Indianapolis, IN 46290 USA

Introduction

We're all friends here, so let's speak openly.

iMovie is simply the best video editing program out there for people who want to learn about digital video. And iDVD is the best DVD program out there for people who want to start making their own DVDs.

The reason I'm so honored to be writing this book (see the "Acknowledgements" section), is that Apple has brought such great products into the world. Not only has Apple led the digital media revolution by delivering amazing software—such as iMovie and iDVD—for people to express their creativity, but it has also made significant contributions in the realm of hardware with innovative technologies and great computers. What other company can claim that they won an Emmy award? That's right! Not Microsoft, not Dell, not Gateway. Good old Apple computer and its wily engineers paved the way for digital video editing by creating the highly acclaimed FireWire standard, which you'll use as you plug in your digital camera and proceed to take up increasing amounts of hard drive space with your very own video clips.

iMovie and iDVD will draw you in, so be prepared to sleep less and have more fun. Stock up on coffee (or some other caffienated beverage), blank videotapes, and blank DVDs!

Who This Book Is For

This book is for everyone who wants to get their feet wet with iMovie, iDVD, or both. You don't need to be a video expert, or even be all that familiar with your Mac. All you need is a desire to have fun and a willingness to explore! You'll also need a Mac with a FireWire port and some free hard drive space in order to transfer your video to your computer for editing with iMovie. If you want to use iDVD, you'll also need a built-in SuperDrive for burning your own DVDs. A digital video camera—your own, borrowed, or rented—will also come in handy!

How This Book Is Organized

This book is divided into two themes. In the first half, you'll become acquainted with iMovie by getting a taste of the way it looks and feels, and walking through each feature you can use to make your iMovie. You'll also be introduced to several ways that you can deliver your iMovie when it's done, including sending it by email, and putting it on the Internet.

In the second half, you'll take a look at the brave new world of making your own DVD, starting with a sample of how DVDs work and moving right into making your own! Toward the end of the section, we review a few sample projects that show some of the different things you can do when making your own DVD.

The book is organized into four parts:

Part I, "Digital Video Basics," introduces fundamental video concepts and basic technical requirements for working with digital video in iMovie.

Part II, "Learning iMovie," explores the iMovie interface, walks you through importing, exporting, and editing video clips, and presents enhancements—including transitions, video effects, titles, and audio—that you can use to spice up your iMovies.

Part III, "DVD Basics," introduces key concepts in DVD production as well as system requirements and constraints of iDVD.

Part IV, "Learning iDVD," explores the iDVD interface, describes the creation and customization of DVD menus and slideshows, and shows sample DVD projects to foster your understanding of DVD design.

Conventions Used in This Book

This book uses the following conventions:

Text that you type appears in bold `monospace` type. Filenames are in regular weight `monospace`.

A **Note** presents interesting information related to the discussion.

A **Tip** offers advice or shows you an easier way to do something.

A **Caution** alerts you to a possible problem, and gives you advice on how to avoid it.

PART I
Digital Video Basics

Hour

HOUR 1

Understanding Digital Video

The goal of this first hour is to equip you with the basics you need to understand key concepts and issues in digital video, which will be helpful to keep in mind as you're working on projects.

iMovie makes it so easy to work with digital video that you don't really have to understand all the nuts and bolts. But getting a better sense of how things work will help you to have more confidence, and will most likely result in better-looking productions.

Throughout this hour, we discuss the following topics:

- Digital video concepts
- Exporting iMovies
- Pixels and screen size
- Frame rate
- File compression
- Timecode

Throughout this hour, there are examples based on files that might be available in the iMovie folder on your computer's hard drive. If you can't find the files, or if they have been erased, try reinstalling the iMovie software from the CD-ROM that came with your computer; it will install tutorial video files into the iMovie folder. You can also order a disc with some sample files from www.idvd.be.

Pixels

One of the fundamental concepts in working with digital video is the system that a computer uses to draw images on the screen. Your Mac divides the screen up into a grid of individual pieces called *pixels*, which are essentially individual dots that make up a picture.

It's possible for a computer to talk to a camcorder in such a way that you never have to deal with the measurement of pixels. When you capture video, iMovie automatically chooses the right settings, and you end up exporting to your camera again. When you're working with iMovie, you might never need to consider pixels, but it can be helpful to understand them, especially if you ever need to export an iMovie at a different size than the original. For example, you might want to save a special version of your iMovie to burn on a CD or put on a Web site, and when you do so, you end up saving it at a smaller size, which involves fewer pixels. Later in the lesson, we take a look at how this is done.

One typical way that you might need to work with pixels on your computer is when you adjust the *resolution* of your screen.

 Resolution is a term that describes how much detail there is in a computer-generated image. A high-resolution image has more detail, and is considered to be a higher-quality image. Conversely, a low-resolution has less detail, and thus is of lower quality. For example, when you choose a different screen size on your Mac, such as 800×600 pixels, or 1024×768, you're changing the resolution of the screen—and you can see that with higher resolution, more can fit on the screen.

On a Mac, you can go adjust the resolution setting in System Preferences area of your computer. If you aren't familiar with pixels already, you might want to try this to get better acquainted.

Task: Tinkering with Display Settings

In this simple example, we'll adjust some system preferences on your Mac. I assume you have Mac OS X. If you aren't sure what you have, watch the Mac screen when you turn on your computer and it will say Mac OS 8.6, Mac OS 9, or Mac OS X.

To get to the display settings in Mac OS X:

1. Click the System Preferences icon in your Dock.

2. In the System Preferences window, click the Displays icon.

3. In Display area, try clicking on the different options for the screen (for example, 800×600 or 1024×768, depending on your computer).

> While earlier versions of iMovie worked in both OS 9 and OS X, the current version of iMovie requires that your computer's operating system be Mac OS X.

The display options on a Mac allow you to change a number of settings, including the number of pixels that your computer uses to draw a screen. In Figure 1.1, you see that the screen is set to 1024×768, which means that it's drawing the screen 1024 pixels wide and 768 pixels high.

FIGURE 1.1

The Display options in OS X, displaying a setting of 1024×768.

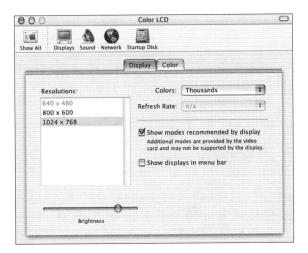

If you switch to a different setting, such as 800×600, your computer will draw a screen 800 pixels wide and 600 pixels high, showing fewer pixels on the screen.

Another way to think of pixels is in terms of individual graphics that you see on the screen, such as when you are looking at a Web page. Figure 1.2 shows an example of an image that might be familiar to you, which I've opened in an image-editing program called Adobe Photoshop. People who work with digital images make adjustments to pixel sizes all the time, such as when they take a large digital picture and make it smaller so that they can put it on a Web page.

FIGURE 1.2

A digital image as seen in Photoshop.

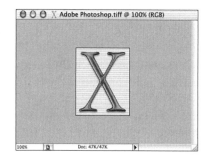

So, even though your overall computer screen size might be something like 800×600 or 1024×768 pixels, individual windows and images on the screen have their own measurements. For example, the image shown in Figure 1.2 is exactly 114 pixels wide and 140 pixels high, and we could resize it if we wanted to by typing a different number in Photoshop (see Figure 1.3).

FIGURE 1.3

The Image Size dialog box in Photoshop, displaying the pixel measurements of an individual image.

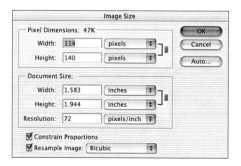

Your Mac draws images in such a way that you don't normally notice that an image is comprised of individual dots, but to get a clearer sense of what pixels actually are, let's take a closer look. In Figure 1.4, you see the same image you've been looking at, but now it's shown at 1200% and you can clearly see how the computer is using individual square-shaped blocks to draw the image.

FIGURE 1.4

A close-up view of an image, showing the individual pixels.

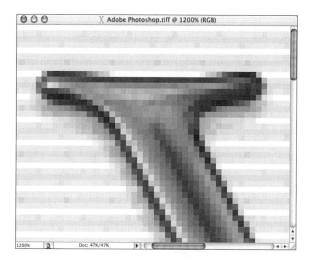

Screen Size

The concept of screen size is related to pixels, because a computer screen or video image is made up of rows of pixels. There are differences between the ways that a computer and a television draws images, but to keep things fairly simple, it's generally okay to think of working with video in terms of pixels.

In the United States, televisions use a system called NTSC (National Television Standards Committee). When you design video on your computer for NTSC televisions, it is 720 pixels wide by 480 pixels high when it's displayed at full size.

When you work with video in iMovie, you can see a reduced-size version of the iMovie in the Monitor window.

If you live in Europe, you probably use the PAL system for working with video, which has a screen size of 768×576. The PAL system also uses a different frame rate, a concept that we talk about later in the hour.

As with pixels, the screen size isn't necessarily something that you need to be concerned about. In fact, you could make hundreds of iMovies and deliver them on VHS tape or through iDVD and never even consider the screen size.

One of the great things about iMovie is that it gives you the flexibility of working with video how you want. You can either let your Mac make educated guesses about how to adjust the settings, or you can go in (if you learn a bit about the kind of concepts that we talk about in this hour) and adjust things yourself. iMovie does have its limits, but as you'll see, it has a lot of flexibility as well.

If you're new to digital video, you might want to try some of these tasks even if you don't think you'll ever adjust settings. Understanding the fundamentals gives you more confidence, and knowing what kind of options you have might open up new creative possibilities.

As I mentioned earlier, one of the most common reasons to change the size of video is if you want to share your iMovie in a variety of ways. In the next example, we take a look at how different screen sizes are used in iMovie.

Task: Saving an iMovie to Different Sizes

In this example, we'll use the Export Movie function in iMovie as the basis for a digital field trip into the world of screen sizes. As you'll see, even when iMovie gives you the ability to make your own adjustments, it often makes the process easier by providing pop-up menus that contain typical choices as an alternative to typing in numbers.

To practice exporting in iMovie:

1. Open iMovie and import one of the sample clips that are included in the iMovie tutorial folder. See Figure 1.5.

 If you have Mac OS X, you might still have an iMovie tutorial folder in the Mac OS 9 area of your Mac or on a CD-ROM that came with the computer. Don't worry if you're not able to find this file—you can always just follow along by looking at the figures.

FIGURE 1.5

The location of the iMovie tutorial folder, as seen in Sherlock after typing in tutorial.

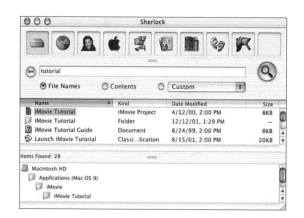

▼   2. Choose File, Export Movie. In the dialog box that comes up, you'll see an Export
       pop-up menu. Set it to QuickTime, and the dialog box will look something like
       Figure 1.6.

FIGURE 1.6

*The Export Movie dia-
log box, set to Email.*

   3. If it isn't already, set the Formats menu to Email.

       The Export Movie dialog box gives you various choices that are typically used to
       share iMovies in different ways.

   4. Now click on the Formats pop-up menu and switch to the CD-ROM setting. See
▲   Figure 1.7.

FIGURE 1.7

*Choosing the CD-
ROM setting, which is
used for exporting an
iMovie that's small
enough to put on
a CD.*

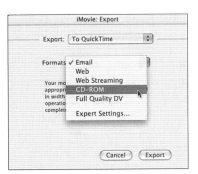

iMovie makes an automatic adjustment to a number of settings, including the screen size.

The Export dialog box enables you to choose a variety of different ways to
share your iMovie. When you export the iMovie, your Mac creates a separate, smaller file.

Frame Rate

The *frame rate* of digital video is the number of images that are displayed in a second as they flash by like frames in a traditional movie. Before television or video existed, moving pictures achieved the simulation of motion by projecting images on movie screens. This effect was achieved by rapidly projecting a succession of images on a screen, and the rate that the images were displayed was called the *frame rate*.

In traditional movies, the individual images and frames are contained in large reels, and they go by at a rate of 24 frames per second. The frames per second measurement has been adopted by digital video, but the measurement depends on a variety of factors, including the country you live in and the way you want to deliver your digital video. For example, if you use the NTSC digital video system, the measurement is most often 29.97 frames per second (fps).

You might notice that the fine print in Figure 1.8 contains the phrase *15 frames per second*, when we want to share an iMovie on CD-ROM. In this CD-ROM setting, in addition to changing the screen size, iMovie changes the frames per second automatically from 29.97 to 15. A reduction in frame rate results in a smaller, lower-quality file.

So, as with other settings, you can let iMovie decide what frame rate setting to use. But if you want to, you can tweak your iMovie and change the frames per second manually.

Task: Adjusting the Frame Rate of an iMovie

To practice adjusting the frame rate of an iMovie:

1. Choose File, Export Movie. If you don't have a movie to work with, you might want to go back to the test movie we worked with earlier in the lesson.

> In general, when you're exporting movies, you'll want to have the Export pop-up menu set to QuickTime.

2. In the Export dialog box, click the Formats pop-up menu and choose the Expert Settings option at the bottom. See Figure 1.8.
3. The Save Exported File As dialog box appears. Choose a location for your file, and then choose the Options button. See Figure 1.9.

FIGURE 1.8

The Expert Settings option in the Export dialog box.

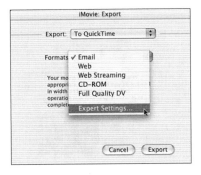

FIGURE 1.9

The Save Exported File As dialog box.

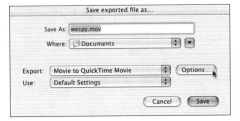

4. In the Movie Settings dialog box (see Figure 1.10), you'll notice that you have more direct access to various settings. In the Video area of the dialog box, click the Settings button.

FIGURE 1.10

The Settings button.

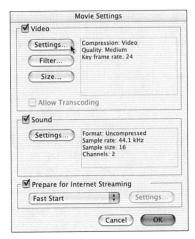

▼   5. In the Compression Settings dialog box, in the Motion area, click in the Frames
            Per Second field, and type in a new frame rate of 15 frames per second as shown in
            Figure 1.11.

FIGURE 1.11

Entering in a new
frame rate.

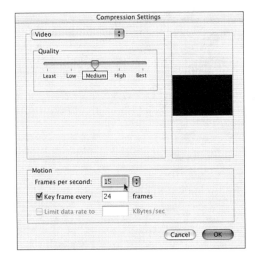

▲   6. Click OK.

> Be careful when experimenting with iMovie because you might find yourself
> having fun before you realize it! There's nothing wrong with opening, sav-
> ing, clicking, and adjusting. You can't hurt anything! But if you're experi-
> menting with settings, keep your eye open for the Cancel button—you
> might want to use it if you just want to get your feet wet when trying a
> particular task.

Compression

Compression is another aspect of video that affects the quality of the image and the
amount of space that digital video takes up on a hard drive or a disc such as a CD or
DVD. Most digital video has some kind of compression already applied. For example,
when you simply capture video from your camcorder into iMovie, iMovie compresses
the video slightly so that it can display your video on the screen and store it on your hard
drive without taking up too much space.

Compression is similar to what people do when they stuff or zip a file to make it smaller so that they can email it. Compression is a kind of digital squeezing.

As with some of the other concepts in digital video, you might not need to think much about compression unless you want to start experimenting with sharing your iMovies in different formats such as email, CD-ROM (if you have a CD burner), and DVD (if you have a DVD burner).

Task: Adjusting Compression

In this example, we'll choose a compression setting other than the one iMovie suggests using the same Expert option that we used to adjust the frame rate in the previous task.

To adjust the compression of an iMovie:

1. Choose File, Export Movie. In the Export Movie dialog box, click the Formats pop-up menu and select the Expert Settings option.

2. In the Save Exported File As dialog box, click the Options button on the left side of the dialog box, in order to display the Movie Settings dialog box. Then click on the Settings button.

3. In the Compression Settings dialog box, click the uppermost pop-up menu in the dialog box, and switch from Animation to Cinepak (see Figure 1.12)—a method of compression commonly used for delivering video on CD-ROM. QuickTime offers a wide variety of compression methods, which are also known as *codecs* (COmpression/DECompression). To learn more about codecs, visit www.idvd.be.

FIGURE 1.12

QuickTime compression methods.

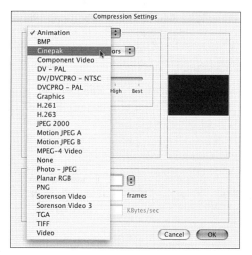

▼   4. Now click the slider in the Quality area of the Compression Settings dialog box
        and adjust the quality to a different setting, such as High or Medium. Doing so can
        result in lesser image quality, but the idea is that sometimes reducing the quality
        can allow you to have a smaller file size—it's always a trade off. See Figure 1.13.

FIGURE 1.13

*Tweaking the Quality
setting.*

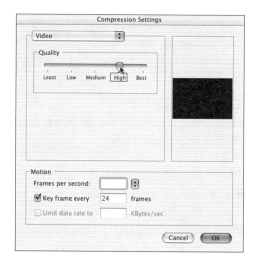

▲   5. Click OK.

As you're experimenting with iMovie, if you get stuck and can't seem to get
out of a window, you can always follow these steps to get out of the situation: First, see whether there's an OK or Cancel button that you can click on
somewhere. If there is, you might not be able to do anything else until you
choose either (Cancel is the safe bet). Second, if you are in Mac OS X, you
can click on the red circle at the tops of many windows to close them. (In
Mac OS 9, there's a small square you can click on to close a window.) Finally,
if your Mac gets flustered and freezes (it's been known to happen), never
fear; you can try holding down the power button to shut it down, or press
Ctrl+Apple key+power button.

Timecode

Timecode is simply a fancy term for keeping track of where you are in your iMovie. At
first glance it doesn't seem like a big deal, but it can come in very handy if you watch
your video ahead of time and mark points where you want to edit it.

Figures 1.14 and 1.15 show an iMovie in which we wanted to go directly to a spot five minutes into the iMovie. The timecode (5:00) is displayed directly to the right of the playhead, and reflects five minutes—the number of minutes and seconds of video.

Figure 1.14

Looking at an iMovie, five minutes in.

Figure 1.15

Looking at the same iMovie in the Timeline Viewer.

A digital video timecode is often displayed with seconds and frames, rather than minutes and seconds, but iMovie makes it easier by displaying minutes and seconds.

Summary

In this hour, you learned about a variety of concepts in digital video that help make up the iMovie puzzle. Becoming familiar with the fundamentals provides confidence and opens up new options for what you can do with your iMovies.

In the next hour, we take a closer look at the iMovie program itself, where some of the concepts we've learned about are turned into exciting, creative possibilities.

Workshop

The Workshop consists of quiz questions and answers to help you to develop a better sense of the material. First, try to answer the questions before checking the answers. (No peeking!) Be sure to read the explanations, even if you get the answers right. You'll come away from the book with more knowledge this way, and you will also be able to help your friends, family, or colleagues to learn iMovie!

Q&A

Q I live in the United States, so I have an NTSC television, and I want to make a tape to send to a friend in England, and he has PAL. Can I just export into PAL from iMovie and make him a tape with my VCR?

A Unfortunately, converting from one TV system to another is a complex process, and is beyond the capability of most video-editing systems. PAL and NTSC have different screen sizes, frame rates, and other characteristics, so the best thing to do would be to export your iMovie to a Mini-DV or Digital-8 tape as you normally would, and send it to a conversion house (see `www.idvd.be` for up-to-date links). The conversion house will charge a (fairly reasonable) fee to convert your video and send you a VHS tape in PAL format.

Q I have a video file I downloaded from the Web. Can I open it in iMovie?

A It depends on what kind of format it's in, but chances are that you won't be able to open it in iMovie. What you can do is get QuickTime Pro, an inexpensive upgrade to the regular QuickTime Player that's available from Apple's Web site, and it can open up just about any kind of file. When you open the video file, you can export it from QuickTime Pro into the DV Stream format, which is iMovie's native format for working with video.

Quiz

1. What's the full screen size of digital NTSC video?
   A. 640×480
   B. 720×480
   C. 768×576

2. What's the full screen size of digital PAL video?
   A. 640×480
   B. 720×480
   C. 768×576
   D. All of the above

3. What's the frame rate of digital NTSC video?

    A. 29.97 frames per second

    B. 15 frames per second

    C. You can set it however you like

1

Quiz Answers

1. **B.** Digital NTSC video is 720×480

2. **C.** Digital PAL video is 768×576

3. **C.** Generally, the frame rate of digital NTSC video is 29.97 for most full-screen purposes, such as exporting back to videotape or DVD, but frame rate can be adjusted for other uses such as exporting to CD-ROM or for the Web.

HOUR 2

Getting to Know How iMovie Works

iMovie is a program from Apple that lets you take video that you've recorded with a camcorder and make your own movies. It gives you the power to be your own movie director. When you go out with your digital camcorder, you might find that you quickly fill up an entire tape shooting scenes of events or people. Similarly, in Hollywood, when they shoot a movie, they take cameras and shoot a considerable amount of footage.

This is where iMovie comes in: the point at which you have your footage and want to do something with it. In Hollywood, the process of deciding which parts of the footage ends up in the final product is called *editing*. If you stay at the movie theater after the movie and pay attention to the credits as they roll by, you'll notice at some point that people are credited with being the editors for a movie. Movie editors are the people who craft the various scenes to fit together—in essence, they're making the same kind of decisions that you'll make for your iMovie.

Throughout this hour, we discuss the following:

- The basic stages of video production: shoot, edit, enhance, share
- Making sure that you have the latest version of iMovie
- Understanding the iMovie system requirements
- Hard drive optimization

Apple's FireWire Innovation Makes It Possible

One of the greatest things about iMovie is that it gives you the ability to use your creativity to easily create impressive, high-quality video productions. Apple has been a part of the desktop video revolution from day one. The reason we can now make such projects in the home or office without a lot of expensive equipment is partly due to Apple's invention of the FireWire interface (also known as iLINK). FireWire is simply the connection on a digital camcorder and computer that enables them to directly connect. It used to be that you had to have special equipment to convert video and edit on your computer. Now almost every computer, Mac or PC, incorporates Apple's FireWire technology. And Apple's iMovie software has had a similar, significant impact, helping people around the world to unleash their creative potential.

Basic Stages: Shoot, Edit, Enhance, Share

Apple explains the process of making iMovies in general stages, which roughly follow the general process that professional movie makers follow: shoot, edit, audio effects, visual effects, and share.

Shoot and Capture

Shooting video is simply the process of using your digital camcorder to record scenes or events for your iMovie. Most people find themselves recording sound with their video using the built-in microphone on their camcorder, but you don't necessarily need to do this—it's possible to record sound separately with the right equipment and then import it into your iMovie. For example, you might shoot some footage of an event and want to record yourself separately, making narrative commentary about the footage.

There are really no limits to what you can do when shooting video—you're limited only by how many blank tapes you have and how well charged your batteries are. (Hint: Extra batteries are definitely a wise investment, and you'll almost surely find yourself in situations in which they come in handy.) One thing to keep in mind, though, is that you're limited to being able to work with only a limited amount of the footage you have shot, because iMovie temporarily stores your production on your computer's hard drive. That means the available free space on your hard drive has a direct relationship to the amount of video you can edit at one time. For example, you can shoot as much video as you like, but you might not be able to edit all ten tapes worth of footage at one time.

As you'll see later, there are some techniques you can use to get good quality video when you're using your camcorder, but ultimately the magic happens in iMovie. The way that you get video into the computer so that you can use it in iMovie is called *capturing* video. Apple makes it so simple to capture video, you don't really need to think of it as a separate stage in the process of making an iMovie. You simply shoot your video, connect your camcorder to your Mac with a FireWire cable, and click a button. iMovie captures the video for you and automatically processes the incoming video into separate clips.

Edit

Some people find that editing video is their favorite part of working with iMovies. This is where you get to make the creative decisions that cause the final product to take form. One way to think of video editing is that it's somewhat like a word processor for video. In essence, you get to copy and paste pieces of a project just as you would when composing a letter or email. But in iMovie, instead of working with words and paragraphs, you move around video clips.

The most common adjustments that iMovie enables you to make when editing video are the *start* and *end* of an individual video clip. For example, when you bring a new video clip into iMovie, let's say it's a scene of a friend standing in front of a building, talking about an event, and the total length of the clip is about two minutes long.

But when you look at the clip in iMovie, you notice that there's a little boy sticking his tongue out at the camera while he's walking by in the background at the beginning of the clip. One option is to leave this type of accidental action in a clip, but ultimately you'll probably find yourself wanting to remove or add things to your iMovie—thus you'll want to learn how to edit.

If you want to edit the boy out of the scene in this example, iMovie gives you the ability to pick a new start for the clip. For example, you could start the clip two seconds later.

As you'll learn in this book, iMovie gives you the ability to make just about any kind of edit that you'd like. One fun thing that you can do as you start to learn about video editing is to start thinking about how editors have made decisions in television shows or movies that you're watching. Ask yourself how each scene leads into the other, and what effect a change in the edit point would have on the movie.

Enhance with Audio and Visual Effects

iMovie gives you a number of tools and special effects that you can use to spice up your iMovie. In traditional video or film production, the stage where audio and visual effects are added is referred to as *post-production*, when a movie or television show is tweaked and developed, special effects are added, and final decisions are made about how the production will turn out.

iMovie is simple to use, but powerful, and one of the places it shines is in the category of effects. iMovie 3 comes with more than 18 built-in effects, including Brightness & Contrast, Adjust Colors, and others. It also enables you to add sound effects, music from your own collection, and recorded audio to your movies.

Share

Sharing is my favorite stage of making an iMovie. A whole new generation of iMovie makers can now have revenge on their parents, who very well may have made them sit through countless hours of slide shows or look at hundreds of individual 4×6 prints. They might have had you looking at VHS tapes, but who wants to fast-forward through all those tapes to find the scene you're looking for? And every time the tape was played, the image quality was worn down just a bit. Now, thanks to iMovie and iDVD, you can share your creations with as many people as you like, and the quality is as good as you'd like to make it.

Computer and video enthusiasts are coming to realize that a combination of a digital camcorder, a Mac, and iMovie/iDVD software becomes a complete *digital-to-digital* system. You no longer find yourself editing your video digitally, only to deliver it on a VHS tape, which is not only poorer quality, but is also *nondigital* or *analog*. Being able to go directly from a digital camcorder into your Mac through FireWire and then to burn a DVD means that you get the best-looking video possible to share with your friends, colleagues, and family.

Which Version of iMovie Do I Have?

If you're not sure which version of iMovie you have, it's a good question to ask because this book focuses on iMovie 3, which has several new features, including integration with other easy-to-use digital media applications from Apple: iTunes, iPhoto, and iDVD.

iMovie and iDVD make a great pair, which is why this book exists, but remember that the use of iDVD requires you to have some special hardware. Specifically, you must have a computer with Apple's built-in SuperDrive—an optical drive that can read and write both CDs and DVDs.

Although the previous version of iMovie could run in the older Mac operating system (Mac OS 9), iMovie 3 requires at least Mac OS X 10.1.5.

Apple occasionally releases a new version of a program that's known as an *update* or *upgrade*. Basically, that means some additional features have been added, and some enhancements might have been added to the stability and functionality of the program.

It's always a good idea to occasionally visit the Apple Web site and check to see whether Apple has introduced any new versions or updates of the program. If a later version—even a minor update—is available, you should download and install it.

Task: Checking Apple Menu for Version

If you're not sure which version of iMovie you have, there's an easy way to tell:

1. Start iMovie.

2. Choose iMovie, About iMovie (see Figure 2.1).

FIGURE 2.1

The About iMovie option, accessed from the Apple menu.

If you've been using iMovie under Mac OS 9, you'll have to go to the Apple Web site and download iMovie 3 and any available updates.

iMovie will bring up a window that displays the version number. Sometimes there are minor updates such as the one shown in Figure 2.2, iMovie 3.0.2.

FIGURE 2.2

The version of iMovie.

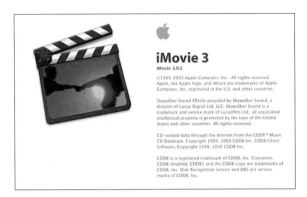

Getting the Latest Version

To get the latest version, try visiting the following links to go to Apple's Web site, where there's a lot of helpful information as well as a number of interesting and helpful downloads:

Mac OS X—www.apple.com/iMovie

Apple Store—www.apple.com/store

If you plan to use iDVD and don't have a brand-new computer, you might want to purchase iLife. iLife contains iMovie 3 and iDVD 3 as well as iTunes 3 and iPhoto 2 on an installation disc. Note that iMovie, iTunes, and iPhoto can be downloaded without fee from the Apple Web site, but only the recent version of iDVD comes with iLife. This is because iDVD is too large to conveniently download.

iMovie System Requirements

Chances are that you don't need to be concerned about the system requirements for iMovie, as it was included with the Mac you purchased. Essentially, if you have a FireWire connection on your Mac, you can run iMovie.

If you purchased a used Mac and you don't find iMovie software on it, it might be that the Mac is an earlier machine that doesn't have a built-in FireWire connection, or someone might have deleted iMovie from the machine for some reason.

The following is the official Apple information on system requirements for iMovie at the time of writing. As always, it's a good idea to check the Apple site (`www.apple.com/iMovie`) for the latest information on new versions.

iMovie 3 requires a Macintosh computer containing a 400 MHz PowerPC G3 processor or faster, a built-in FireWire port, CD or DVD drive, 256MB or more of memory, 2GB of available hard disk space, Mac OS 10.1.5 or later, and a monitor that supports at least 1024×768 resolutions. QuickTime 6.1 is also required.

2

Task: Verifying Available Memory

▲ TASK

As with any other digital video program, the more RAM you have in the computer, the better. RAM is different from hard drive space: RAM is the chip memory that your Mac can use while it's turned on. Think of it as being the conscious memory of your computer—when you turn off your Mac, the contents of the RAM goes away. But just as your own short-term memory helps you to perform daily tasks while you're awake, the RAM in your Mac helps it to perform its own tasks, especially with digital video.

RAM, which is measured in megabytes, is getting cheaper all the time, and you might want to add some memory to your Mac. To expand this short-term memory in your computer, you buy and install extra chips. While the computer is turned on, the RAM helps it to process information more efficiently. Then, when the computer is turned off, the RAM is empty again.

Hard drive space, usually measured in gigabytes, is the long-term memory on your computer. To expand the hard drive memory, you typically purchase an additional hard drive unit, such as an external FireWire hard drive. Expanding the hard drive memory would enable you to work with more video at one time. You can always erase something you've stored in your hard drive when you're done, but unlike RAM, the file will stay there even when the computer is turned off.

To check how much RAM you have, first you must make sure that you're in the Finder. The Finder on your Mac is like the main hotel lobby; so, if you have several programs running, the Finder is the central place in your Mac.

To switch to the Finder:

▼   1. Click on the Apple menu in the upper-left corner of the screen (see Figure 2.3).

FIGURE 2.3

The Apple menu.

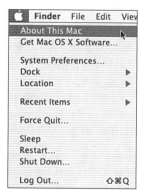

2. Choose About This Mac (see Figure 2.4).

FIGURE 2.4

The About This Mac window, displaying memory information.

Hard Drive Space

Another consideration in working with digital video when making your iMovies is the question of how much hard drive space you have. Unlike RAM, memory on your hard drive is long-term storage. That is, when your Mac turns off, information such as the video that you're working with stays there.

Digital video takes up a lot of space. Each second of digital video in iMovie takes up approximately 4 megabytes of space, so a minute of video takes up 240 megabytes, which is a significant portion of a gigabyte (1GB = 1,000MB).

The amount of space taken up by a specific time period of video depends on the format and compression used for the video. In the earlier example, we're keeping things simple. Technically speaking, we're referring specifically to NTSC-DV video, but the numbers would be similar for PAL-DV video.

When you're considering how much hard drive space you need, keep in mind that iMovie makes copies of your original video files. When you add additional effects, and other enhancements, they take up additional hard drive space—so, in the end, it's best to have as much hard drive space as you can reasonably afford. Start out with the built-in hard drive space, and add more when you can afford to—you'll always use it. When working with limited space, one thing you can do is get in the habit of emptying the trash and deleting unused clips as soon as you know you won't need them.

Task: Checking Free Hard Drive Space

To check your available hard drive space , follow these steps:

1. Go to the main hard drive icon on your Mac in the upper-right corner of your screen, hold down the Ctrl key on your keyboard, and single-click the icon to select it.

2. Select the Get Info option as shown in Figure 2.5. The Hard Disk Info window (see Figure 2.6) will appear and display information about your hard drive, including the amount of free space you have.

FIGURE 2.5
The Get Info option gives you the low-down.

A hard drive icon might not necessarily be named *hard drive* because you can change the name of your hard drive. To do so, click once on the letters

beneath the icon; let go of the mouse button but hold the mouse pointer in
position. When the text becomes selected, you can just type in the new
name.

FIGURE 2.6

The Info window.

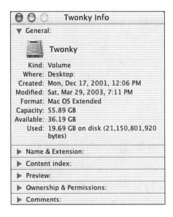

To help you monitor the space consumed by your iMovie project as you
work, iMovie also has a built-in capacity to determine how much free space
you have on your hard drive.

Task: Calculating Video Capacity

The built-in calculator on your Mac can be a convenient way to calculate how many minutes of video you can fit on your hard drive after you know how much free space you
have.

Let's say you have 1.5GB of free space on your hard drive. Translated into megabytes,
this turns out to be 1500MB.

To determine your video capacity (based on how much free space you have to work with
video):

1. Open the calculator (which should be located inside the Applications folder on
   your hard drive) and enter the number of megabytes of free space you have. See
   Figure 2.7.

If you have a very large hard drive, the free space might be given in giga-bytes (GB) rather than megabytes (MB). In that case, multiply the gigabytes by 1,000 to convert them to megabytes before continuing with your cal-culations.

2

FIGURE 2.7

36.19 GB = 3,619,000 MB of free space.

2. Divide that number by 4, and you end up with an approximate number of seconds of video you can work with at a time. See Figure 2.8.

FIGURE 2.8

Divided by 4, you end up with the number of seconds available (904,750). When you divide the number of seconds by 60, you get the number of avail-able minutes (15,079.17).

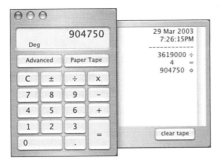

Optimizing Your Hard Drive

Whether you're working with the built-in hard drive on your Mac or using an external hard drive to store your video, it can improve the performance of your system if you reg-ularly optimize your hard drive.

In the course of normal use of your Mac, the computer is constantly writing various files, deleting others, and fitting them in to various leftover spots on the hard drive. Like a cluttered room, the hard drive can end up becoming *fragmented*, where part of a file is on one spot on the hard drive and another part of the same file is stored on a different spot.

This isn't because you've done anything wrong, it's simply the way that hard drives store data. But because of the demands that digital video places on the hard drive, this fragmentation can have a significant impact. *Defragmenting* basically takes the various bits of each file from various spots on the hard drive and reassembles them into contiguous, nonfragmented files. That means the computer can read the file without having to jump around the hard drive.

To optimize your hard drive, you must purchase a tool, such as Norton Utilities. This suite contains a number of useful tools for maintaining your system (www.symantec.com).

> One of the beautiful things about using a DVD burner (aside from being able to make your own DVDs with iDVD) is the ability it gives you to permanently store digital video files. This is one way to free up more space on your hard drive—each DVD disc can hold about 4.5 gigabytes' worth of digital video files.

Summary

In this hour, you became acquainted with how iMovie works, and you had a chance to consider the stages of making an iMovie: shoot, edit, enhance, and share. Each of these stages is an important part of making an iMovie, as you'll learn throughout the book.

We also took a look at a few of the things you can examine as you work with iMovie. If you have the budget, the question of the day probably is, "when can I get some more hard drive space?" because your available hard drive space will fill up fairly quickly.

In Hour 3, "The iMovie Workspace," you'll take a closer look at the iMovie interface, including the monitor window, the shelf, and the timeline views.

Workshop

The following questions will test your knowledge of the iMovie moviemaking process, and how iMovie's performance relates to your Mac's hardware resources. Answers are provided for your reference.

Q&A

Q I'm running out of hard drive space on my Mac and I need to be able to work with more video than I can fit on my hard drive. How do I add more space?

A One option is to go back into your hard drive to search for digital video files that you're no longer using, drag them to the Trash, and empty the Trash. You might be able to find video files in the Media folder within an iMovie project folder, which would be located wherever you saved your iMovie. Another option is to purchase an external FireWire hard drive that you can connect to your Mac and use specifically for video.

Q How do I add RAM to my Mac?

A You can look in the Yellow Pages for a local Apple authorized reseller, check the Web for area resellers, or order RAM directly from one of the Mac mail-order catalogs such as MacMall (www.macmall.com) that can send you the chip. You can put the chip in yourself if you feel inspired. This is one way to save some money, and it's not that difficult. When you buy RAM to install it yourself, it usually comes with directions, but you can ask the salesperson to see whether you need any special tools.

Quiz

1. Your hard drive has 5GB of free space on it. How many minutes of digital video can you fit on it?

    A. Approximately 20 minutes

    B. Approximately 5 minutes

    C. Approximately 600 minutes

2. What are the basic stages of making an iMovie?

    A. Copy, paste, move, delete

    B. Shoot, edit, enhance, share

    C. Share, share alike, shoot, edit

    D. Lather, rinse, repeat.

3. What's optimizing?

    A. When you take video clips and put them back together

    B. When you take memories and put them back together

    C. When you take computer file fragments and put them back together

Quiz Answers

1. **A.** Five gigabytes equals 5000 megabytes. Using the approximate value of 4 megabytes per second of video in iMovie, you divide 5000 by 4 and get 1250 seconds; divide this by 60 to get minutes and you end up with about 20.

2. **B.** First you shoot the video, edit it, enhance it with effects and so on, and then share it with your friends, colleagues, and family!

3. **C.** Optimizing is the process of running a program that finds fragments of files and combines them.

Exercises

1. Check your version of iMovie. Compare that version to the latest version from Apple's Web site. If you don't have the most current version, download and install the updates.

2. Check the free space on your hard drive and calculate the number of minutes of video you will be able to store.

HOUR 3

The iMovie Workspace

iMovie is a simple yet powerful video editor that enables you to develop your video project with three main tools: the Monitor, where you look at the video clip; a shelf, which gives you the ability to look at all the clips you have to work with at a glance; and a special area at the bottom of the screen known as the Timeline Viewer, where you can put together your clips, and make decisions about when you want them to start and end. Many people have found the iMovie interface to be so easy to use that the Mac ends up becoming like a helpful friend.

Throughout this hour, we discuss the following topics:

- iMovie Monitor
- Timeline Viewer
- Shelf

iMovie Monitor

You'll find that the iMovie workspace is easy and fun to work with, like a well-planned playroom (see Figure 3.1)—and the iMovie monitor will end up being the center of activity. See Figure 3.2. After you've created a new project, the action happens in the Monitor window, which is used both to capture and preview video in iMovie. The deceptively simple Monitor window is a powerful tool that enables you to switch between looking at video that's coming from your camcorder and the clips that you already have on your Mac by toggling the import/edit control (labeled with a camera-and-scissors icon) below the window.

FIGURE 3.1

The overall iMovie workspace: the Video Monitor, Shelf, and Timeline Viewer.

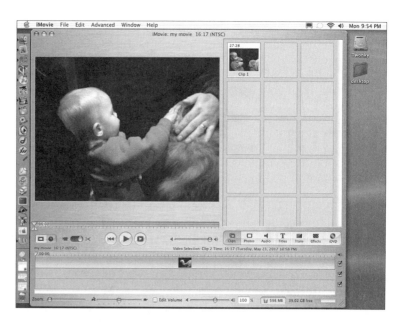

FIGURE 3.2

The Monitor window with VCR-style controls to navigate through a clip.

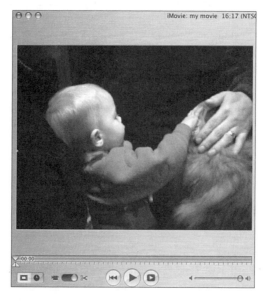

The controls in the Monitor window are much like you use on a DVD player and VCR, enabling you to quickly move through your video or jump to a specific location.

Shelf

The value of the shelf (see Figure 3.3) quickly becomes apparent when you connect your camcorder to the Mac for the first time and start capturing clips. It almost seems like alien technology at work as you watch the video clips from your tape start to appear in the shelf. The shelf is like a pantry for video—when you capture video, you load up the shelf with clips and you can take a quick glance to see what you have to work with.

FIGURE 3.3
The shelf.

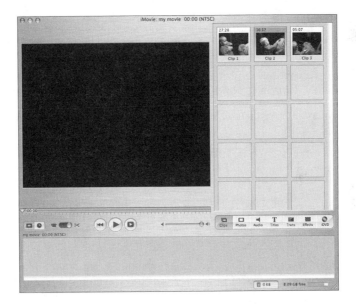

3

As you'll see in later hours, the shelf shares space with several additional tools to enhance your video productions, including transitions, titles, and effects, as well as a place to put audio if you've recorded it separately from your video.

Timeline Viewer

The Timeline Viewer enables you to make adjustments to your video clips, such as adjusting the start and end times of each clip, as well as adjusting effects and other things that you might add to a clip.

The Timeline Viewer (see Figure 3.4) enables you to see things as they progress over time.

FIGURE 3.4

The Timeline Viewer.

The Timeline Viewer makes it easy to make more specific adjustment to your project based on situations in which you might want to go to a specific location in a clip. It also enables you to work easily with multiple audio clips, so if you want to add different sounds that you've recorded, it's as easy as clicking and dragging.

Clip Viewer

The Clip Viewer (see Figure 3.5) is an alternative to the Timeline Viewer, representing another way of looking at video clips that some people might prefer. In the Clip Viewer, video clips are treated more like icons. You can easily click and drag an individual clip to position it differently and thus have a different order for your video production.

Shuffling video clips in iMovie is kind of like playing a card game such as Solitaire, where you lay cards down in a particular order, and then come back later and move them into different positions. We'll talk more about the Clip Viewer in the next hour.

> If you're new to digital video, try imagining iMovie as your "word processor for video." You can re-arrange, delete, and add material, but instead of working with paragraphs, you're working with video clips!

FIGURE 3.5

The Clip Viewer offers an alternative way to look at your clips.

Other Important Controls

At the very bottom of the iMovie window is a row of controls and status indicators, which are visible in Figure 3.1. Some of these controls are visible only in Timeline View.

The first is a slider labeled Zoom that enables you to zoom in on the Timeline to see more detail. As you add more and more scenes to the Timeline, the proportion of the whole that each takes up shrinks, and so do the rectangles representing those clips. Use the Zoom slider to focus in one part of the Timeline by selecting a clip and dragging the Zoom controller to the right.

Next is the Speed slider, labeled with icons of a rabbit (or hare) and a turtle (or tortoise), which might call to mind Aesop's fable about the fast hare and the slow tortoise. (To refresh your memory, the slow-but-steady tortoise wins the race.) This slider controls the speed of the selected clip. If you want a clip (or other element in the Timeline) to be sped up or slowed down, drag the slider toward the appropriate side.

> If a slider control button moves sluggishly when you try to drag it, you could instead click on the spot along the slider path where you want to set it. The button will jump precisely to that spot with ease.

Near the middle of the bottom row are controls for audio. Checking the box for Edit Volume makes a volume level appear in each of the elements in your Timeline. You can then adjust the volume of each clip or sound file so there aren't unpleasant volume changes. The slider next to the check box controls the overall volume of the movie. We'll some additional features, especially of the Edit Volume check box, in Hour 11, "Adding Sound to iMovies."

The bottom row also includes a couple of helpful things to manage your iMovie project: the free space indicator, and a miniature trash can so that you can easily get rid of video clips that you don't need any more. These controls are visible from both the Timeline and Clip Viewer.

Task: Create a New Project

Before you can begin working on making iMovies, you must know how to create a new project. iMovie makes this easy by bringing up a special screen (shown in Figure 3.6) if you don't already have a project started.

FIGURE 3.6

A startup screen appears if you haven't already started a project.

To create a new project:

1. Start iMovie. If you get the window shown in Figure 3.6, click the New Project button.

▼   If you don't get this window when you start iMovie, you can choose File, New
         Project from the menu bar to get the same thing.

2. When you create a new project, iMovie asks you where you want to put the project
    on your hard drive by bringing up the Create New Project dialog box (see Figure
    3.7). Type in a name for your movie and click Create if you want iMovie to simply
    save the file directly to the hard drive.

FIGURE 3.7

*The Create New
Project dialog box.*

When iMovie creates a project, it puts all your video material in one location
on the hard drive, sort of like a suitcase, making it easy to have everything
for your iMovie in one place. When you capture video, all the clips end up in
the project, and even though there are separate files, everything stays
together.

3. You might want to switch to a more convenient location than the one iMovie sug-
    gests (such as the desktop), by clicking the pop-up menu at the top of the Create
▲   New Project dialog box. See Figure 3.8.

FIGURE 3.8

Switch to the desktop.

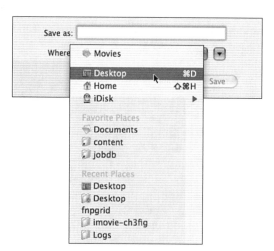

Importing Video

In Hour 5, "Capturing Video with iMovie," we'll get into the process of actually capturing video from your camcorder into your Mac using iMovie. But in this hour, we'll import a file that has already been captured into iMovie.

> iMovie is designed primarily to work with video that's captured directly from a camcorder on a Mac, but it's possible to take video from a PC and use it in iMovie. One way to do this is simply to ask whoever is giving you the video from a PC to save it in DV format (NTSC or PAL or SECAM, depending on what country you live in) to a portable FireWire hard drive, and to import it from there.

3

Task: Import a Video File

To get to the sample file, you must find the iMovie Tutorial folder, which is located in the iMovie folder on your hard drive.

1. Open iMovie and choose File, Import File. The Import File sheet will appear from the top of the iMovie window.

2. Click the pop-up menu at the top of the dialog box and navigate to the video file you want to import.

3. Select the file and click Import (see Figure 3.9). iMovie opens the clip and you'll see it in both the Monitor and the shelf, as shown in Figure 3.10.

FIGURE 3.9
The Import File dialog box.

FIGURE 3.10

A clip selected in the shelf, previewed in the Monitor.

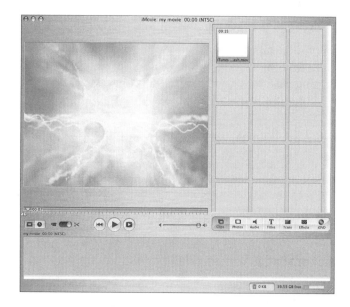

Moving Around in a Clip

One of the most enjoyable parts about playing with footage in iMovie is the way that you can easily move around in a clip in the same way that you might use the remote control on your VCR or DVD player to find a spot in a movie. In iMovie, as you're editing your creation, you'll often want to move through various parts of individual clips or the overall movie as it takes shape. Instead of playing through the entire movie, you can quickly get to the spot that you want, with a control called the *playhead*, which is located at the bottom of the Monitor window (see Figure 3.11).

FIGURE 3.11

A close-up view of the playhead along with the timestamp for that spot in your video clip.

Task: Go to a Specific Spot in a Clip

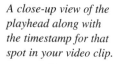

To go to a specific spot in a clip:

1. Click on the playhead, and hold down the mouse button.

2. Drag the playhead horizontally to the left or right to find the spot that you want. The number of minutes and seconds are displayed next to the playhead as you drag it, indicating how far into the clip you are, as shown in Figure 3.12.

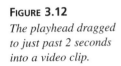

FIGURE 3.12

The playhead dragged to just past 2 seconds into a video clip.

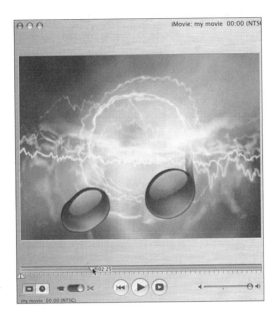

Making Basic Edits

To get a better taste of how the iMovie interface gives you the power of video editing, we'll take a look at how to make a very basic edit using a combination of the shelf, the Monitor, and the Timeline Viewer.

Preparing a Clip

In this section, we go through the process of making an adjustment to a clip. To prepare the clip, click on it in the shelf and, holding the mouse button down, drag it diagonally down and to the left into the uppermost row of Timeline Viewer, which is where you add video clips to your iMovie. See Figure 3.13.

Figure 3.13

Before: dragging a clip into the Timeline Viewer.

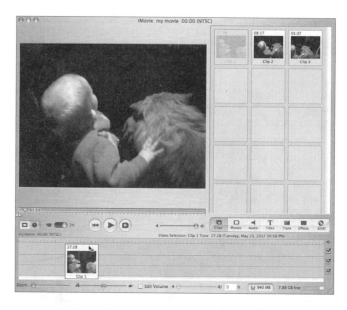

After you drag the clip, it now appears on the Timeline Viewer instead of the shelf, as illustrated in Figure 3.14.

Figure 3.14

After: the clip as it appears in the Timeline Viewer.

Task: Deleting Extra Footage

Now that we have a clip added to the Timeline, we can make an adjustment to it. In our scenario, the adjustment we want to make is to delete some extra footage at the end of the clip.

To delete extra footage:

1. Drag the playhead in the Monitor to somewhere close to the end of the clip —to the point just before the clip switches to another scene. See Figure 3.15.

2. Choose Edit, Split Video Clip at Playhead (see Figure 3.16) to mark the spot so that iMovie knows where one clip ends and the next begins. In essence, you've just created two separate clips from one original clip (see Figure 3.17).

FIGURE 3.15

The playhead in the Monitor and Timeline Viewer.

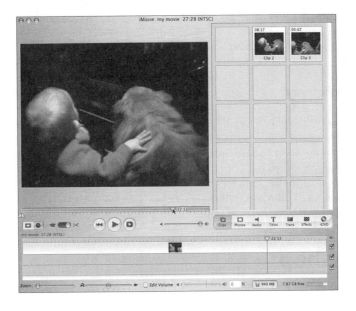

FIGURE 3.16

Splitting a video clip at the playhead.

Edit	Advanced	Window	Help
Undo			⌘Z
Redo			⇧⌘Z
Cut			⌘X
Copy			⌘C
Paste			⌘V
Clear			
Select All			⌘A
Select None			⇧⌘A
Crop			⌘K
Split Video Clip at Playhead			⌘T
Create Still Frame			⇧⌘S

FIGURE 3.17

The newly split clip with both pieces selected.

3. In the Timeline Viewer, click the second clip and choose Clear from the Edit menu. The unwanted footage will be removed.

Notice in Figure 3.18 how the overall length of the new clip is shorter than in Figure 3.14, as shown by the numbers that appear in the upper-left corner of the Timeline.

FIGURE 3.18

The remaining clip now expands to fill the entire width of the Timeline.

Summary

Congratulations, you've taken a step further into the world of making your own iMovies by becoming better acquainted with the iMovie interface. In this hour, you took a closer look at the shelf (where video clips are stored), the Monitor (which lets you see the clips), and the Timeline Viewer (which gives you another way to interact with clips).

In Hour 4, "The Clip Viewer," we'll ease into things by covering the basic tasks you can accomplish in iMovie using the Clip Viewer.

Workshop

The Workshop consists of quiz questions and answers to help you to develop a better sense of the material as you develop your digital video skills. First, try to answer the questions, before checking the answers. Then check out the explanations, even if you get the answers right. You'll gain more knowledge this way, and you'll also be able to help your friends make their own iMovies.

Q&A

Q I tried to drag a clip from the shelf into the Timeline Viewer, but it wouldn't let me. What did I do wrong?

A To be able to drag a clip into the Timeline Viewer, remember that it must be dragged into the topmost row of the Timeline Viewer. So, when the arrow that you're moving on the screen with the mouse ends up in that row, let go of the mouse button. You know you're in the right spot to drop the clip when a + appears next to your mouse cursor.

Q I can't see the Timeline Viewer. Where did it go?

A To get the Timeline Viewer, click the clock icon on the lower-left corner of the screen in iMovie, just below the film frame icon that represents the Clip Viewer.

Quiz

1. Which area of the interface can contain a video clip?

    A. The shelf

    B. The Clip Viewer

    C. The Timeline Viewer

    D. All of the above

2. What does the playhead enable you to do?

    A. Clicking the playhead starts a clip playing.

    B. Dragging the playhead moves you to a certain spot in a clip.

    C. Dragging the playhead moves you to a certain spot in a clip and it starts playing.

3. How can you import a video file?

    A. You can't import a video file; you can only capture from a camcorder.

    B. Through File, Import File.

    C. Through Edit, Import.

Quiz Answers

1. **D.** Any area of the iMovie interface can contain a video clip.

2. **B.** You can use the playhead to go to a certain spot in a clip.

3. **B.** File, Import File brings up the Import dialog box. There's no Import command in the Edit menu.

Exercise

Open iMovie and acquaint yourself with the interface elements discussed in this hour. Be sure to note the location of the Timeline and the Shelf. Also note the amount of free space iMovie says is available on your hard drive.

3

PART II
Learning iMovie

Hour

HOUR 4

The Clip Viewer

In this hour, we take a look at the Clip Viewer, which is an alternative to the Timeline and might be preferable for some as a way to work with clips. The Clip Viewer is different from the Timeline; it's basically something more like dragging icons around on your desktop.

In some ways, the Clip Viewer is the "lite" version of iMovie. If you want to have a simplified way of working with iMovies, you might want to start in the Clip Viewer and then move on to the Timeline. Also, children might find it easier to play with iMovie in the Clip Viewer because there are fewer skills to master—just clicking, dragging, and dropping.

Throughout this hour, we discuss the following:

- Adding clips
- Previewing
- Effects
- Transitions
- Titles
- Rearranging clips

Understanding the Clip Viewer

The Clip Viewer is an alternative that you might prefer if you want a simplified way to work with video clips. Although the Timeline view provides an excellent way to work with clips and is easy to use, the Clip Viewer is even easier to use, and it might be a good starting place for some people. For example, because there are fewer options to work with in the Clip Viewer, a person who's new to computers or digital video might enjoy it more at first. Then, when confidence is gained and creativity is sparked, the Clip Viewer user will naturally want to investigate the Timeline, where there are more things to play with.

> In the Clip Viewer, you can do just about everything you can in the Timeline, including adding transitions, effects, and titles (which we'll discuss in depth in later hours). One of the only major differences is that you can't work with audio in the Clip Viewer. When you try to drag a sound effect into the Clip Viewer, it switches you back to the Timeline.

Figure 4.1 shows the Timeline with three successive video clips that are arranged from left to right. Time is represented on the Timeline by the leftmost part of the Timeline being the beginning of the movie, and the rightmost part of the Timeline being the end of the movie.

FIGURE 4.1

Three clips in the Timeline view.

Now let's take a look at the Clip Viewer in Figure 4.2, which is accessed simply by clicking on the film frame symbol at the left corner of the screen.

FIGURE 4.2

The same three clips in the Clip Viewer.

The video clips represented in Figure 4.2 are the same video clips that you saw in Figure 4.1. If you have iMovie open, take a moment to click back and forth between the Timeline and the Clip Viewer to investigate the differences.

Some people might prefer to think of the Clip Viewer as being like a *slide sorter* (a device that enables you to easily sort slides that have been developed from traditional camera). If you've ever seen slides that were developed from traditional film, you'll notice that the icons in Figure 4.2 that represent the video clips look a lot like slides.

Task: Adding Clips

Adding clips is very simple in the Clip Viewer. You can basically handle things in the same way that you learned how to do in the Timeline: by dragging clips into the Clip Viewer from the Shelf.

1. Open an iMovie project that has several clips in it.

2. To access the Clip Viewer if it's not already open, click on the film frame icon in the lower-left corner of the screen. The iMovie window should look something like Figure 4.3.

FIGURE 4.3

Clips in the Shelf, ready to be dragged and dropped to the Clip Viewer.

▼　　3. Choose a clip for your iMovie by single-clicking on one of the clips in the Shelf, holding the mouse button down, and dragging it down toward the Clip Viewer area as shown in Figure 4.4. When you have the mouse arrow over the Clip Viewer area, you can let go of the mouse button and drop the clip there.

FIGURE 4.4

After Clip 1 is dragged to the Clip Viewer, its first frame will appear in the Monitor.

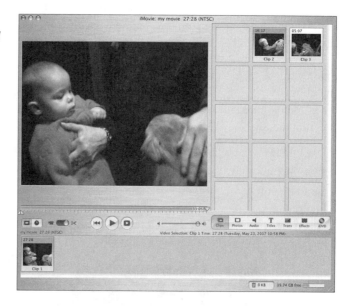

▲　　4. To add an additional clip, repeat steps 2 and 3 to drag the additional clip down and drop it to the right of the first clip (see Figure 4.5).

FIGURE 4.5

Dragging the second clip to the Clip Viewer.

When you've finished dragging clips into the Clip Viewer, it'll look something like Figure 4.6. If one of the clips is a blue color, that simply means it's selected. If you want to deselect it, you can click somewhere other than on the clip in the Clip Viewer.

FIGURE 4.6
Three clips, dragged and ready to go.

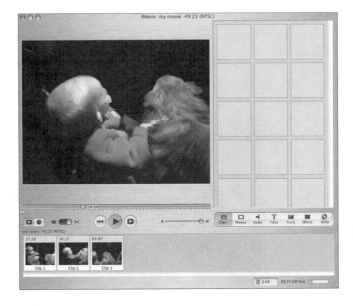

Previewing Clips

When you want to watch one of the clips you're using in your iMovie, you simply select it by clicking the clip, and then click the Play button. And when you want to preview the entire movie, you click the Play button without any clip selected, and iMovie will play all the clips in succession.

Task: Previewing a Single Clip

It's easy to take a look at a single clip in iMovie, when you want to see what it contains.

1. Open an iMovie project with clips that have been dragged into either the Timeline view or the Clip Viewer.

2. Click the film frame icon to display the Clip Viewer.

3. Click once on a video clip to select it in the Clip Viewer (see Figure 4.7).

FIGURE 4.7
Clip 2 is selected and turns a blue color.

▼   4. Click the Play button under the Monitor to watch the clip, or click the playhead
         and drag it to the left and right to rapidly review what's going on in the clip (see
▲   Figure 4.8).

FIGURE 4.8

*The playhead is at the
end of the clip after it
plays.*

Notice how, in Figure 4.8, iMovie displays how much time each video clip takes up at
the upper-left corner of the each clip. By the time you reach the end of the clip, the playhead is to the far right of the blue bar, telling you how many seconds have elapsed. In
video, there are 30 frames per second, so the farthest number on the right reflects the
frame, and the number to the left of the colon represents the number of seconds.

Task: Previewing an Entire Movie

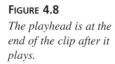

Previewing an entire movie is as simple as previewing a single clip; you just have to
remember not to have any one clip selected when you click the Play button.

1. Open an iMovie project containing more than one film clip.

2. Click the film frame icon to select the Clip Viewer.

3. Click somewhere other than on a clip to make sure that you don't have any clip
   selected—they should all be a white color (see Figure 4.9).

4. Click the Play button below the iMovie Monitor, and iMovie plays through all the
▲   clips, giving you a preview of your entire iMovie (see Figure 4.10).

Figure 4.9

Clicking outside of the clips to deselect.

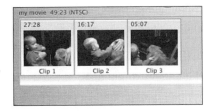

Figure 4.10

Previewing—seeing the entire movie, clip after clip.

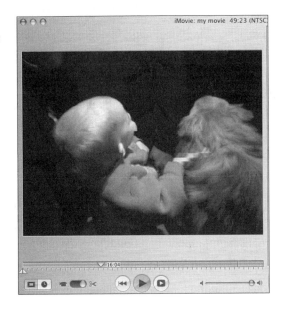

Notice how, in Figure 4.11, iMovie draws a small red marker that moves slowly to the right in the Clip Viewer area as you watch your movie. The position of the red marker in Figure 4.11 corresponds to where the playhead is positioned in the Monitor window in Figure 4.10. Both the playhead and the red marker are essentially ways of keeping track of where you are in your movie project.

Figure 4.11

The Clip Viewer has a red marker that goes through the clips when previewing, like a little red fire ant, to indicate where you are in the iMovie.

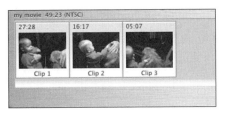

The folks at Apple, in their typical subtle elegance and imaginativeness, have built a helpful way of seeing where one clip starts and one clip ends directly into the Monitor window. The small vertical lines in the scrubber bar below the Monitor correspond to where one clip ends and another begins. This feature is sort of like having a timeline even when you're in the Clip Viewer.

Enhancing Clips with Transitions

Adding transitions, or effects is also simple. In many cases, you simply click a button to display the right palette, drag your transition onto the Clip Viewer, and you're there!

Task: Adding a Transition

It's easy to add a transition in the Clip Viewer:

1. Open an iMovie project with clips.

2. Click the film frame icon to select the Clip Viewer if it's not already visible.

3. Click the Trans button in the main iMovie window to display the Transitions palette.

4. Click a transition and drag it to a spot in the Clip Viewer. Try clicking Fade Out and dragging it into position after the last clip in your iMovie—see Figure 4.12.

▲

If you have more clips than will fit on the screen at one time, click-and-drag the blue scrollbar at the bottom of the screen all the way to the right to get to the end of your clips, and then drag the transition down to the spot after the last clip.

After you drag the transition into place, iMovie attaches a small indicator to show you how the processing is going, with a small red line that moves to the right (see Figure 4.13). When it gets all the way to the right, the transition is officially processed and you can preview the clip.

Task: Adding an Effect

Effects have a few more options, as you'll learn more about in Hour 9, "Advanced Video Editing—Effects," but adding them to a clip is an easy enhancement.

Figure 4.14 shows a project in which the second clip is a bit too dark and we decide that we want to brighten things up a bit. No problem!

1. Open an iMovie project and click the film frame icon to look at the Clip Viewer.

2. Click the Effects button to display the Effects palette.

FIGURE 4.12

Dragging a Fade Out transition to the Clip Viewer.

FIGURE 4.13

The new Fade Out transition is processing, making a preview of what the fade out will look like.

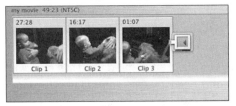

▼

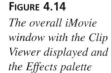

FIGURE 4.14

The overall iMovie window with the Clip Viewer displayed and the Effects palette open.

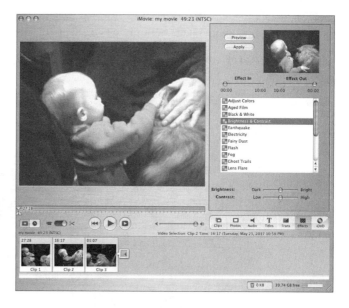

3. Choose a clip and click it to select it (see Figure 4.15).

FIGURE 4.15

Selecting a clip.

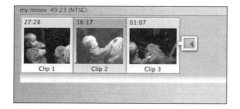

4. With the clip selected, go into the Effects palette and click the Brightness & Contrast Effect to select it.

5. Drag the Brightness slider a bit to the right. Then play with the Contrast setting as well if you have some similarly dark footage (see Figure 4.16).

6. Click the Apply button in the Effects palette to tell iMovie that you've decided you want to use this effect.

After iMovie processes the clip, you can select the clip and press the Play button to preview it.

FIGURE 4.16

Selecting and adjusting the effect.

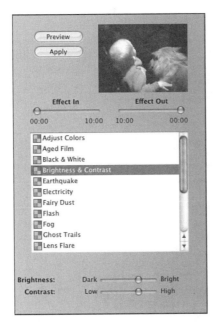

While in the Clip Viewer, you can easily see which clips have had effects applied to them because they're marked with a small checkerboard icon. If you add more than one effect, a number will appear next to the checkerboard to tell you how many have been applied.

If you don't like your settings, you can choose Edit, Undo (or hold down the Command key on your keyboard and then press the Z key—another handy way to undo). This will undo your last step. If you Undo again, you'll undo the step before that.

Task: Rearranging Clips

One thing that the Clip Viewer comes in particularly handy for is rearranging clips if you want to reposition one clip after another or easily try different combinations of scenes. Open an iMovie project with a few clips in it, and before looking at the Clip Viewer, try the Timeline view as shown in Figure 4.17 (click the clock icon). Notice how things look. For comparison, you might want to try clicking on a clip to try moving it around.

FIGURE 4.17

The Timeline: a bit more powerful, but not as useful for rearranging.

Now you're ready to reposition:

1. Open an iMovie project with at least three clips in it, and click on the film frame icon at the lower left to see the Clip Viewer.

2. Click the first clip, and holding the mouse button down, drag the clip to the right, until a space opens up between the second and third clips (see Figure 4.18).

FIGURE 4.18

The Clip Viewer: a bit more convenient; rearranging is as easy as dragging back and forth.

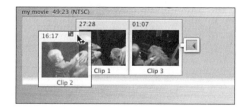

3. Let go of the mouse button to drop the clip in place. See Figure 4.19 for the completed arrangement.

FIGURE 4.19

The repositioned clip.

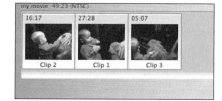

In addition to repositioning clips, the Clip Viewer is also good for putting clips back on the Shelf if you've decided not to use them for the time being. Simply click on a clip to select it, and drag it back into an empty square in the Clips palette.

Summary

In this hour, you learned about the Clip Viewer, the "lite" version of iMovie, an alternative to the Timeline, and a place that some people might enjoy starting at or even continuing to use right up until they accept their first Academy Award. (Don't laugh! Okay, maybe not an Oscar, but someday there'll be a person —maybe *you*—who wins an award at an independent film festival and reveals that instead of using Final Cut Pro or Avid, he or she did it in iMovie.)

In Hour 5, "Capturing Video with iMovie," you'll learn how to capture video from a camcorder directly into iMovie, and you'll see how the control buttons in the Monitor actually enable you to control the camcorder as it is connected through FireWire to the Mac.

Workshop

The Workshop consists of quiz questions and answers to help you to develop a better grasp of the Clip Viewer. First, try to answer the questions *before* checking the answers. Then read the explanations, even if you get the answers right—the explanations will help you to get a better sense of iMovie and digital video in general.

4

Q&A

Q Is it okay to switch back and forth between the Clip Viewer and the Timeline?

A It's no problem. The two views are simply two ways of looking at the same thing; it doesn't change anything in the project to look at it one way or the other. Remember, some tasks can be done in only one view or the other—rearranging clips works only in the Clip Viewer and audio can be added only in the Timeline Viewer.

Q How do I delete a clip in the Clip Viewer without deleting everything else?

A Just click the clip, and then press the Delete key on the keyboard.

Quiz

1. How do you get to the Clip Viewer?

   A. Choose View, Clip

   B. Click the film frame icon

   C. A and B

2. How do you add an effect to a clip?

   A. Drag the effect onto the clip

   B. Select the clip, then select the effect and click Apply

   C. A and B

3. How do you preview a clip?

   A. Click somewhere in the Clip Viewer outside of the clips and then click Play

   B. Select a clip and then click Play

   C. A and B

   D. Neither A nor B

Quiz Answers

1. **B.** The film frame icon represents seeing the movie; the clock icon represents seeing the movie over time.

2. **B.** Effects work a little differently than transitions and titles. You can't drag them into the Clip Viewer, nor into the Timeline Viewer.

3. **C.** A trick question. **B** is the preferred method, but **A** plays the whole movie and therefore plays the clip (heh, heh).

Exercises

1. Open iMovie and click between the Clip Viewer and the Timeline Viewer to see the differences.

2. Open a project containing several clips or create a new project and add clips. Then practice adding clips in the Clip Viewer and rearranging them.

HOUR 5

Capturing Video with iMovie

In this hour, you learn the way that a camcorder can be connected to your Mac and the process of capturing video through that connection. Capturing video, simply put, is the process of importing digital video footage from a camcorder into a computer.

iMovie makes it easy to capture video—all you have to do is hook up your camcorder to the computer, find a spot in the tape you want to capture, and away you go!

Throughout this hour, we discuss the following:

- Connecting camcorders
- Cueing video (finding a spot in a tape)
- Capturing video

Connecting Camcorders

Nowadays, virtually every video camera that you can purchase in a store includes a FireWire connection, an award-winning technology developed by Apple Computer. FireWire is the magic behind being able to make your own digital movie and DVD projects.

Understanding the FireWire Cable

When you want to connect your digital camcorder to your Mac, you must use a FireWire cable. A camcorder often comes with such a cable, but you can also purchase it separately.

The cable that you need to use has two different kinds of connectors: a smaller end that's known as a 4-pin connector and a larger one on the other side that's known as a 6-pin connector (see Figure 5.1).

FIGURE 5.1

The smaller, 4-pin connector (left) is the kind most often found on camcorders, and the larger 6-pin connector (right) is most often found on computers. This small-to-large cable is the kind used to connect a camera to a computer, whereas a large-to-large cable (6-pin to 6-pin) is used to connect computers to external hard drives and so forth.

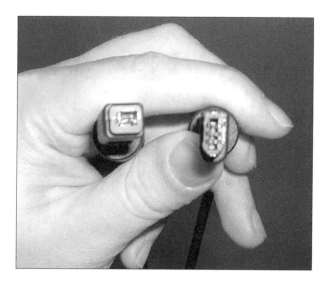

Understanding the FireWire Connections

Your Mac has one or more of the larger 6-pin FireWire connections. If you haven't tried it yet, you can connect a wide variety of devices to your Mac through the FireWire connection including devices like Web cams and additional hard drive storage, such as the unit in Figure 5.2, which is produced by all4DVD (www.all4dvd.com).

On your Mac, the FireWire connection is similar to the connection on the back of your stereo or VCR. The connector on the cable is *male*, while the connector on the computer is *female*. (The male connector on the end of the cable is inserted into the female connector on your Mac.)

FIGURE 5.2

A typical external FireWire hard drive, suitable for video storage (120GB model from www.all4DVD.com).

5

If you take a look at the hard drive in Figure 5.2, you'll notice that a FireWire cable is connected into a port at the top of the drive, but there's still a port open below that one. One of the nice things about FireWire is that you can connect a series of devices.

If you seem to be running out of hard drive space on your Mac, an external FireWire hard drive can be a convenient way to *store* your iMovies. But you need to *capture* video to the hard drive *inside* your Mac. iMovie is not set up so that it can capture video to hard drives outside the computer. Therefore, in order to get the most available free space inside your computer for capturing iMovies, when you are done with a project, you can copy it to an external hard drive. (You can also copy it to the external hard drive immediately after capturing the video, and work with it on the external hard drive. Since iMovie creates a copy of video clips when you make adjustments to them, it may be advantageous to work with the iMovie project where you have the most space.)

After you connect the FireWire cable to your computer, you can connect the other, smaller end into the camcorder. The location of the FireWire port on a camcorder varies, but it's usually located behind some kind of protective cover. Figure 5.3 shows the smaller 4-pin end of a FireWire cable and the corresponding port on a digital camcorder.

FIGURE 5.3

Getting ready to plug the smaller end of the FireWire cable into a camcorder.

Task: Connecting Your Camcorder

In this section we are going to go through the process of how you set up iMovie and connect a camcorder so that you can capture video.

1. Open iMovie and choose File, New Project to create a new project.

2. Click the Camera/Edit Mode switch to switch to the camera (DV) mode (see Figure 5.4).

When you plug in most cameras on your Mac, iMovie will automatically switch to Camera Mode, but you can always use the switch mentioned previously if it doesn't happen.

FIGURE 5.4

Switching to Camera (DV) Mode.

3. Turn on the camera, and insert the smaller (4-pin) end into the FireWire connector on the camcorder as shown in Figure 5.5. (Insert a tape that you've recorded video on into the camcorder if you haven't already.)

FIGURE 5.5

Plugging FireWire cable into the camcorder.

5

4. Insert the larger (6-pin) end into the FireWire connection on your Mac as shown in Figure 5.6.

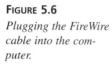

Figure 5.6
Plugging the FireWire cable into the computer.

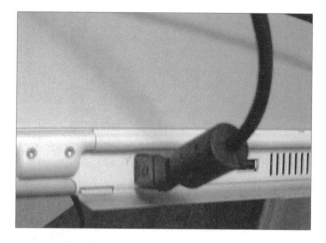

After you've connected your camera, iMovie displays a message confirming that your camera is connected, as shown in Figure 5.7.

Figure 5.7
iMovie confirms when a camcorder is turned on and plugged in.

It's easy to record video to a tape and then forget to rewind it—so you might put the tape in your camcorder and press Play to preview it, but not see anything or see a blank blue screen! The material is still there, earlier on your videotape; you just have to rewind to get to it. The only ways you can actually erase video from a digital videotape are to record over it or subject the tape to strong magnetic fields. For the latter, consult "Task: Subjecting Your Tape to Strong Magnetic Fields." Just kidding.

Working with Video

If you're new to working with digital video on your Mac, all you really need to keep in mind is that you're using your camera and your computer like they were a TV and a VCR.

In essence, iMovie becomes your computer VCR, but instead of recording a program from the television, iMovie records video from your camcorder, and that's what capturing video is all about.

Understanding Cueing: Play, Stop, Fast Forward, Rewind

When working with video on your Mac, you use familiar controls to capture and access your video, such as play, stop, fast forward, and rewind.

When you want to capture video, one of the things that you need to do is find a spot in your video where you want to start capturing, and that's where cueing comes into play. Depending on where you left off in the tape, when you use your camcorder to record your video, you might need to play, rewind, and so on to position and review your footage.

A camcorder is essentially like a miniature portable VCR. And just like a VCR, it has typical controls for moving through a tape (see Figure 5.8).

FIGURE 5.8

The play controls on a camcorder, also known as transport controls.

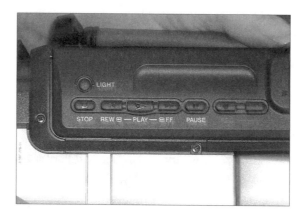

This positioning can be done with the camera itself, by looking at its miniature screen. But one of the most enjoyable things about working with digital video through FireWire is that you can control your camera using buttons in the iMovie screen. So, when you connect your camera, you don't necessarily have to use the buttons on the camera itself.

When connected through FireWire, iMovie can actually control the camera, so you can use the Play/Fast Forward/Rewind buttons (see Figure 5.9) right in iMovie to go through your tape.

Figure 5.9

The play controls in iMovie.

Task: Finding a Spot on Your Videotape Using iMovie

Assuming that you performed the task "Connecting your Camcorder" earlier, follow these steps:

1. Click the Rewind button to rewind the tape (see Figure 5.10).

Figure 5.10

The Rewind button.

2. Click the Play button (see Figure 5.11) to begin playing your video.

> You might need to adjust the sound on your computer.

Figure 5.11

The Play button.

3. While the video is playing, try clicking the Fast Forward button (see Figure 5.12) to fast forward through the video while you're watching it. Click again to stop the tape.

Figure 5.12

The Fast Forward button.

▼ 4. If your video is still playing, click the Stop button (see Figure 5.13), and then click either the Fast Forward or Rewind button. This method of moving through a tape is faster, but you can't see the video moving by.

FIGURE 5.13
The Stop button.

▲ 5. Using the play controls, find a spot in your videotape that you want to start capturing at.

There's no official term for fast-forwarding or rewinding from a complete stop. But if you're new to video, you could think of it as *step starting*, where the tape isn't moving and you have to take a step in a particular direction (backward or forward) to get things going. Step starting is the fastest way to get to a certain point on your tape. In contrast, watching footage going by when you're fast-forwarding or rewinding could be thought of as *play previewing*. In other words, you press the Play button, and then press Fast Forward or Rewind. The disadvantage is that things go slower, but you can see exactly what's going on.

Wear and Tear: The internal parts in a digital camcorder are sturdy, and designed for regular use, but you can extend the life of the camera by using other devices to preview your video when possible. For example, you may want to make a VHS tape of your footage after you shoot it, and view it on the television, marking down spots where you want to capture—this also is a nice way of coming up with ideas. There's nothing wrong with doing this same previewing by hooking your camcorder up to the TV, but over the life of the camera, it can be nice to cut down on the wear and tear. Chances are that your camcorder cost five times as much as the VCR, so that's another way to look at it.

It can sometimes be helpful to start just a little before where you want to start capturing video so that you can make a fine adjustment to the starting point of your video clip in iMovie. For example, if you have footage of a short clip and you want to capture the entire thing, you can start a little bit before the action in your short scene begins. Perhaps the footage includes someone jumping off a diving board—you could position the tape a second or two before the jump so that when you capture the video, you can fine-tune exactly when the clip starts so that you don't miss anything.

5

Capturing Video

When you capture video, one of the nice things that iMovie can do is separate your clips for you. After you shoot video with your camcorder, wherever you pressed Stop and then started shooting a new clip, iMovie is able to separate the clips automatically.

For example, in Figure 5.14, you see two separate clips that were automatically created by iMovie. When this video was shot, the camera ran for about 15 seconds, and then the recording was stopped, and the next thing on the tape was a different scene that's about 5 minutes long.

FIGURE 5.14

iMovie brings in separate clips whenever it encounters a break between scenes.

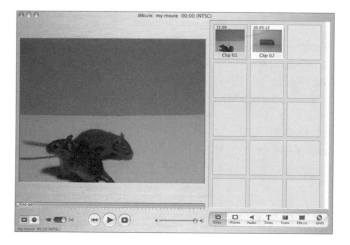

Task: Capturing Video from Your Camcorder

After you've completed the two previous tasks (connecting your camcorder and finding a spot in your tape to start recording), follow these steps:

1. Open iMovie and start a new project.

2. Switch the Camera/Edit Mode switch to the Camera position (DV). See Figure 5.15.

FIGURE 5.15

Switching to Camera mode to connect with the camera.

3. Click the Import button to start importing footage. (Refer to Figure 5.7.)

4. When you've captured your video, click the Stop button.

▲

5. Now click the Camera/Edit Mode switch (see Figure 5.16) and drag it to the right to switch back to Movie mode so that you can begin to work with your clips.

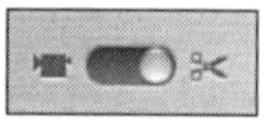

FIGURE 5.16

The Camera/Edit mode button back in Edit Mode position.

One thing to keep in mind when capturing video is that you must keep an eye on the amount of space available on your hard drive. A common technique is to capture more footage than you think you'll use, and then as you're editing your iMovies, you can delete clips you don't need, which frees up space. Another thing to consider if you're planning to export your iMovies to use in an iDVD project (see Hour 7, "Exporting iMovies") is that when you export the file, you need just as much space as your project is taking up—in other words, when you export for iDVD, you need more space.

So, when you get hooked on iMovie (not *if*, but *when*—it's inevitable), you'll probably need to start thinking about ways of backing up your projects or expanding the amount of hard drive space you have available. One option is to obtain an external FireWire hard drive. Another option is to store projects on individual DVD discs as data. In other words, instead of burning an iDVD project, you burn all your files to a blank DVD disc so that you can free up hard drive space (see official Web site).

At the time of writing, FireWire hard drives range anywhere from 10 gigabytes to 120 or even 160 gigabytes of storage space, and current iMacs are shipping with 40-80 gigabytes of internal storage. Because of the way iMovie needs to capture video to an internal hard drive, if you have an iMac with space for only one internal hard drive, one option to consider is to go to an Apple authorized reseller in your area and make arrangements to swap out the hard drive in your computer and put it in an external case, and put a bigger hard drive inside the computer, so that you can still use your older hard drive, but have more space for capturing video.

5

Summary

In this hour, you learned how to get video into your Mac through the process of capturing it using the FireWire interface. Thanks to Apple, FireWire technology has become the standard way to work with digital video around the world.

In the next hour, we'll take a look at where most of the fun happens in iMovie, when you begin to combine and adjust clips at the stage of basic video editing. When you start making these creative decisions about editing, your movie begins to take shape, and this will probably be one of the most enjoyable things about working with iMovie.

Workshop

The Workshop consists of quiz questions and answers to help you to develop a sense of issues that can come up when capturing video. First, try to answer the questions, *before* checking the answers. Then you'll want to read the explanations, even if you get the answers right. Reading through this section will help to paint a clearer picture in your mind with digital video.

Q&A

Q I have a camcorder, but it's not digital and it doesn't seem to have a FireWire connector. How do I hook it up to my Mac so that I can capture video using iMovie?

A To do this, you must purchase an accessory for your Mac that enables you to hook up what's known as an *analog source*. The equipment you need is known as an *analog-to-digital converter*. Practically speaking, it means you have the ability to capture video from nondigital cameras and other devices. An example of this type of device is the Hollywood DV-Bridge from Dazzle Multimedia, (www.dazzle.com), which enables you to plug in an older camera, a TV, VCR, or other source to the DV-Bridge, and the DV-Bridge plugs in to the FireWire port on your iMac. For more information see the official book site.

Q Are all digital camcorders compatible with iMovie?

A Most digital camcorders are compatible with iMovie. For a list of compatible cameras, go to http://www.apple.com/imovie/compatibility.html.

Quiz

1. To capture video, which position should the mode button at the bottom corner of the iMovie window be set to?

    A. Camera mode

    B. Edit mode

    C. A and B

2. Which button do you click in the iMovie window to start capturing video?

   A. The Capture button

   B. The Import button

   C. The Record button

3. How can you tell how much free space you have left when working on a movie?

   A. By choosing Project, Free Space

   B. By looking at the Disk Gauge underneath where the clips are stored in iMovie

   C. By calling Apple customer service

Quiz Answers

1. **A.** Switching to Camera mode tells iMovie to try to connect to your camcorder through the FireWire cable.

2. **B.** When you're ready to start capturing and if your tape is at the spot that you want to begin the capture, you can simply click the Import button. You can also start the tape playing, and click Import right before the spot you want to start capturing from.

3. **B.** The Disk Gauge is a convenient way of keeping track of how much space you have. If you're trying to figure out how gigabytes or megabytes translate into actual minutes of available capture time, you can roughly figure on digital video taking up about 10MB a second, which is about 600MB a minute, or about .6 GB/min (1GB = 1,000MB).

Exercises

If you have video to import from a camera, follow the steps outlined in this chapter to import it. Remember, you can import it as several short clips by pausing the import.

5

Hour 6

Basic Video Editing with iMovie

In this hour, we investigate how to edit video with iMovie by trying out some of the tools that iMovie gives you for making adjustments to video clips.

If you haven't yet tried playing with video clips in iMovie, you'll quickly discover how much fun it can be. iMovie gives you the power to make good-looking movies without a lot of confusing or intimidating options. One of the ways that iMovie accomplishes this is by providing a collection of commonly desired features you can add to movies. Those features are the elements that many people want to add, such as titles, effects, and transitions.

On your way toward adding all the flashy stuff, the fun starts in what's known as basic video editing. Don't worry if you haven't done anything more than use the controls on your VCR to *watch* a movie. Now, with iMovie, video editing is easy enough for anyone to *make* his own movie.

Throughout this hour, we discuss the following:

- Adjusting clips
- Adding and deleting clips
- Restoring a clip

Adding and Deleting Clips

If you're new to digital video, you can think of iMovie as a word processor for video. In a word processing program, you initially type in a lot of words, forming your sentences and paragraphs, but no one is a perfect writer *<cough>*, so you eventually end up going back to what you've typed to spruce things up a bit. Similarly, you might take a video camera out and shoot some scenes for a short movie you're working on and then capture all of your footage into iMovie, but it's very likely that you'll want to make some adjustments and that's where basic video editing comes in.

Task: Adding Clips to the Timeline

To start adjusting your video (now it's time to graduate to thinking of this adjustment as *video editing*), you must add clips to the Timeline. The Timeline view is simply a way of looking at movies over time so that you can easily pick spots in your movie to make adjustments.

1. Open a new or existing iMovie project with video clips in it, and click the Clips button in the iMovie window so that you can see the clips that you have to work with. Those clips are located in the shelf. You might also need to click the Timeline tab so that your screen looks something like Figure 6.1.

2. Click one of the clips. While holding the mouse button down, drag the clip down into the top row of Timeline. You'll know you've reached the right place in the iMovie window when you see a small plus sign appear next to your cursor (see Figure 6.1).

3. Drop the clip in the Timeline by letting go of the mouse button.

    Figure 6.2 shows how a clip looks after it has been dragged into the Timeline.

    Now it's time to add another clip to the Timeline.

4. Click another clip and drag it on top of the preview frame of the first clip that you dragged into the Timeline, as shown in Figures 6.3 and 6.4. Remember, you need to release the clip when the small plus sign appears next to your cursor; otherwise, the clip remains in the shelf.

FIGURE 6.1

Adding clip 03 to the Timeline using a drag-and-drop technique.

FIGURE 6.2

Clip 03 has been transferred to the Timeline and now shows up on the iMovie Monitor window.

6

FIGURE 6.3

Dragging clip 04 to the Timeline.

FIGURE 6.4

A second clip has been added to the Timeline.

Congratulations—you've successfully performed a basic video editing task!

If you're still a bit confused about what's going on, consider our word processing analogy for iMovie and think of the video editing task you just performed as if you were doing it in AppleWorks or Microsoft Word (see Table 6.1). This might help you to see how simple video editing can be in a program such as iMovie when you realize that the adjustments you're making—such as adding two video clips to the Timeline—are pretty straightforward. Video editing has some similarities to writing on a computer. Putting two video clips together in iMovie is kind of like combining paragraphs in a word processor.

TABLE 6.1   Comparison of Editing Video and Writing Text

Two sentences, as if they were separate video clips:	Two sentences, now in a paragraph, as if they were separate video clips that have been added to the Timeline:
In scene one, the gerbils are frisky and running around.	In scene one, the gerbils are frisky and running around. In scene two, the gerbils are looking for some sunflower seeds.
In scene two, the gerbils are looking for some sunflower seeds.	

Task: Deleting a Clip from the Timeline

One thing you might find yourself wanting to do is to delete a clip from the Timeline. You might want to delete a clip because you've decided you no longer want it in your movie, or as a result of splitting video clips (a helpful task that you learn about later in this hour).

One thing to keep in mind when you're about to delete a video clip is that it won't go back into the shelf that you originally dragged it from. If you want to return a clip to the shelf that you just dragged into the Timeline and use it later, try choosing Edit, Undo instead. This backs you up a step. To return a clip to the shelf after you've made other changes to your project, switch out of the Timeline into the Clip view and drag the clip into an empty space on the shelf.

1. Click directly on a clip in the Timeline to select it. A clip changes to a blue color when you select it (see Figure 6.5). If you want to deselect a clip, you can simply click underneath a clip somewhere else on the Timeline.

FIGURE 6.5
Selecting a clip.

2. Choose Clear from the Edit menu to delete the clip that had been selected (see Figure 6.6).

FIGURE 6.6
The final movie without the deleted clip.

Task: Deleting a Clip from the Shelf

One of the more common tasks in basic video editing is deleting unwanted video footage. Doing so is very easy in iMovie:

1. Click on a clip in the shelf to select it (see Figure 6.7).

FIGURE 6.7
Use your cursor to select the clip to be deleted (clip 03).

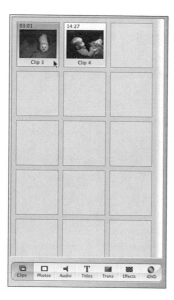

6

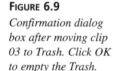 2. Either drag the clip into the Trash until the Trash well darkens or select Clear from the Edit menu. Figure 6.8 shows the shelf after the unwanted clip has been deleted.

FIGURE 6.8

The remaining shelf contains only clip 04.

You'll probably want to get into the habit of emptying the Trash after you've deleted a clip, or at regular intervals, so that you can keep the maximum amount of hard drive space available to work on your movie.

3. Choose File, Empty Trash to empty the Trash.

4. Click OK in the Confirm dialog box that comes up (see Figure 6.9). Then see how much space you have freed up by checking the free space indicator shown in Figure 6.10.

FIGURE 6.9

Confirmation dialog box after moving clip 03 to Trash. Click OK to empty the Trash.

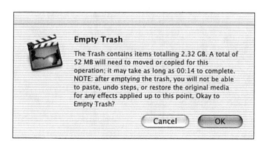

Empty Trash

The Trash contains items totalling 2.32 GB. A total of 52 MB will need to moved or copied for this operation; it may take as long as 00:14 to complete. NOTE: after emptying the trash, you will not be able to paste, undo steps, or restore the original media for any effects applied up to this point. Okay to Empty Trash?

Cancel   OK

Adjusting Clips

When you're working on iMovie projects, you'll probably develop a style of working
with clips that's most comfortable to you.

For example, some people like to preview and rename every clip that's been captured
before they ever drag anything into the Timeline to put the clips together. You could think
of this style as *clip editing*, where special attention is given to individual clips before
combining them.

Other people simply want to start dragging clips into the Timeline view and making
adjustments there. This style could be thought of as *Timeline editing*.

Both styles work just fine, although you'll eventually have to drag the clips to the
Timeline to put your iMovie together.

One of the basics of video editing is the process of *trimming* clips, which consists of
removing unwanted footage from what you've captured. In essence, when you capture
video, you might want to change where a clip begins and ends. In iMovie, you can simply go to a spot in a clip, and delete everything before that spot so that you end up with a
new start point for the clip. This is easy to do in either the shelf or the Timeline view.

Task: Adjusting a Clip in the Shelf

After you've captured video, the first thing that you must do is to acquaint yourself with
the clips you've captured to get an idea of what you have to work with. Playing with
clips in the shelf is a good way to accomplish this.

1. Select a clip in the shelf by clicking it; the selected clip turns blue.

2. Move the mouse over the text in the clip and click. The area behind the text turns
   white and you can type a new name in for the clip (see Figure 6.11).

> Another way to see the clip name is to double-click a clip in the shelf, which
> brings up the Clip Info dialog box.

▼ **TASK**

6

▼

FIGURE **6.11**
Renaming a clip: 1) select a clip; 2) click on its name; 3) replace the sample text with new text.

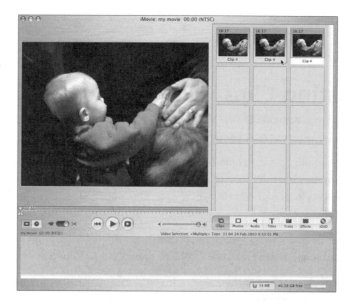

3. Click the playhead in the Monitor window (see Figure 6.12) and drag it to the left and the right to preview the clip.

4. Choose a spot that you want to be the new beginning of the clip.

FIGURE **6.12**
Positioning the play-head in the Monitor.

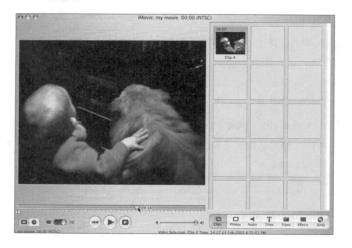

▼ 5. Choose Edit, Split Clip to split the clip into two pieces (see Figure 6.13).

FIGURE 6.13

The clip is now split, and the second clip begins at the point selected in Figure 6.12.

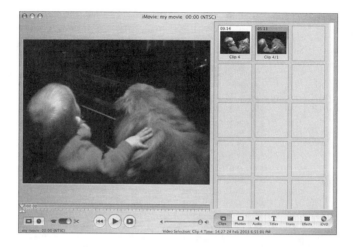

6. If you want to remove the first portion of the clip you split into two pieces, either drag the unwanted clip into the Trash or select the clip in the shelf and choose Clear from the Edit menu (see Figure 6.14).

FIGURE 6.14

The remaining footage, in the adjusted clip.

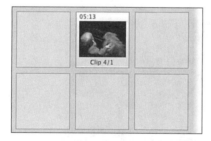

Task: Adjusting a Clip in the Timeline

▼TASK

If you take the clips directly to the Timeline as soon as you capture them, you can make adjustments there just as easily as in the shelf:

1. Click on a clip in the shelf. Drag it down and to the left into the Timeline until a small plus sign appears near your cursor (see Figure 6.15).

2. Click on the playhead in the Timeline, and drag it to a desired spot in the clip (see Figure 6.16).

6

▼

FIGURE 6.15
Dragging Clip 4 into the Timeline.

FIGURE 6.16
The blue triangle pointing downward to the timeline is the playhead. Click and drag it to select the point where you want to split your clip.

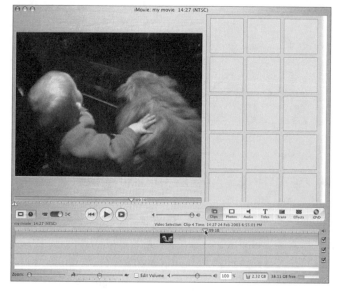

3. Choose Edit, Split Video Clip at Playhead.

When the clip is split into two parts, you might want to delete either everything before this point or everything after (see Figure 6.17).

▼

FIGURE 6.17

*The playhead is posi-
tioned between the two
clips after splitting,
and both are selected.*

4. Click somewhere on the Timeline underneath the clips to deselect them, as shown
   in Figure 6.18.

FIGURE 6.18

*Click underneath the
clips to deselect them.*

5. Select the clip you want to delete by clicking it.

6. Choose Clear from the Edit menu to remove the unwanted clip, as shown in Figure
   6.19. This leaves the other clip in the Timeline (see Figure 6.20).

FIGURE 6.19

Deleting a clip.

6

FIGURE 6.20

*The remaining clip
with a new starting
point.*

Task: Restoring Clip Media

No video editor is perfect, and sooner or later you'll decide that you want to start over again when adjusting clips. One way to back up is to go through a repeated series of undo steps by pressing Ctrl+Z on your keyboard or choosing Edit, Undo.

Another way is to use the Restore Clip option, which enables you to start over again by bringing clips back to their original state.

> You can restore split clips only to the condition they were in up until the last time you emptied the trash, so be careful to save or clean up only after you're happy with your edits.

For example, you might have recorded a friend talking at great length about an important topic, and toward the end of her monologue, she realizes that another friend has been standing behind her doing a strikingly realistic impression. So, you capture the video clip and make a few adjustments, but accidentally trim the clip too close to the humorous scene at the end. You want to start over again, but aren't sure how. iMovie to the rescue!

1. Click one of the clips in the Timeline that you made by splitting the original clip.

2. Choose Advanced, Restore Clip as shown in Figure 6.21.

▲ 3. Click OK in the dialog box that appears to restore the original clip (see Figure 6.22).

Figure 6.23 shows the clip in its restored state.

> Restoring a clip won't merge the pieces of the original clip back together. If you split a clip and then restore one of the pieces, the restored clip will contain some of the same footage as the unrestored clip.

FIGURE 6.21

*A clip in the Timeline
view.*

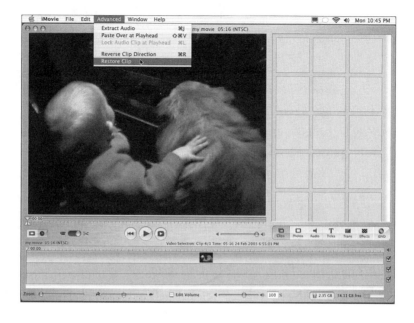

FIGURE 6.22

*iMovie asks whether
you want to restore the
modified clip to its
original state.*

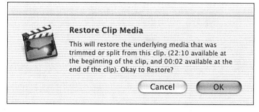

FIGURE 6.23

*The restored clip at its
original length,
unedited and uncut.*

6

Task: Checking the Size of an iMovie Project

Just about the time you start getting hooked on iMovie, you might realize that your Mac
doesn't have an endless amount of storage space on the hard drive, and you need to think
a bit more about how much space your projects are taking up.

Chances are that you'll have enough space on your hard drive to work on a few projects
at the same time, unless you're working on full-length movies from day one. When
you're done and have exported your iMovies to tape or iDVD, you can burn the raw files
in your iDVD project folder to CD or DVD or move them to an external hard drive.

▼ Whichever way you go, it can be helpful to learn how to see how much space your project is taking up. It's good to keep an eye on things so that you can decide when you have to delete your collection of accumulated media files (the video clips, animations, video games, and MP3 audio files that you've downloaded from the Internet for purely educational reasons as a part of your ongoing studies in sociology).

1. Locate the folder with your iMovies—when you created a new iMovie project, you named it something.

2. Select the folder and choose Get Info from the File menu, as shown in Figure 6.24. A window will appear.

In Mac OS X, this folder is probably in the Movies folder within your home folder.

FIGURE 6.24

Getting information about your movie.

The Get info window gives you a variety of information, including the size of your folder (see Figure 6.25).

▲

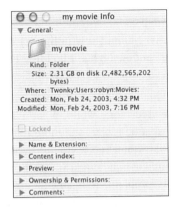

FIGURE 6.25

The Info window shows you how much space your project takes up on the hard drive.

Summary

In this hour, you learned about some introductory, basic video editing tasks, such as adding clips to the Timeline, making adjustments, and deciding to do it all over again to make it perfect. That's what it's all about!

In the next hour, we'll consider what you can do with an iMovie after you make it and as you recover from the initial surprise of how much fun it is, and realize suddenly that you need to share your iMovie with the world. You can share it on the Internet, on CD, on Video CD, on DVD, and more!

These basic tasks provide a foundation for having fun, but they should be performed very carefully. You might already have started losing sleep, shunning civic responsibilities, and eating more bananas (potassium for the brain)—all toward the end of fun.

Workshop

The Workshop consists of quiz questions and answers to help you to develop a better grasp of the landscape of digital video you've been traveling through this hour. First, try to answer the questions, *before* checking the answers. And you'll probably want to read the explanations, even if you get the answers right, because they'll help you have the kind of confidence that you'll certainly enjoy.

6

Q&A

Q **I'm getting tired of fast forwarding and rewinding my camcorder to put it in exactly the right position to input each clip. I feel like I'm editing on the camera. Are there any other options?**

A One thing you can do is to rewind your tape to the beginning, click the Import button, and let iMovie capture the video for a while. When you start using the playhead more, you'll see that it might be easier (and more fun) to look through your video after it's captured. iMovie automatically creates suggested clips based on whenever you stopped and started the camera again while recording, but even if you shot continuously, it's not a problem. You can take the one long clip in iMovie and split it into a number of smaller clips with the Split Video Clip at Playhead command.

Q **I left the camcorder running while I was capturing video, and got distracted in the other room watching *Wallace and Gromit* videos. But when I came back, iMovie had stopped capturing at 9 minutes and 28 seconds for no reason and started another clip. What can I do?**

A You're probably running into the 2GB capture limit for iMovie. iMovie won't capture continuously for longer than 2GB worth of video. Your only real option is to drag the clips into the Timeline and piece them together—iMovie does a pretty good job of rejoining clips.

Quiz

1. How do you get a video clip to show up in the Monitor in iMovie?

    A. Click on it in the Clip window

    B. Click on it in the Timeline

    C. A and B

2. Why is Bill Gates spending so much time at home these days?

    A. Working on a new business plan

    B. Playing secretly with iMovie on his new iMac

    C. Making the switch (`www.apple.com/switch`)

    D. Playing DOOM over the Internet with Steve Jobs, cofounder of Apple Computer

    E. All of the above

3. Why is Steve Jobs spending so much time at home these days?

    A. Working on a new business plan

    B. Playing secretly with iMovie on his new iMac

    C. Watching the *Pirates of Silicon Valley* over and over

    D. Playing DOOM over the Internet with Bill Gates, cofounder of Microsoft

    E. All of the above

4. How do you restore a clip after you've trimmed it?

    A. Choose Clip, Restore

    B. Click on the Clip Restore button

    C. Choose Advanced, Restore Clip Media

Quiz Answers

1. **C.** Any time you select a clip, it shows up in the Monitor window in iMovie (unless you forgot to take the lens cap off, in which case you won't be able to tell).

2. **E.** Bill Gates is actually a nice guy. He has a nice foundation called the Gates Library Foundation (www.glf.org). Little does he know that GLF also stands for Gerbil Liberation Front, but if he read this book, he would find mention of it in Hour 21, "Example Project—Multiple Screens."

3. **E.** Steve Jobs is one of my heroes, along with Steve Wozniak. Thanks to their persistence and unique vision, and the people they drew together in California and around the world, we have programs like iMovie. Thanks Steve.

4. **C.** It's great that you can play and not worry if you need to go back and change something.

Exercises

1. Give meaningful labels to any clips you've imported.

2. Practice splitting clips at the playhead as described earlier. If you don't like the result, remember that you can either undo a recent action or choose Restore Clip from the Advanced menu.

6

HOUR 7

Exporting iMovies

In this hour, you take a look at what you can do with your movies after you complete them—prepare them for email, Web, and disc delivery. You look behind the scenes at how you can export in different directions, and take a brief look at how an iMovie can be delivered with programs such as AOL (for emailing), Roxio's Toast (for CD-ROM and Video CD), and PlayStream's Content Manager (for putting iMovies on the Web). We'll also look at exporting your iMovies to iDVD for delivery via DVD.

When your iMovie is edited and ready to share, there are two ways that you can deliver it. Each method can be easily accessed from iMovie. You can deliver your iMovie using either tape (using a camera) or a file (when you'll be delivering by email, the Web, or disc such as CD or DVD).

When you're going back out to tape, some of the main considerations are how much time you have left on the tape and how long your iMovie is. But you'll generally want to put your iMovie at the beginning of the videotape so that it's easy to get to.

When you want to share an iMovie as a file, the file size could be more of a consideration. When you share an iMovie through email, the Web, or on disc (CD/DVD), each method of delivery results in a file that has a particular amount of compression. To get an appropriate file size that fits the delivery method, iMovie has to squeeze the file. So, you might notice a considerable difference in the image quality between what you see in iMovie and what you see when you send the file.

As with some other aspects of iMovie, you can take its advice, and when you choose a way to share your iMovie, you can accept the suggested compression settings that Apple engineers have calculated as the appropriate settings for typical situations. Doing so makes it easy to take your iMovie in a number of different directions. (You can also use the Expert settings that were mentioned in Hour 1, "Understanding Digital Video" to accomplish advanced adjustment of your iMovie.)

Throughout this hour, we discuss the following topics:

- Sharing your iMovie
- Exporting to different formats
- Making videotapes from iMovie
- Putting iMovies on the Web
- Burning iMovies to CD
- Putting iMovies on DVD

Choosing a Way to Share Your iMovie

When you're ready to export your iMovie, simply choose File, Export Movie from iMovie's menu bar. Then choose one of three options in the Export Movie dialog box: To Camera, To QuickTime, or To iDVD.

Exporting to Camera

When you export to camera, you're connecting the same camcorder that you used to capture your video, and are sending the finished iMovie back out to Mini-DV or Digital-8 tape. From there, you can watch the finished product by connecting the camera to the television, recording from the camera to your VCR, or sending the tape off to have a number of copies duplicated.

Exporting to QuickTime

When you export to QuickTime, the method you choose to share your iMovie results in a particular kind of file, based on the settings that are chosen and iMovie uses to conform the file to a particular format. For example, when you export an iMovie that you want to email to someone, it creates a relatively small file because it has to travel over the Internet and you don't want the person on the other end to have to wait too long to download the attachment. Or, when you want to burn a CD with an iMovie, the CD can hold a much larger file than an email could handle, so the movie quality is much better, but still not as good as the original iMovie.

Exporting to iDVD

Film clips imported into the current version of iMovie are compatible with iDVD, so while you can choose the option in the Export dialog box, you can just as easily drag the video clips into iDVD.

Besides exporting to iDVD from the Export dialog box, there's an iDVD palette that lets you add chapters to your movie in iMovie and then create an iDVD project from within iMovie. We'll talk about how later on in the hour.

Making Videotapes from iMovie

To view an iMovie on television from a tape, the first step is to export the movie to your camcorder. Then you can either connect your camcorder to your television, or make a VHS tape from your digital tape (Mini-DV or Digital-8).

Task: Exporting to Camera

When you've finished your iMovie and are ready to take it to the next level, exporting to a camcorder will allow you to display it on the television. With a few simple steps, you can make the video ready to share in a one-time event, where you play the video only from the camera. Or, after you have exported the video from iMovie to your camcorder, you can then go on to make a tape from there.

1. Load a blank tape into your camcorder and turn it on. (Make sure that you aren't about to record over something you want. Keep a pen around just for labeling tapes—and label those tapes!)

2. Connect your digital camcorder to your computer with a FireWire cable.

3. In iMovie, choose File, Export Movie, and choose Export to Camera from the Export pop-up menu. See Figure 7.1.

4. Click Export.

7

Figure 7.1

Exporting an iMovie to a camera.

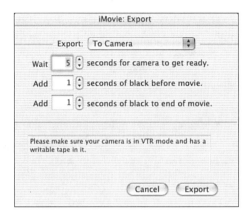

If you want to make VHS copies of the digital tape that you just made, you can connect your camcorder to your VCR using standard RCA cabling, where you connect a series of cables to the Video Out and Audio Out jacks of your camera. The video connector is usually indicated by a yellow color. Two cables carry the audio, where each cable carries half of a stereo signal (the left audio channel is the white connector; the right audio channel is the red connector). See Figure 7.2.

Figure 7.2

The Video/Audio Out connectors on a typical camcorder.

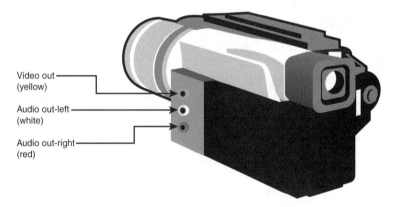

Then you connect the cables to the Video In and Audio In jacks of your VCR. See Figure 7.3.

FIGURE 7.3

The Video/Audio In connectors on the back of a typical VCR.

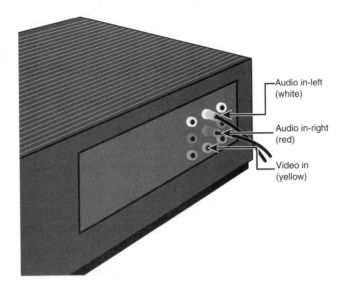

Audio in-left
(white)

Audio in-right
(red)

Video in
(yellow)

Emailing iMovies

When you want to email an iMovie, you export it from iMovie and save it to your hard drive. Then you connect to the Internet and use your email program to attach the iMovie file to an email. If you've never emailed an attachment before, keep in mind that it can take a few minutes for the attachment to upload, depending on whether you are using a 56K modem or a higher-speed DSL or cable modem connection.

Another thing to keep in mind is that it will probably help you to choose a special name for the email version of your iMovie, such as my movie-email. Save it in a place that you can easily find on your hard drive, so that when it comes time to send it via email, you know which file to send and right where it is. (What you *don't* want to do is try to send your original iMovie via email. It'll be several hundred megabytes large, and would probably take a few weeks to send via modem.)

Task: Exporting to Email

You don't have to do any special preparation of your iMovie to send it via email—that's what the Export function is for: to save it in a format that can be emailed.

1. Choose File, Export, and then choose To QuickTime from the Export pop-up menu.

2. Choose Email in the Formats pop-up menu. (See Figure 7.4.)

7

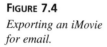

FIGURE 7.4

Exporting an iMovie for email.

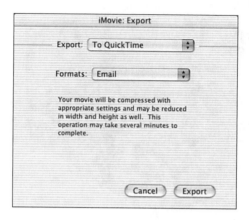

3. Click Export and save your iMovie to a spot on your hard drive.

4. Open the program that you use to send email (such as America Online).

5. Compose a new email and click the appropriate button to add an attachment to the email. (In AOL for OS X, you click on the Attachments tab, and then click Attach.)

6. Locate the iMovie that you want to send by email and attach it to your email. (AOL: Find the file and click Enclose.) See Figure 7.5.

FIGURE 7.5

Attaching an iMovie to an email in AOL.

Figure 7.6 shows the iMovie attached to the email.

7. Connect to the Internet and send the email. See Figure 7.6. You don't necessarily have to connect to the Internet *before* you attach the email. You can compose an email and attach a file before connecting with many email clients, and then you send the email when you do connect.

Figure 7.6

Looking at an email that has an iMovie attached.

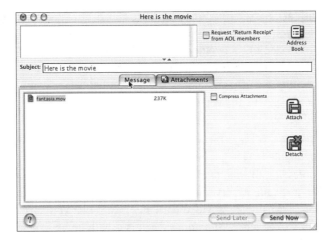

Some email programs have file size limitations. For example, at the time of writing, you probably can't send a file larger than 10 megabytes through AOL. (And it would take quite a long time to upload or download that large a file anyway if you're using a 56K modem.)

Putting iMovies on the Web

Putting iMovies on the Web is a bit more involved than putting them on tape or sending them via email, but taking the time to figure out how to do it can make for an ideal way of sharing your iMovies with people who are far away.

There are two ways that iMovie can save your movie for delivery on the Web: as a Web movie or a streaming Web movie. A Web movie is uploaded to a standard Web server and a streaming Web movie is uploaded to a streaming Web server.

Here are some terms and concepts that are helpful to consider; there are entire books and series of books that have been written about each item, but just starting to take a look at each can be helpful down the road when you start to put more things of your own up on the Internet.

- **Server:** A *server* is the name for the computer that's used as the central storage location for Web pages. When you create a Web page on your computer, you have to upload the files to a server. Then, when people view your Web page, the Internet basically functions as a network connection to the server computer. When people hit your Web page, all they're really doing is downloading a series of files (text, graphics, HTML, and so on) from this Web server (the same place that you uploaded the files) to their computer.

7

- **Standard server (for Web movies):** This is the most common type of server. When you put your Web page file on the server and a person clicks on the file, it's downloaded like any other file, and then the person double-clicks the file to view it. A standard server is basically any server that doesn't have QuickTime streaming capability. So, if you're not sure what kind of server you have and you don't know that it's specifically capable of streaming QuickTime, chances are that it's a standard server.

- **Streaming server (for streaming Web movies):** True streaming video is when you're able to watch a video without downloading the entire file. Streaming video enables you to watch video in *real time*, meaning that you establish a connection with a streaming server and watch the video as if it were a miniature television show. True streaming video basically means that you have a smoother, higher-quality experience. Streaming video is usually more expensive and more complicated to set up, but many companies and individuals find that the effort and expense is worth it. In addition to QuickTime, other forms of streaming video that you might recognize include RealMedia and Windows Media. All forms of streaming video require some kind of player application, such as QuickTime, to be present on a person's computer.

Keep in mind that even true streaming video is still dependent on how fast your connection is—video can be streamed on typical 56K modems for example, and the streaming version is smoother than a non-streaming version, but the quality is not as good as you would have on a higher-speed connection such as DSL.

Task: Exporting a Web Movie for Use on a Standard Web Server

You'll probably want to save your iMovies using the Web Movie option, unless you specifically know you'll be using the file on an official QuickTime streaming server. In the next section, we'll take a look at the streaming server as well as investigate an easy-to-use method of streaming video provided by PlayStream.

1. Choose File, Export, and then choose To QuickTime from the Export pop-up menu.

2. Choose the Web option in the Formats pop-up menu (see Figure 7.7).

3. Click Export and save your iMovie to a location on your hard drive from which you can then upload it to a Web server.

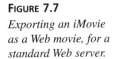

FIGURE 7.7

Exporting an iMovie as a Web movie, for a standard Web server.

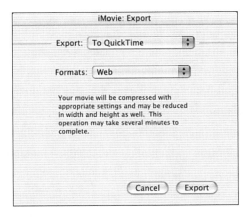

4. Using an FTP application or a Web page creation and upload program such as Dreamweaver, upload your file to your Web site. See Figure 7.8.

FIGURE 7.8

Uploading an iMovie to a Web site using Dreamweaver, a powerful and popular Web page creation tool.

5. Using a Web page creation tool, make a link to your iMovie, as shown in Figure 7.9. Here's some sample HTML link code:

```
Click<A HREF=http://www.psrecords.net/stdwebmovies/fantasia.mov>here</a>
to see Fantasia, a cat who thinks she's a kitten
```

Figure 7.10 shows the Web page with a linked iMovie playing on top.

Even though this isn't a true streaming server, QuickTime has the capability to play as much of the movie as you've downloaded. If you have a very fast connection, it can be almost as if it were a streaming clip.

When you are sharing your iMovies with people on a Web site, you might want to include instructions for people visiting your Web page to describe how they can actually download the file to their hard drive instead of

7

watching it on the Web page. Instruct Mac users to hold the Ctrl key down on their keyboard, click the movie link, and choose Save Link As or Download Link to Disk option. See Figure 7.11.

FIGURE 7.9

A sample Web page with simple links to the iMovies that we were uploading in Figure 7.8.

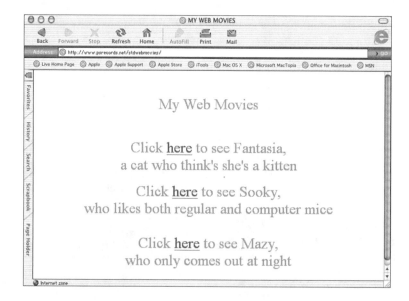

FIGURE 7.10

The iMovie plays when you click on the link.

FIGURE 7.11

Holding the Ctrl key down on a Mac while clicking on a link for an iMovie in Internet Explorer.

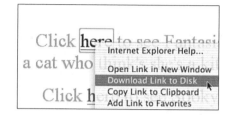

Instruct Windows users to right-click the link and choose the Save Target As option to save the file to disk. See Figure 7.12.

FIGURE 7.12

In Windows, right-clicking on the iMovie link in Internet Explorer.

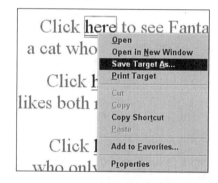

You might also want to instruct people that, in order to view your iMovie, they might need to download and install the latest version of QuickTime, which is a free download available from www.apple.com/quicktime/download.

Task: Exporting for Streaming Server

Exporting your iMovie as a streaming Web movie for use on a streaming server is similar to exporting your iMovie as a Web movie for use on a standard server.

1. Choose File, Export, and then choose To QuickTime from the Export pop-up menu.

2. Choose the Web Streaming option in the Formats pop-up menu. See Figure 7.13.

TASK

7

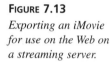

FIGURE 7.13

*Exporting an iMovie
for use on the Web on
a streaming server.*

3. Click the Export button and save your file on your hard drive in a location you can find later to upload to the streaming server. You might want to name the file so that you can easily distinguish it later as a streaming file, something like `my movie-streaming.mov`.

4. Use your FTP program or Web page creation and upload tool to upload the iMovie to the streaming server.

As mentioned earlier, setting up a QuickTime file for a streaming server can be more complex and might require some experimentation and research. At the minimum, you must set up a Web page account and address (`www.websitename.com`) with a host company that's capable of QuickTime streaming (example: `www.metric-hosting.com`).

But you might also want to investigate a company such as PlayStream, whose mission is to make the process of streaming video as easy as possible. PlayStream has special accounts that exist only to host streaming video. So, if you already have a Web page, you can put your video on a PlayStream account and link to it from your current Web page. Or you may simply want the increased quality of streaming video without the typical hassles, so a service like PlayStream might be a worthy option.

One reason PlayStream is nice is that it offers a free 15-day trial, and its accounts enable you to host the major three forms of streaming video—QuickTime video, Real Media, and Windows Media—so that you can reach the maximum audience. Preparing your video for the different formats can require downloading or purchasing additional software, but it might be worth it because most people usually either have the ability to view video encoded for the Real Player or Windows Media Player. For some people, it might actually be easier to try a service such as PlayStream and using full streaming video, rather than getting Web creation software and so on. PlayStream enables you to simply use your browser to upload files, and you don't even need your own Web page—when you upload files, you're given a link that you can email to people to get them directly to your video.

FIGURE 7.14

The PlayStream Web site,

www.playstream.com.

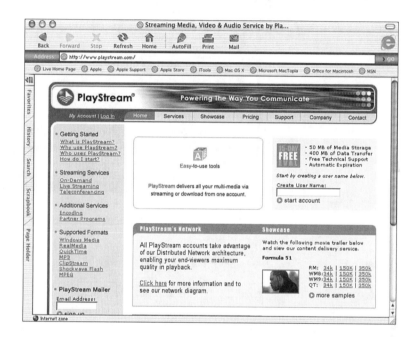

Task: Uploading a Streaming Web Movie iMovie for PlayStream

▼ TASK

If you want to try the PlayStream option, you can sign up for a free 15-day trial at www.playstream.com. It's a way of getting right into putting your iMovie on the Web without spending any money.

1. Go to www.playstream.com and log in, and then click on the Content Manager link.

2. Click the Browse button (as shown in Figure 7.15) to locate the streaming Web movie file you saved earlier to your hard drive.

3. Click the Upload File button in the Content Manager on the PlayStream Web page to upload the file to your space on PlayStream. A window pops up (see Figure 7.16) that gives you a progress indicator of the upload.

▼

7

▼

FIGURE 7.15

Using the Browse button right in the Web page to upload your video file—no special software required.

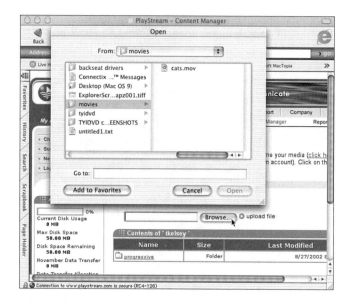

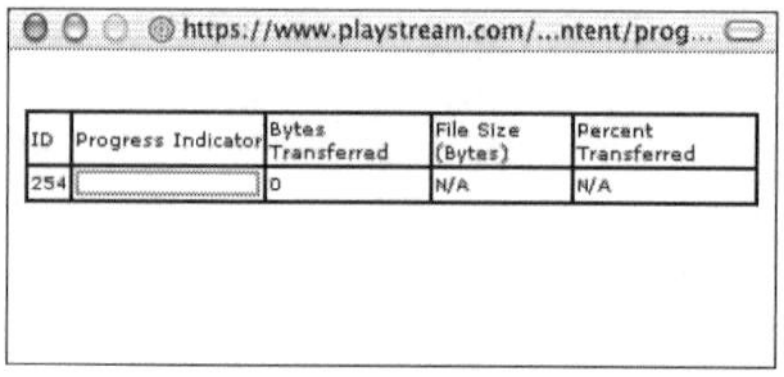

FIGURE 7.16

The Progress Indicator window showing the file being uploaded.

4. After the file is uploaded, select the text in the Stream Link field (see Figure 7.17) and copy the link into memory by going to the Edit menu at the top of the screen and choosing Copy.

FIGURE 7.17

An automatic link is generated that you can either email to someone, put in a Web page to link to your streaming Web movie, or simply save for later use and paste directly into a Web browser window to see the movie play.

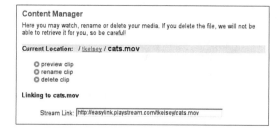

▼

5. Paste the link text somewhere you can get it later, such as in an email to yourself, a text document, and so on.

6. To allow access to the movie, insert the Stream Link text in an email, use it as a link on a Web page, or just paste it right in your Web browser.

You might want to include in your instructions that to see your iMovie, some people might have to download and install the free QuickTime software from www.apple.com/quicktime/download. Doing so installs a special plug-in file for the person's Web browser (Internet Explorer/Netscape/AOL) that enables them to view the streaming video file.

Burning iMovies to CD

If you have a CD burner and want to share your iMovies via CD, you can simply save as a CD-ROM movie, which generates a QuickTime movie file that you can then burn to CD. If a person is on a Mac, she can see the movie without installing special software. Many Windows PCs have QuickTime software installed, but if it's not on your recipient's computer, she can download and install it for free from www.apple.com/quicktime/download.

Another fun option for burning iMovies to CD is called Video CD, where you can actually put the resulting disc in most DVD players. The quality is only a little better than VHS, but you can fit about an hour's worth of video on the disc and it's cheaper than burning DVDs.

Task: Exporting iMovie for CD-ROM

If you want to share the CD-ROM iMovie, you must investigate how to burn a CD that's compatible with the computer owned by the person you're sharing the iMovie with. If you burn your CD on a Mac, it's compatible with other Macs. But if you want to share it with someone on a Windows PC, you must learn how to burn a PC-compatible CD-ROM or a hybrid CD-ROM that works on both Macs and PCs. We'll take a look at burning with Roxio's Toast (www.roxio.com), a popular program that enables you to burn in just about any format you want.

To export an iMovie for CD-ROM:

1. Choose File, Export, and then choose To QuickTime from the Export pop-up menu.

2. Choose the CD-ROM option in the Formats pop-up menu (see Figure 7.18).

7

FIGURE 7.18

Exporting an iMovie for delivery on CD-ROM.

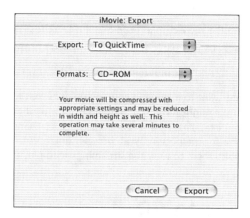

3. Click Export and save your file in a location on your hard drive where you can find it later.

4. Using your CD-burning software (such as Toast), drag your CD-ROM movie file into the program and burn a data CD (as opposed to an audio/music CD). Choose a format that's compatible with the computer of the person you're burning it for, such as the Mac OS/PC Hybrid CD option in Toast, which makes the CD-ROM compatible with either Mac or PC.

Putting iMovies on DVD

Exporting your iMovies for DVD is the ultimate in digital video. You start by recording your footage digitally, editing in iMovie, and retaining the digital quality by going directly to DVD. iMovie makes creating DVDs simple by integrating with iDVD.

> Be aware that you can't use iDVD unless you have a Mac with Apple's SuperDrive, which can read and write both CDs and DVDs.

Although there is an Export To iDVD option in the Export dialog box, the message shown in Figure 17.19, tells you that it is no longer necessary to export to iDVD because iMovie prepares projects for iDVD every time they are saved. You can still choose to "export" your project this way.

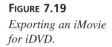

FIGURE 7.19

Exporting an iMovie for iDVD.

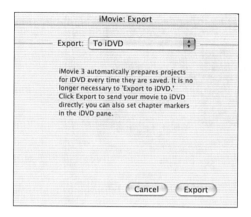

Alternatively, you could open the iDVD palette on the right side of the iMovie interface and click the button for Create iDVD Project. It will take a moment for your movie to open in iDVD where you can customize the menus and add additional movies.

Task: Adding Chapters to Your Movie

Besides maintaining video quality, DVDs offer another benefit: chapters. Adding chapters enables you to segment your video project so that people viewing the completed DVD can skip straight to the part they want to see.

Follow these steps to add chapters to an existing iMovie:

1. Open a finished iMovie project and make sure you are in Timeline view.

2. Click on the iDVD button in the main iMovie window to display the iDVD palette.

3. In the Timeline viewer, move the playhead to the point in your movie at which you want to start a new chapter.

4. In the iDVD palette, click the Add Chapter button.

5. A row for the newly created chapter will appear in the iDVD palette, where you can type in a chapter title, as shown in Figure 7.20.

   A small yellow diamond will appear in the Timeline viewer to mark the location of chapters, as shown in Figure 7.21.

6. You can repeat steps 4 through 6 until you've added up to 36 chapters to your iMovie.

7. When you are through adding chapters, click the Create iDVD Project button to open your iMovie in iDVD, as shown in Figure 7.22, where you can choose themes to customize the menu that displays your chapters. (We'll talk about using iDVD in the second half of this book.)

FIGURE 7.20
Type a descriptive title for your chapter.

FIGURE 7.21
Chapter markers will appear in the Timeline.

FIGURE 7.22
This is an iMovie with chapters after export to iDVD.

Summary

In this hour, you learned how to take your iMovies and share them in a number of different ways. Some methods, such as streaming Web video, might require more effort than others, but learning how to put an iMovie on the Web can open up new audiences for your creative works. You literally gain the ability to go worldwide with your iMovies!

In the next hour, we'll take a look at some intermediate-level techniques for editing your iMovies, including the use of special effects and transitions, which can add a whole new dimension to your productions.

Workshop

The following questions will test your knowledge of the process of exporting iMovies. Answers are provided for your reference.

Q&A

Q I want to make iMovies and share them by CD, but I don't have a CD burner or software. What should I get?

A If you haven't purchased a Mac system yet, get one with the SuperDrive, which also includes the iDVD software—the SuperDrive is capable of burning CDs and DVDs. If you have iMovie software on your current Mac but no CD burner, you can purchase an external CD burner that will connect via a FireWire, USB, or SCSI cable. Try visiting www.macmall.com. A Mac with a built-in SuperDrive contains integrated software for burning CDs, but you might still want to investigate purchasing Toast for maximum flexibility (www.roxio.com).

Q I want to share my iMovies on the Web, but I don't have a Web page. How do I get started?

A It depends on how far you want to go. If you just want to be able to give people a link, you could use PlayStream's service to upload and host your files. If you want to learn how to make your own Web pages, try downloading a free 30-day trial version of Macromedia's Dreamweaver (www.macromedia.com) or Adobe's GoLive (www.adobe.com). You can go to literally thousands of companies to start an account up to host your own Web page, and you can consult a number of helpful online resources and books.

7

Quiz

1. To export an iMovie from your camcorder to a VCR, where do you connect the cables?

   A. From the Audio In jack on the camcorder to the Audio In jack on the VCR

   B. From the Audio and Video Out jacks on the camcorder to the Audio and Video In jacks on the VCR

   C. None of the above

2. Which program can be used for burning iMovies to CD?

   A. Photoshop

   B. Toast

   C. iDVD

   D. A and B

3. Which is the best quality video?

   A. Email attachment

   B. CD-ROM

   C. Video CD

   D. DVD

Quiz Answers

1. **B.** Audio and Video Out jacks carry the signal out of the camcorder, and the Audio/Video In jacks carry the signal into the VCR so that you can record to tape.

2. **B.** Toast is a program available from from Roxio (www.roxio.com). (In case you're wondering, the latest Mac operating system integrates disc burning within the Finder, and iDVD burns only DVDs, not CDs.)

3. **D.** In ascending order of quality, an email attachment has the lowest quality image (but has the smallest file size, and is the only format appropriate for emailing); CD-ROM is better for watching on a computer; Video CD is even better and can be watched on many DVD players; DVD is the best.

Exercises

1. Locate a video clip that you'd like to share with a friend. Export it for email and send it as an email attachment. (If your friend isn't a Mac user, don't forget to include instructions to download and install the QuickTime Player.)

2. If you have the option to export your iMovies to iDVD, open an iMovie project and practice adding chapter markers. When you've added a couple, click the Create iDVD Project button to launch iDVD and see how the chapter markers are used.

Hour **8**

Intermediate Video Editing—Transitions

In this hour, we pick up where we left off in Hour 6, "Basic Video Editing with iMovie," and move on to transitions, which enable you to enhance your iMovies with features such as fade in, fade out, cross dissolve, and others.

Using transitions is like every other part of iMovie—it's as simple as drag and drop. After you've tried adding, adjusting, and removing transitions from an iMovie, you'll be well on your way toward making a great video project.

Throughout this hour, we discuss the following:

- Transitions
- Fade ins and fade outs
- Adjusting transitions
- Adding transitions
- Removing transitions

Transitions

Transitions could be thought of as the bread and butter of video editing. Or, perhaps, as the peanut butter that makes scenes stick together.

When you capture and edit video, there's no rule that you really have to do editing of any kind. You could literally let the camera tape for 30 minutes, and then capture that same 30 minutes and use it as a single clip.

But video editing enables you to refine and focus your video project, making scenes out of the raw footage. You start to see things you don't really want to leave in that you filmed, so you eventually end up splitting your footage into a series of clips.

When you deal with clips, if you choose wisely, one clip can in many cases cut to another without anything between the clips. To get a better understanding of the concept of a *cut*, just try watching any few minutes of television or a movie and looking for the spots where the camera switches from one view to another—this usually happens most rapidly in music videos. Some people prefer cutting from one scene to another without any blending.

But there are times when you want to find a way for one clip to lead smoothly to another, and a transition is a perfect way to accomplish this. The following is a list of standard transitions:

- **Circle Closing**   The first clip appears in gradually shrinking circle, behind which the next clip is revealed.

- **Circle Opening**   The first clip disappears behind a gradually increasing circle containing the next clip.

- **Cross Dissolve**   Blends one video clip into another.

- **Fade In**   Brings the desired video clip slowly into view from nothing.

- **Fade Out**   Fades the video clip slowly out of view to nothing.

- **Overlap**   One clip slides over the other until it completely replaces it on screen.

- **Push**   One clip "pushes" another off of the screen in the direction chosen, (left/right/up/down).

- **Radial**   One clip "sweeps" another away in a motion like the second-hand on a clock.

- **Scale Down**   Reduces the size of the first clip, while revealing the next clip.

- **Warp Out**   The first clip is split at the center by the next clip in a gradually increasing circle.

- **Wash In** Brings the desired video clip slowly into view from bright white.
- **Wash Out** Lightens the video clip slowly out of view to bright white.

Figure 8.1 shows the Transitions palette in iMovie, which can be easily accessed simply by clicking the Transitions button. The Transition palette enables you to choose a transition to use in your iMovie, as well as make some simple adjustments to the way the transition appears.

Figure 8.1

The Transitions palette.

The Transitions palette is an excellent place to start enhancing your iMovies. Experimenting with transitions leads naturally to some of the other enhancements that we cover in upcoming hours, including titles, effects, and audio.

Sample Transition—Cross Dissolve

To get a better understanding of transitions, let's take a look at the Cross Dissolve transition. Simply put, a cross dissolve is a standard tool that's used all the time in television and films to blend one scene into another. You probably see hundreds of cross dissolves every week without even realizing it.

In Figure 8.2, you can see the beginning of an iMovie project, with a single video clip in the Timeline and the Cross Dissolve transition selected in the Transitions palette.

FIGURE 8.2

A clip in the Timeline, and a transition selected and ready to drag.

Figure 8.3 shows the same project, but now an additional video clip has been inserted before the original one. The playhead has been dragged to the right to reveal what happens toward the end of the opening clip.

FIGURE 8.3

The playhead is set to show what you see at the end of clip 1.

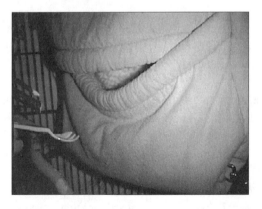

Now, in Figure 8.4, we've moved the playhead to the very beginning of the second clip.

If we watched the movie as is, when one video clip ends, it simply cuts from one video clip to another. But a cross dissolve could help the scenes blend.

iMovie gives you the ability to drop a transition between the two clips, and Figure 8.5 shows the transition. The transition appears between the clips.

8

FIGURE 8.4

The playhead is set to show what you see at the beginning of clip 2.

FIGURE 8.5

A transition appearing between two clips in the Timeline.

Essentially what happens over the course of a Cross Dissolve transition is that you see less of the first clip and more of the second. Compare the images you see in Figure 8.3 and Figure 8.4, and then look at Figure 8.6, which represents the blending of two video clips.

FIGURE 8.6

Cross dissolve—at this stage, both clips are semi-transparent.

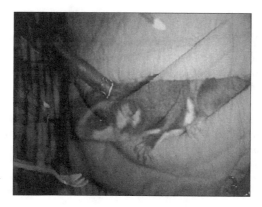

Working with Transitions

Transitions are very easy to work with. Just as with other enhancements that you can add to an iMovie, a transition takes a few moments to process, and if you add a lot of transitions to your iMovie, you might have to wait a few minutes. But when the processing is done, you have a nice way to spice up your iMovie. It's worth experimenting to find and develop your own style.

In general, there are three ways of working with transitions: adding, adjusting, and removing.

Task: Adding a Fade In

Adding a transition is as simple as clicking to select it, dragging it into the Timeline, waiting for a moment while it processes, and then watching it to see how you like it.

Keep in mind that to try a transition, you must have at least one video clip in the Timeline. Some transitions are better suited to be before or after a clip (rather than in between), such as the fade in transition, which is a good way to start off your iMovie.

1. Open an iMovie project and drag a video clip from the Shelf into the Timeline.

2. Click the Trans button in the main iMovie window to access the Transitions palette.

3. Click the Fade In transition. After a transition is selected, a mini-preview of it will play in the window at the upper right.

4. If you are satisfied with the select transition, drag it to a point in the Timeline window to the left of the current clip's preview icon. When you are in the right region, the current clip will move aside to make room for the transition, indicating that you can let go of the mouse button to drop the transition in place (see Figure 8.7).

Which side of a clip you drag a clip to depends on the transition being added. Fade In must come before a clip, so you drag it to the left side of the affected clip. Fade Out must follow the clip, so you would drag it to the right side. If you try to place a transition on the wrong side of a clip, an error message will tell you whether the transition you have chosen must be placed before or after a clip.

Transitions that require two clips to work—such as Cross Dissolve, Overlap, and Push—will give you an error if they aren't sandwiched between two clips. Somewhat confusingly, this error message is the same one that appears when you place a transition on the wrong side of a single clip—the one that tells you to place the transition on the opposite side of where you've placed it. If you follow that advice with only one clip in the Timeline, the next error will again tell you to place the transition on the opposite side.

The red processing indicator bar will show you how transition is processing. The thin red indicator line travels to the right underneath the transition until it's done (see Figure 8.8).

FIGURE 8.7

Dragging a Fade In transition to the beginning of a clip, and therefore to the beginning of an iMovie.

8

You can click on the Zoom slider at the bottom of your iMovie window to switch to a larger view of the transition and the thin red indicator line.

FIGURE 8.8

After a transition is dragged into place, your Mac must think about it for a few moments to make sense of it and deliver the video you're asking for.

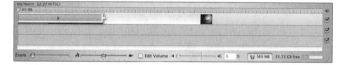

5. When the processing is done, try dragging the playhead through the transition to see how your iMovie now starts black and the video clip slowly fades in (see Figure 8.9).

Task: Adding a Fade Out

A fade out is like a fade in, but is used mostly at the end of an iMovie or at the end of a clip.

If you're following along with the example, try considering a situation where you want a quick fade in, such as the one earlier, but a lengthier, slower fade out at the end of a clip.

1. Click in the Transitions palette.

2. Click once to select the Fade Out transition.

3. Before clicking anywhere else, click and drag the blue Speed slider button above the list of transitions to change the speed of the transition, setting it to something like four seconds (4:00). See Figure 8.10.

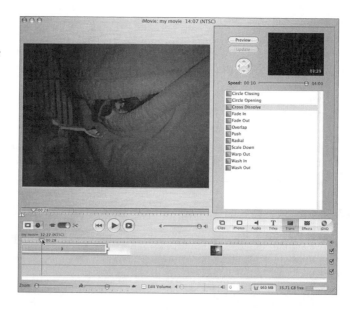

FIGURE 8.9

After the processing is done, you can drag the playhead back and forth to get a quick preview of the transition.

Transitions work by transforming the video frames to which they are applied—if a video clip isn't long enough for the duration of the transition you've selected, iMovie will display a message to let you know it just won't work out.

4. Click and drag the Fade Out transition down and to the left from the Transitions window to the end of a video clip, as shown in Figure 8.11.

5. To get a closer view of the transition, select the transition in the Timeline view and drag the Zoom slider button at the bottom of your iMovie window to the right. In this larger view, shown in Figure 8.12, you can easily see the red line indicating its processing status.

6. When the processing is done, trying dragging the playhead to position it to the left of where the transition starts. Then either click on the Play button in the iMovie Monitor window to watch a preview, or click and drag the playhead through the transition to see how it fade from the video clip to black—just like in the movies!

FIGURE 8.10

Changing the Speed setting.

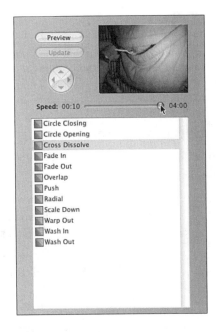

8

FIGURE 8.11

Adding a Fade Out transition to the end of a clip.

FIGURE 8.12

Close-up view of the Fade Out transition.

One thing you might want to experiment with at this point is to add fade outs and fade ins in between clips: You could have a clip fade out to black, and then have the next clip fade in—consider how this effect is different from a cross dissolve.

When you choose a transition and make speed adjustments, it can be helpful to watch the mini-preview at the upper right in the Transition palette before you drag it to the Timeline view. To do this, simply make your adjustments and click again on the selected transition. The mini-preview will automatically play.

> If you want to see a larger preview, click on the Preview button at the top of the transition palette and the transition will play in the Monitor window. When you're happy with the settings you can drag the clip as you normally would to the Timeline View.

Task: Changing and Updating a Transition

At some point, you might want to change a transition that's already been added, and doing so is easy to accomplish:

1. Open your iMovie project in which you have a clip with a transition that you want to change. In Figure 8.13, we see a sample project. In this scenario, we've decided that we want the fade out to be longer; that is, we want the fade to start earlier in the clip.

2. Click on the transition to select it; a translucent box will appear around it.

FIGURE 8.13

Selecting the transition.

3. Click on the Speed slider in the Transition tab to adjust the Speed setting, and change it to four seconds (4:00). See Figure 8.14.

> The higher the Speed setting, the more seconds of space the transition will take up. So, if you want a longer transition, you want a higher Speed setting—toward 04:00. For a shorter transition, you want a lower setting—toward 00:10.

4. Click the Update button in the Transition palette. When the processing is done, drag the playhead back and forth on the Timeline to see the effect of the adjusted transition, or position the playhead to the left of the transition and click the Play button below the Monitor window (see Figure 8.15).

Compare the relative lengths of the transition and video clip in Figures 8.13 and 8.15. Notice how the transition in Figure 8.15, which has been adjusted to 4:00, is longer and therefore takes up more space in the Timeline than the original transition shown in Figure 8.13. The transition begins earlier in the video clip.

Figure 8.14

Adjusting the selected transition.

Figure 8.15

Viewing the results of the adjusted transition, which has to process first.

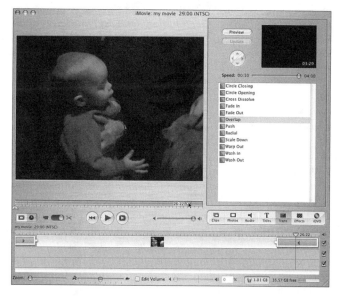

Task: Replacing a Transition

Figure 8.16 shows two clips with a transition in between them. We added a fade out in the previous task, but now we've decided to add another clip to our iMovie and we don't want to fade out anymore—we've decided to replace the fade out with a more blending transition.

FIGURE 8.16

The former end of the movie, a fade out transition, now falls between two clips.

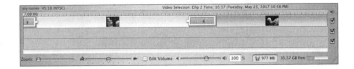

1. Click the transition to select it. Remember, a translucent box will appear around a selected transition, as shown in Figure 8.17.

FIGURE 8.17

Selecting the fade out.

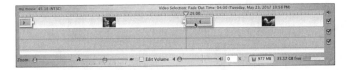

2. In the Transitions palette, click a new transition (such as Overlap) and click the Update button (see Figure 8.18).

FIGURE 8.18

The new transition has been inserted between the clips.

iMovie processes the new transition, and as shown in Figure 8.19, the old transition is officially replaced! But don't worry, if you decide you don't like the results, you can hold down the Command key and press the Z key to undo your last action. (You can also press Command+Z several times to undo a series of changes you've made.)

FIGURE 8.19

Feed your Mac lots of RAM and treat it kindly—it's hard work processing all that digital video.

Finally, when all the processing is done, you can click and drag the Timeline's scrollbar to get a preview, and thus see the effects of the processing.

Task: Removing a Transition

If you decide you don't want a transition you've added, you can easily remove it altogether by following these steps:

1. Open your iMovie project in which you have a clip as well as a transition that you want to remove.

2. Click on the transition to select it; a translucent box will appear around it.

3. From the Edit menu, select Clear, and the transition will be removed.

Summary

In this hour, you learned how iMovie enables you to add professional-looking transitions to a project, which can help digital video to look and feel more like a real movie. In fact, when you use iMovie to edit your digital video, you *are* making a real movie—a *digital* movie.

In the next hour, we'll take a look at effects, another useful and enjoyable feature of iMovie that you might have noticed.

Workshop

The Workshop consists of quiz questions and answers to help you to develop a better grasp of transitions. First, try to answer the questions, *before* checking the answers. Then you'll want to read the explanations, even if you get the answers right—the explanations will contribute in a small way to your overall understanding, and help paint a clearer picture in your mind with digital video.

Q&A

Q **I'm working on an iMovie and I want it to look as good as it can, but I'm not sure how long to make the transitions between the scenes in my movie. Is there any way to figure out the best length for transitions?**

A It's probably best to deal with each transition that you place in your movie separately because the action that happens before and after the transition might have an effect on what settings will feel right. You might simply want to go into the Transitions palette, and if you're using a cross dissolve (for example), select the transition before you drag it into your iMovie, and set it to a speed of two seconds (2:00). Doing so places the Speed setting in the middle so that you can drag this one between all of your clips. Then try adjusting things clip by clip, adjusting each one higher and lower until it feels right. In other words, there aren't really any true rules on the matter, but when you actually watch the video through and then try changing the Speed setting higher or lower and comparing how the transitions feel, you'll start to get a sense of what seems right to you.

Q **I'm sleep deprived because I've been watching too many episodes of *Trading Spaces*, and I realized that I put the wrong transition between all of the clips in my movie. Is there any way to easily replace them?**

A You'll have to update transitions one-at-a-time by selecting them in Timeline or Clip View, then selecting replacement transitions in the Transitions palette. Click Update to start your computer processing the new transition.

Quiz

1. How do you add a fade in to a movie?

   A. Choose Edit, Add Fade

   B. Drag a Fade In transition into the Timeline

   C. A and B

2. With regard to transitions in an iMovie, how much is too much (expressed in number of transitions per minute)?

   A. <5

   B. Between 5–10 transitions

   C. 30 tps (transitions per second)

   D. Completely subjective

3. Which will result in the longest, slowest transition?

    A. Setting the Speed value to 4:00

    B. Setting the Speed value to 00:10

    C. Setting the Speed value to 2:00

Quiz Answers

1. **B.** It's as easy as drag and drop, baby!

2. **B.** This is a bit of a trick question, and fairly subjective, but it's definitely a good question to ask yourself. Probably the best thing to do is to keep the length of transitions reasonably short, and to focus on how you edit the underlying video so that you aren't relying on transitions too much.

3. **A.** A setting of 4:00 results in a 4-second transition.

Exercise

In this hour, we looked at basic transitions: Fade In, Fade Out, and Cross Dissolve. Now, open a project containing at least two clips and try out the other possibilities. (You won't have to apply every transition—simply clicking on a transition will preview it in the mini-preview window in the Transitions palette.)

HOUR 9

Advanced Video Editing—Effects

In this hour, we pick up where we left off with transitions by starting to take a look at the effects in iMovie, which represent some of the most powerful and useful features of iMovie. The wonderful thing is that effects are just as easy to use as any other feature of iMovie.

It's almost as if Apple took the simplicity and fun of a Fisher-Price toy, and combined it with the power of a spaceship. What you end up with in iMovie is a tool that can take you to the moon, yet is easy enough for anyone to use (with a spaceship, you might have to get a driver's license). This combination of power and fun is especially true with effects, where you get to use professional-quality tools, such as Brightness/Contrast and Adjust Color, in an environment in which you don't have to worry at all about making a mistake. In fact, there might not be such a thing as a mistake in iMovie because you could join a host of other video makers who occasionally do something accidentally, whether in shooting or adjusting video, and then decide that they like it: "Yeah, thanks, I like how that turned out too, just the way I intended it."

Throughout this hour, we discuss the following:

- Effects
- Adjusting an effect
- Updating iMovies
- Brightness/Contrast
- Adjusting colors

Effects

Effects represent another way that you can enhance your iMovies by adding something to them. You take plain video and make it stand out or spice it up to create your own movie-making style.

For example, if you want to give a historic feel to a portion of your iMovie, you could use an effect to make the movie either black-and-white or a sepia tone to give it the feel of an early moving picture.

Sometimes the video you use might give you ideas. For example, there might be a scene in a movie that's supposed to represent a person's dreams, and you could use the Fog effect to give that scene a surreal feeling. Maybe you could even combine it with another effect to change the colors around, and when the person in your iMovie wakes up, everything returns to normal and you don't see the effects anymore.

In essence, to add an effect, you simply choose a clip in the Timeline and then choose and apply an effect —you can make your adjustments anytime you want. If you want to add an effect to only a portion of your iMovie, you use the Split Video Clip at Playhead command (refer to Hour 6, "Basic Video Editing with iMovie") to separate a portion of your video, and then apply the effect to it.

Effects are similar to transitions and titles in that the magic happens in the relevant palette in iMovie (see Figure 9.1); the Effects palette gives you a convenient place to try out different things.

If you like to keep things as simple as possible, you can choose and apply an effect without altering its defaults; but iMovie also enables you to completely customize each effect if you choose to. You might find that you start by adding effects with their default settings, and then end up coming back to the Effects palette to try different options when you get ideas for how some adjustment could work better for a particular clip. Table 9.1 lists the effects available in iMovie.

FIGURE 9.1

The Effects palette in iMovie.

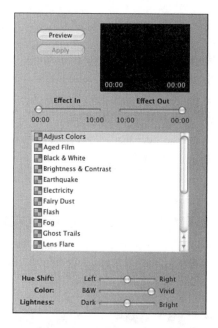

TABLE 9.1   List of Effects in iMovie

Effect Name	Description
Adjust Colors	Enables you to adjust various aspects of color, as if you were shining different colored light on your video
Aged Film	Adds dust and scratches to a clip
Black and White	Enables you to take a step backward in time before color television or movies
Brightness & Contrast	Very helpful for adjusting video when you want to make it look better, such as video that was shot in low-light situations
Earthquake	Makes the image shake and blur is if the video were shot during an earthquake
Electricity	Adds a blue zap of electricity, which you can rotate for better placement
Fairy Dust	Adds a trail of sparkles to the clip
Flash	Adds an instant of bright white to the clip
Fog	Adds an overlay of moving fog to the clip
Ghost Trails	Faint impressions of the clip echo the motion in the real clip
Lens Flare	Gives the feel of an old photograph
Letterbox	Displays the clip in letterbox format, with black space in the open area at the top and bottom of the screen

TABLE 9.1   continued

Effect Name	Description
Mirror	Mirrors half of the clip on the other side of the screen
N-Square	Splits the screen in N equal squares containing the selected clip
Rain	Adds an overlay of moving rain to the clip
Sepia Tone	Gives the feel of an old photograph
Sharpen	Can enhance video that's slightly out of focus
Soft Focus	Adds a soft feel to video

Sample Effect—Brightness & Contrast

When you use an effect in iMovie, you choose a clip, such as the one in Figure 9.2, and decide you want to do something to it. In this case, we have a video clip that came out a bit dark.

FIGURE 9.2

A dark clip before the Brightness & Contrast effect is applied.

But with a bit of tweaking, using the Brightness & Contrast controls, we can improve the clip so that you can see the singers a bit better (see Figure 9.3).

Because they can be so simple to add, it can be very easy to overdo effects, making things so "effected" that they look worse than when you began. So, if you want to preserve the quality of the video, you have to keep things somewhat balanced by not going overboard and using the most extreme settings in each effect.

FIGURE 9.3

The clip after the Brightness & Contrast effect is applied.

Working with Effects

When you try out effects, you can experiment without waiting for iMovie to process—or render—an effect, which can take several minutes. When you've made a decision, you can apply the effect and allow iMovie to render it, and you can continue to add other effects to that clip if you want.

In general, the options when working with effects are Preview, Apply, and Restore Clip.

Previewing

The Preview button enables you to see an effect on the main Monitor area in iMovie. It becomes active when you select an effect in the Effects palette.

When you first click on an effect in the Effects palette in iMovie, there will appear a small preview window that contains a miniature version of your iMovie, and it's helpful to get a general sense of what the effect does. But ultimately it's nicer to see how the effect looks at normal size, in the main iMovie Monitor area.

> In some versions of iMovie, the Preview feature isn't functional for Effects. To see an approximation of the chosen effect with the changes you've made to the settings, watch the mini-preview space at the upper right closely as you click the control settings.

Applying

Applying an effect is simply the process of going beyond the preview stage and actually having iMovie change your video clip by employing the effect on the clip you have currently selected. At this point, iMovie will process (or render) the effect, which might take several minutes. The status of the processing will appear as a red bar at the top of the affected clip in the Timeline (see Figure 9.4).

FIGURE 9.4

If you're happy with the preview, you can click Apply to render the effect.

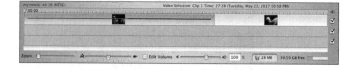

Restoring Clips

After you apply an effect, if you want to go back to how the clip originally was, you can use the Restore Clip function available under the Advanced menu (see Figure 9.5).

FIGURE 9.5

An effect has been applied and now the same clip can be updated or restored to its original state.

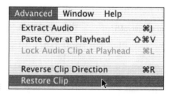

Undo/Redo

The Undo/Redo option in iMovie is a handy thing to keep in mind when working with effects. The top portion of the Edit menu changes to display which of the standard editing functions are currently available, such as in Figure 9.6, where an effect has just been updated.

FIGURE 9.6

The Undo Update Effect command is your emergency management system for undoing unwanted changes to clips. If you used the Undo feature after a commitment, you can choose Redo Commit Effect in this same menu.

Task: Enhancing a Clip with Brightness & Contrast

In this example, we take a video clip that came out dark and use the Brightness/Contrast effect to tweak the video so that we can see the people in the video better.

1. Open an iMovie project, and if you haven't already, drag a clip into the Timeline.

2. Click once on the clip you want to use in the Timeline in order to select it, as shown in Figure 9.7.

FIGURE 9.7

A very dark clip in the iMovie Timeline.

9

3. Click the Effects button in the main iMovie window to display the Effects palette. Then click the Brightness & Contrast effect, as shown in Figure 9.8.

FIGURE 9.8

The Brightness & Contrast effect with the Brightness setting adjusted to be midway between Dark and Bright, and the Contrast setting adjusted to midway between Low and High.

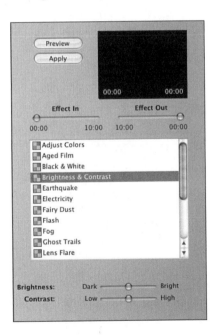

4. Start adjusting the clip through increasing the contrast by clicking the blue slider button, holding the mouse button down, and dragging a small bit to the right to bring out the brighter colors and distinguish the darker colors from them (see Figure 9.9).

▼   5. Now click the Brightness slider button and slowly drag it to the right, keeping an eye on the video clip (see Figure 9.10). Watch the mini-preview window as you adjust the settings.

FIGURE 9.9

Moving the Contrast slider toward the higher setting helps to give you a brighter clip.

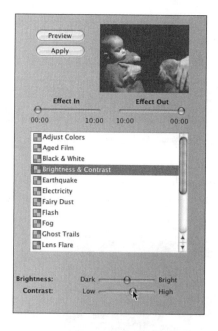

FIGURE 9.10

Moving the Brightness slider from Dark to Bright also enhances the brightness of the clip.

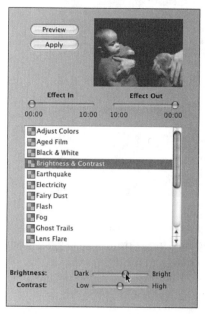

▼

6. When you like how the previews look, click Apply and iMovie begins to process the video (see Figure 9.11).

FIGURE 9.11

The clip with the Brightness & Contrast effect renders in the Timeline.

When iMovie is done processing your clip, you can play the movie to see how the effect looks.

Sometimes after you apply an effect and iMovie begins to render it, you change your mind. What do you do to stop iMovie from rendering the rest of the clip? If you press the Command key and the period on your keyboard at the same time while iMovie is rendering any element, the process will be cancelled and the clip will remain as it was before you started.

Task: Enhancing a Clip with Adjust Colors

The Adjust Colors effect can come in handy when you want to make certain colors stand out, or want to give the clip a distinct imaginary feel of some kind. It gives you three subsettings that you can play with: Hue Shift, Color, and Lightness.

- Hue Shift—Shifts the entire video clip to a different color
- Color—Changes the amount and vividness of color, from no color (black-and-white) to Vivid (as much color as possible, which is how the effect starts out with no changes made)
- Lightness—Similar to the Brightness & Contrast effect

In this example, we want to give the video a washed-out feeling by taking out the color (also known as *desaturating*) and increasing the brightness/lightness.

1. Open an iMovie project, and with a clip selected in the Timeline, choose the Adjust Colors effect in the Effects window (see Figure 9.12).

2. Click the Color slider and drag it to the left to make the video black and white (B&W). See Figure 9.13.

FIGURE 9.12

The Adjust Colors effect with the as-yet-unchanged, default settings.

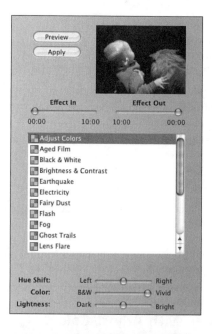

FIGURE 9.13

The Color slider in the Black and White position turns the clip into a black-and-white movie.

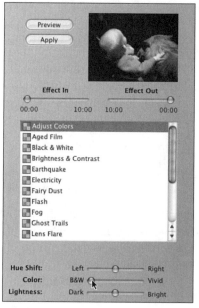

▼ 3. Click the Lightness slider and drag to the right to make the video brighter (see Figure 9.14).

FIGURE 9.14

Adjusting the Lightness setting.

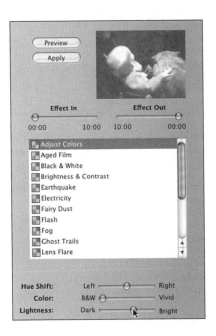

▲ 4. Click the Apply button in the iMovie window to set iMovie going on processing your video. Figure 9.15 shows the effect during processing.

FIGURE 9.15

The Adjust Colors Effect being applied.

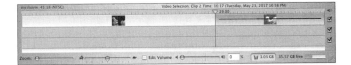

The Hue Shift option changes the overall tone of the clip. Dragging the slider from one end to the other should give you nearly the full range of the spectrum, from warm reds to cool blues.

Keep in mind that the colors available in the Hue Shift option depend somewhat on the colors, brightness, and other features of your original video.

Making Changes to Effects

After you've tried effects by simply applying them to successive clips, you'll probably discover that you want to make things more interesting or customized.

 You can drag and drop transitions, but the drag-and-drop feature doesn't work with effects.

Because you've already applied an effect to a clip, you must reapply the changed effect. To do so, select the clip you want to work with, choose the same effect you applied, make the changes, and then click Apply. In some cases, a dialog message sheet window will appear to let you know that the new effect invalidates the previous one. You must choose OK for your new effect to be processed.

Effect In, Effect Out

One of the options you have for customizing for an effect is how suddenly the effect appears in a clip. For instance, consider the Fog effect. If you apply the Fog effect to a scene in your iMovie, you could have it appear from the beginning to the end of a clip as if the fog were thick during the actual filming. Alternatively, you could have the fog drift appear briefly, as if a small patch blew past the camera.

You can achieve the first kind of Fog effect by simply applying Fog to a selected clip. To get the second kind, you must use the Effect In and Effect Out controls, which control when an effect begins and ends within a clip.

Task: Effect In, Effect Out

We've decided that we want to slowly increase the impression that the effect has on our clip over the space of a few seconds by bringing in the effect to give the clip a unique feel and then fading out the effect.

1. Select a clip in the Timeline that you want to apply an effect to (see Figure 9.16).

2. Click the blue slider in the Effect In area of the Effects palette, and drag a bit to the right to choose the length of time that it takes for the effect to develop to full strength (see Figure 9.17).

▼ TASK

▼

FIGURE 9.16

The Effects palette showing the settings of an effect that's applied to a clip.

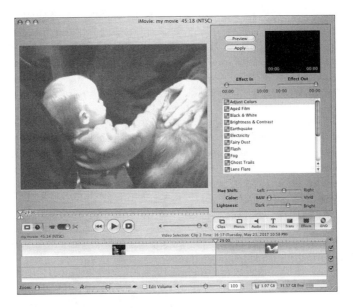

FIGURE 9.17

Instead of simply turning on, the effect now fades in over the course of a few seconds.

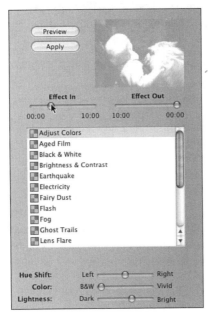

9

▼   3. Now click the Effect Out slider and drag it to the left (as shown in Figure 9.18) to choose how long it takes for the video to return to normal.

FIGURE 9.18

The effect will fade out over the course of a few seconds.

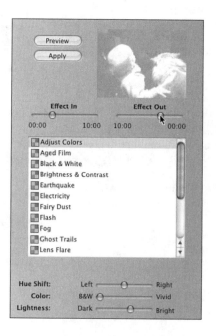

▲   4. Click the Apply button to reapply the effect with these new settings.

When you click the Apply button, iMovie starts to process the video: In a short while, you can preview it to see the final version of the video. Of course, if it isn't finished yet, you can continue steps 1–4, trying out different adjustments until you're happy with the effect.

Summary

In this hour, you learned how you can bring your iMovies one step closer to their Hollywood (or living room) debut. You saw how, in certain situations, an effect such as Brightness & Contrast can actually help you to see your video better if it was shot in a setting where there wasn't much light, also known as a *low-light situation* (such as a karaoke bar).

In the next hour, we'll take a look at how you can enhance your iMovie with titles. iMovie makes it easy to add titles and credits to your movie to give it that extra professional look!

Workshop

The Workshop consists of quiz questions and answers to help you to develop a better grasp of the material. First, try to answer the questions, before you check the answers. You may also want to read the explanations, even if you get the answers right. The more you investigate the world of Effects, the more interesting your iMovies will become.

Q&A

Q I shot some video and want to use the Brightness & Contrast effect to make it look better, but it just keeps appearing completely black in iMovie. What went wrong?

A Chances are that one of two things happened. You might have left the lens cap on your camcorder when you were shooting the video, or there might have been so little light that there might not really be much you can do to fix it. The next time that you go out trying to film nocturnal lizards in low-light conditions, you might want to see whether you have a Nightshot feature on your camera, which uses infrared technology to enable you to shoot video in even extremely dark situations. Nightshot is a feature on most Sony camcorders, and more recent models have a Super Nightshot feature that's even better for this type of thing. Otherwise, you'll have to find some way of lighting the situation so that you can bring the video closer to the point where iMovie can make use of it. Even though iMovie has the Brightness/Contrast feature, it's ultimately better, if possible, to have the video lighted well in the first place.

Q I'm confused by the similarity of the Fade In/Fade Out transitions and the Effect In/Effect Out feature. What's the difference, and when's the best time to use each one?

A The Fade In transition is normally used when you want to fade in video from black for the beginning of your iMovie, and the Fade Out transition is commonly used at the end of a video to fade to black. The difference with fading effects in and out using the Effect In/Effect Out feature of iMovie is simply that iMovie enables you to slowly change your video with an effect by fading in that effect. Instead of fading in video itself, you're simply adding (Effect In) or removing (Effect Out) something like brightness to a video over time. This gives you the creative freedom to slowly change the effect, rather than having it switch on completely at once.

Quiz

1. How many effects are there in iMovie?

    A. 7

    B. 18

    C. Unlimited

    D. B and C

2. Which effect enables you to try to fix video that was shot in low-light conditions?

    A. Adjust Colors

    B. Brightness/Lighting

    C. Brightness & Contrast

    D. Fix Video

    E. A and C

3. How do you perform color correction in iMovie?

    A. Adjust Colors

    B. Brightness/Lighting

    C. Brightness & Contrast

    D. Fix Video

Quiz Answers

1. **D.** At first glance, there are only 18 effects if you go by how many individual effects appear in the list in the Effects palette when you first install iMovie. But the number increases when you consider the individual adjustments that you can make within an effect (such as the Hue Shift/Color/Lightness options in the Adjust Colors Effect). Add on how you can fade in and fade out each effect, and you get even more possible combinations. Ultimately, the number of iMovie effects could be said to be unlimited because you can download additional ones from the Internet.

2. **E.** There's no real substitute for good lighting, but Adjust Colors and Brightness & Contrast are the next best things.

3. **A.** It's great that you can have an advanced tool like Adjust Colors in a program such as iMovie. People who want to go as far as they can in digital video will find that features like this are a great place to start, and provide a foundation of experience that can acquaint the tinkerer with some of the most relevant issues in digital video. Welcome to the world of color correction!

Exercises

1. In this hour, we looked at basic effects: Brightness & Contrast and Adjust Color. Now open a project containing at least one clip and try out the other possibilities. You won't have to apply every effect—simply selecting a clip and clicking on an effect will preview it in the mini-preview window in the Effects palette.

2. Choose an effect that would look best gradually phased in and phased out, and practice using the Effect In and Effect Out settings.

9

HOUR 10

Titles

In this hour, you learn how iMovies can be enhanced by using the built-in Titles feature in iMovie. Whether you're looking for a traditional Hollywood-style intro credit or a flashy animated flying title, iMovie makes it easy and fun to try out the various options. It's deceivingly simple to add titles to your iMovies, but when people see the titles in your movie, they might be surprised that you did them in iMovie. In theory, your titles can look as professional and/or playful as you want them to be.

Throughout this hour, you learn about

- Selecting titles
- Adding titles
- Adjusting titles
- Typing in new text for a title

Titles

When you're ready to try adding a title to your iMovie, you'll be working in a new area of iMovie: the Titles palette.

When the Titles palette comes up, you'll see a number of options, including ways to adjust the size and color of the letters in your title, as well as a list from which you can select different titles (see Figure 10.1).

Figure 10.1

The Titles palette.

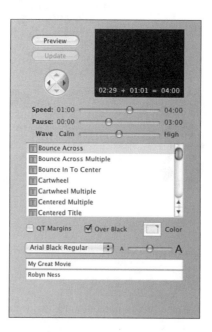

For now, don't worry about all the options. You can add a title to your iMovie simply by choosing one (such as Bounce In To Center) from the list, clicking on it, and dragging it into the Timeline.

Sooner or later, you'll want to take advantage of all the things you can do to spruce up and modify titles to give your productions a customized touch. To get our feet wet, let's take a look at a couple of the sample titles that are included with iMovie. Later on, we'll dive into adjusting and customizing titles.

Sample Title—Bounce In To Center

Near the top of iMovie's title list is Bounce In To Center, and it's a great starting place to play around with titles. Looking at Figure 10.2 to a sense of how the text moves in from the top and bottom of the screen to meet in the middle.

Notice how the text you see on the screen in Figure 10.2 corresponds to the text entered in the bottom portion of the Titles palette that you saw in Figure 10.1—this is where you can change the text for the title. iMovie fills it in for you, based on combining the name of your project (for example: My Great Movie), with the computer name or username on your Mac.

FIGURE 10.2

A sample title from left to right.

Sample Title—Centered Multiple

At first glance, Centered Multiple might sound like an abstract algebraic principle, but after you start playing with it, its value becomes apparent.

Centered Multiple is an example of a title to which you can add multiple lines of text. In essence, iMovie makes it easy to create multiple "screens" by enabling you to add additional lines of text to some titles.

On the top in Figure 10.3, we see the first screen (imagine the text fading in, pausing, and then fading out), and on the bottom we see the next screen, where the same thing happens again.

If you're having difficulty picturing what's going on, don't be concerned. When you start playing in the program, it'll become clear, and you'll see the nice effect that this kind of title has.

iMovie makes it easy to enter text in titles like this one. As with the previous title we examined, the text you enter in the bottom of the Titles palette is what appears in the title (see Figure 10.4).

With a multiple line title, you can click-and-drag the blue scrollbar down (the blue scrollbar to the right of the text) to reveal more lines of text. Notice how the text in the lower pair of text boxes in Figure 10.4 corresponds to the second screen in Figure 10.3.

If you haven't tried them (although we aren't officially in the middle of a task), the + and - buttons to the right of the title text enable you to add and remove lines of text, which generates more screens. This particular title is a nice way to have introductory screens fade in and out before a movie starts.

FIGURE 10.3
Two moments from a multipart fade title.

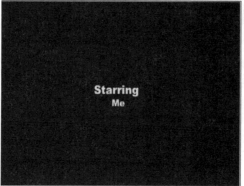

FIGURE 10.4
The text input area in the Titles palette.

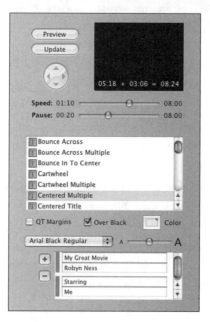

Now that you've gotten a taste of our two basic titles, take a moment to consider all the titles you have available. See Table 10.1.

TABLE 10.1 Titles in iMovie

Title Type	Description
Bounce Across	Two lines of text appear from either the left or right and move like a wiggling worm toward the center of the screen.
Bounce Across Multiple	Like Bounce Across but with multiple screens of text.
Bounce In To Center	Two lines of text appear and move towards the center of the screen.
Cartwheel	Two lines of text, each letter rotating, move diagonally toward the center of the screen.
Cartwheel Multiple	Like Cartwheel but with multiple screens of text.
Centered Multiple	Multiple titles fade in and out in sequence, one after another. It's a nice movie-style effect.
Centered Title	A single title fades in and out.
Converge	Two lines of text with broadly spaced letters gradually move to the left to form words.
Converge Multiple	Like Converge, but with multiple screens of text.
Converge to Center	Two lines of text with broadly spaced letters gradually move to the center to form words.
Converge to Center Multiple	Like Converge to Center, but with multiple screens of text.
Cross Through Center	Two lines of text start out with letters and lines reversed and rotate until correctly positioned.
Cross Through Center Multiple	Like Cross Through Center, but with multiple screens of text.
Drifting	Multiple lines fade in from different directions.
Flying Letters	Letters of title fade into the screen to form words of title.
Flying Words	Entire lines of title fly in at one time. Nice effect.
Gravity	Two lines of text fall into place from one edge of the screen.
Gravity Multiple	Like Gravity but with multiple screens of text.
Music Video	Enables you to put a music video–style paragraph of text that can appear in the corner of the screen. Useful.
Rolling Centered Credits	Enter multiple lines of text to get the effect you see at the end of movies. Very nice.
Rolling Credits	Similar to centered credits; different formatting.

10

TABLE 10.1   continued

Title Type	Description
Scroll with Pause	Titles roll on to screen, pause, roll off; helps with being able to read individual credits.
Scrolling Block	Will scroll an entire paragraph of text by; something like the original *Star Wars* credits.
Spread from Center	Two lines of text appear from a pile of letters at the center of the screen.
Spread from Center Multiple	Like Spread from Center, but with multiple screens of text.
Stripe Subtitle	A nice title to put in the corner of a screen to introduce a new section of a video.
Subtitle	Gives you the ability to add text to the screen to simulate the subtitle effect of a DVD.
Subtitle Multiple	Multiple subtitles.
Twirl	Two lines of text appear at the center of the screen with each letter rotating.
Typewriter	Creates the effects.
Unscramble	A jumble of letters separates into two lines of text.
Unscramble Multiple	Like Unscramble, but with multiple screens of text.
Zoom	Creates a zoom effect, moving close in on video.
Zoom Multiple	Multiple zooms.

Using Titles over Black

One simple way to have titles appear is against a black background so that the titles appear against a solid color and your attention is focused on the title itself, as shown in Figure 10.3. To accomplish this, you simply click on the Over Black option in the Titles palette.

Overlay Titles (over Video)

Another method you might want to try is to uncheck the Over Black option so that your title appears over a video clip, as shown in Figure 10.5. The only requirement is that you have a video clip in the project!

You can actually layer different titles in iMovie. For instance, you can add one long-duration title that's set over black, and have other titles that aren't set over black cross over the top of it.

FIGURE 10.5

Clicking on a title with Over Black unchecked to see a mini-preview with the title displayed over a video clip.

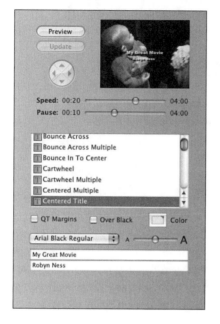

10

Task: Selecting a Title

To begin working with titles, you'll want to know how to find a particular title that was listed in Table 10.1.

1. Click on the Titles button in the main iMovie window to display the Titles palette.

2. Click the blue scrollbar, and drag it down so that the title you're looking for is revealed.

3. When you find the title you want to try, click to select it, as I've done with the Typewriter title near the end of the list (see Figure 10.6).

FIGURE 10.6
The blue scrollbar has been dragged down, revealing more titles.

Adjusting Titles

As soon as you start trying out the different titles, you'll want to know how you can adjust them, and Apple has done an excellent job yet again of making things easy and intuitive, yet flexible. Essentially, you can do no tweaking at all or as much as you want.

Task: Adjusting a Title

In this task, we look at how to make adjustments to a title. iMovie makes it easy to try things out with titles and then go back and expand or change them, all without having to type in the text over again.

1. Follow the steps in the previous task to select a title. In this example, we're using Typewriter.

2. Try clicking the Text Size slider, marked with a small and a large capital A, and dragging it to the left or right to change the size of your title text (see Figure 10.7).

3. To choose a different color for the text, click once on the Color button (see Figure 10.8). A pop-up menu of colors will appear.

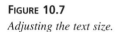

FIGURE 10.7
Adjusting the text size.

FIGURE 10.8
Clicking on the Color option to change text color.

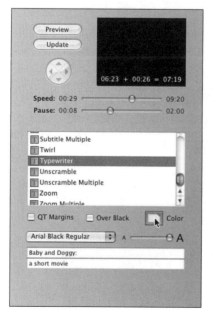

10

▼   4. Click on a color that you want to use for your text (see Figure 10.9), and then click
          somewhere outside the pop-up menu to deselect it.

FIGURE 10.9

*Selecting a new text
color.*

5. Try clicking and dragging the blue Speed slider to the left or to the right to see
   how it affects the behavior of the title text. (see Figure 10.10).

FIGURE 10.10

*Adjusting the Speed
slider.*

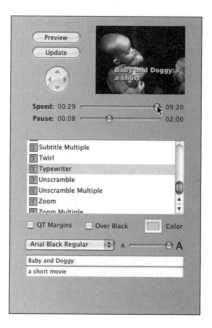

▲   6. To see the miniature preview of a title again, just click on the title, and it will
          appear again in the preview area.

If you've been following along with the example, try clicking on the Preview button in the Titles palette, and your title should appear in the Monitor area, something like what's shown in Figure 10.11.

FIGURE 10.11
The adjusted title in icy blue.

Task: Typing In a New Title

It's very simple to change the text for a title; just click and type away.

1. Locate the text input field for the title you're using (see Figure 10.12).

FIGURE 10.12
The title text field.

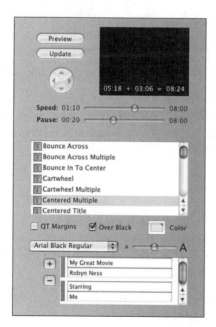

▼   2. Move the mouse arrow and click once on the line you want to change.

   After you single-click it (as opposed to a double-click), the line of text will change
   color to indicate that it's selected (see Figure 10.13). You'll also see a flashing text
   insertion cursor, just as you'd have in a word processing program.

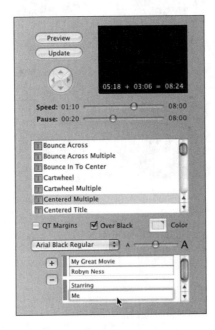

Figure 10.13

*After clicking once on
the text, it's selected
and you can start
typing.*

   3. With the text selected, you can just type in new text to replace the old.

   4. Repeat steps 2 and 3 to change an additional line of text.

   5. To see the title in the Monitor in iMovie, click the Preview button in the Titles
      palette. You'll see the changes you've made to the text reflected in the animated
▲   title.

Adding Titles

The ultimate goal of making titles is to introduce or otherwise enhance your movie. You
could have a title at the beginning, a rolling credit at the end, and any number of titles in
between to introduce different scenes (reminiscent of silent movies?) or sections (such as
a training video).

If you think back, earlier in this hour we talked about the two different ways that titles
can work: either displayed against a black screen (Over Black), or as an overlay

displaying directly over video. Either approach can be fun and work in different situations, but you might want to start out with a standard Over Black title (by clicking the Over Black box).

Task: Adding a Title to a Movie

Adding a title to a movie is as easy as adding a clip to a movie; it's a very similar, almost identical process. In fact…it is identical. As Austin Powers might say, drag and drop, baby!

1. Open an iMovie project and drag a clip into the Timeline. If the Clip Viewer tab is visible, just click the Clock icon in the lower-left corner of the screen to display the Timeline.

2. Click on a title of choice in the Titles palette, and drag it down into the Timeline until your video clip moves aside to make room for the title (see Figure 10.14). Drop the title into the open space.

FIGURE 10.14

Dragging a title from the Titles palette down to the Timeline in front of the video clip.

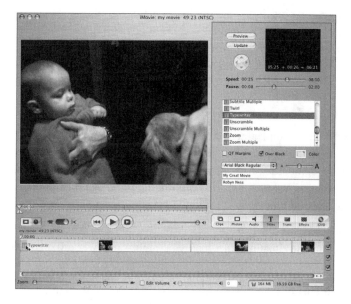

3. Notice in Figure 10.15 how the small red bar travels from left to right underneath your title to indicate that the title is being processed.

4. Now that your title is in the Timeline, try clicking on the playhead and dragging it through your title to get a quick glance at how the title animates.

FIGURE 10.15

A little red bar going to the right underneath the title in the Timeline indicates that your Mac is processing your title.

To experiment with a title that you've created, try changing a setting in the Titles palette, and then clicking the Update button in the Titles palette.

When you've dragged a title into the Timeline, you can click in the Timeline to select it (it'll change to blue) and make adjustments to it. Then you need to click Update for iMovie to process it and give you a preview.

iMovie can quickly build a miniature preview in the Titles palette when you make changes. But digital video takes a lot of processing power. So, in order for it to catch up with changes when you place it in the Timeline, it has to be processed before you can get the final preview of how it'll look on a television.

Summary

In this hour, you learned about how easy it is to make and adjust titles in iMovie. If the bug hasn't caught you yet and you're not sure what to do next, you might want to break out the camcorder, film the next four or five people you encounter, and then make an iMovie that introduces each one of them. Then, to get extra credit, try the Rolling Credit title and add it to the end, and give your actors and actresses credit.

If you haven't done so already, try out each title just to get used to it; play with it a little, and imagine situations in which you might want to use such a title.

In general, when you've created and edited an iMovie, ideas about how to make titles will probably suggest themselves, so it's probably something you can add as a final touch if you want to. Certain titles might stick out to you when you consider the subject material.

But if you feel like it, there's no reason you can't start with titles and imagine different scenes—you could even use titles as a way to plan scenes for your iMovie!

In the next hour, we'll take a look at the world of working with sound in iMovie. You'll see that you're only a point and a click away from adding sound effects and recorded sounds to your iMovies, beyond what you record with your camera.

Workshop

The Workshop consists of quiz questions and answers to help you to develop a better grasp of titles. First, try to answer the questions. Then read the explanations, even if you get the answers right—the explanations will contribute to your overall understanding of iMovie.

Q&A

Q I made a title on a black screen using the Over Black option, but I'd like to try displaying it over a video clip now. How do I do it?

A To see your title over video when you've already dragged your title to the Timeline, click in the Timeline to select the title. Then click the Titles button to display the Titles palette, and uncheck the Over Black option. Now, click the Update button in the Titles palette. This causes iMovie to reprocess your title so that the iMovie is updated.

Q I'm having fun using the Scrolling Block title, and I've been typing the text into iMovie, but it's kind of hard to type it in the little window. Can I import text somehow?

A You can't import a text file in the present version of iMovie, but what you can do is compose your paragraphs of text that you want to use in a program such as AppleWorks or Microsoft Word, and then select the text in the word processing program (choose Edit, Copy to copy the text into memory). Then switch to iMovie, select the Scrolling Block title, and choose Edit, Paste to paste the text right into the title.

Quiz

1. How do you get a preview of a title?

   A. Click on the title in the Titles window

   B. Select the title and click the Preview button

   C. Click on the title in the Monitor window

   D. A and B

2. Where do you adjust a title?

   A. In the Adjust palette

   B. In the Titles palette

   C. In the Adjust Titles palette

3. Which is the coolest title?

    A. The Centered Multiple title because it fades nicely

    B. The Scrolling Block title because you can make your movie look like the beginning of *Star Wars*

    C. The Stripe Subtitle because you can make your own infomercial

Quiz Answers

1. **D.** Both A and B will get you a preview.

> A third previewing option is to click the Preview screen itself.

2. **B.** The Titles palette is where the action happens!

3. **A.** The Centered Multiple title is definitely the coolest title. Okay, okay, this question wasn't particularly objective. But the moral of the question is that titles are very subjective. They're a great way to express yourself and can have a profound effect on the identity of your iMovie.

Exercises

1. Click through the list of titles available in the Titles palette to see what each looks like on screen.

2. Choose a title, customize it for your project, and apply it.

HOUR 11

Adding Photos to iMovies

iMovie is only for people with video cameras, right? Wrong. Still images with accompanying sound can be used to create high-impact presentations and documentaries, and can be used to spice up live-action films with professional title and credit backgrounds. Even if you're a digital photographer who is completely satisfied with iPhoto, you'll find that iMovie can create new and exciting ways to display your masterpieces.

In this hour, you learn

- How to import still images into iPhoto
- How to add photos to iMovie
- About different options available for displaying still images in your iMovies

Photos and iMovie

iMovie is known for the ease of use with which it enables you to import and manipulate digital video with special effects and transitions. iMovie 3
integrates completely with iPhoto 2, providing instant access to your photograph library.

Photographs can be worked with very much like video clips—you can apply the same effects and transitions, as well as use a very special effect designed specifically for digital photographs and dubbed the *Ken Burns effect*. This effect, which we'll discuss later, can add motion and depth to otherwise still images. Figure 11.1 shows a still image within the Timeline; it appears identical to a video clip.

FIGURE 11.1
Still images work virtually identically to video clips within iMovie.

iMovie supports a number of native image formats through QuickTime's media framework. TIFFs, JPEGs, and even PDF files can be dragged into an iMovie project as a source of still images.

Importing into iPhoto

The best and cleanest way to handle importing images into iMovie is to import them into iPhoto first. iMovie automatically connects to your iPhoto library and provides access to all of your digital images in the same way it does with digital music and iTunes. The drawback to this is that even if you want to insert only an image or two into iMovie, it's best if they're added to your iPhoto library.

> You should start iPhoto at least once before using iMovie. Otherwise the iPhoto/iMovie integration won't be complete, and iMovie might behave strangely when attempting to access photo features.

There are two straightforward methods for getting images into iPhoto. The first method is to connect a supported camera to your computer, and follow your camera's instructions to place it in playback or transfer mode. Your computer will sense the connected camera, launch iPhoto, and present you with the Import pane shown in Figure 11.2.

FIGURE 11.2

Images in iPhoto are imported directly from the digital camera.

Clicking the Import button transfers files from your camera. Thumbnails of the transferring images appear in the image well of the Import pane along with the number of photos remaining to be transferred. When the import is complete, the new images will appear in the photo viewing area along with any other images you've imported. If the box for Erase Camera Contents After Transfer is checked, you'll be asked to approve the deletion of the original photo files from the camera.

Imported images are stored in groupings called *rolls* in the photo library. Any image, in any roll, can be added to an arbitrary album by first creating the album (choose New Album from the File menu), and then dragging from the photo library into the album name displayed along the left side of the iPhoto window. This helps you keep track of your images, and provides a convenient means of accessing them in iMovie.

The second method of importing images assumes that you already have a group of image files on your computer but not in iPhoto. In this case, you can select them in the Finder and drag them into the iPhoto library.

Adding Photos to iMovie

As mentioned previously, there are two ways to add photos to iMovie, either from files on your desktop or via iPhoto integration. Because iPhoto is the preferred method, we'll start there.

Task: Achieve iPhoto Integration

To add a photograph that you've previously stored within your iPhoto library:

1. Click the Photos button on the icon bar in the lower-right portion of the iMovie window. The Photos palette should appear, as seen in Figure 11.3.

   At the top of the palette are the controls for the Ken Burns effect, followed by the library of available iPhoto images. The pop-up menu at the top of the image catalog can be used to limit the images being displayed to any of the iPhoto albums you've created or two special categories:

   iPhoto Library—All images in the iPhoto library

   Last Import—The last group of images you imported into iPhoto

11

▼ TASK

▼

Figure 11.3

The Photos palette provides direct access to iPhoto images.

2. Choose the album or category that contains the image you want to use, and then scroll through the image catalog to find the exact picture you want to add.

3. Finally, drag the image to the Timeline or Clip view at the bottom of the iMovie window. iMovie will behave *exactly* as if you were adding a video clip with a 5-second duration. Figure 11.4 shows a collection of three images that have been added to the Clip view in iMovie.

Figure 11.4

Just think of still images as video clips without much video.

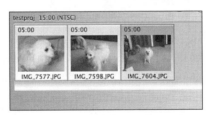

Unfortunately, this is the point at which some of Apple's user-friendliness gets in the way. The software will immediately try to render the Ken Burns effect within your image. Because we don't even know what the Ken Burns effect *is* yet, we probably aren't that anxious to use it! To cancel the rendering, simply add the image to the Timeline, select it within either the Timeline or the Clip view, and press the escape (Esc) key, or Command+. iMovie will stop trying to add the special effect and we'll get exactly what we want: a 5-second still clip of the photograph.

The Ken Burns Effect

So, what is the Ken Burns effect that Apple so desperately seems to want us to use? It's a method of bringing life to still images that was pioneered by the filmmaker Ken Burns, who has created many award-winning documentaries, and whose work has even been nominated for an Academy Award.

 For a complete background on Ken Burns and his work, visit
http://www.pbs.org/kenburns/.

The effect is really quite simple. Rather than just putting a photograph onscreen while someone narrates, a virtual camera pans over the image, zooming in or out as it goes. A photograph of a bouquet of flowers, for example, could start zoomed in on one particular flower, and then zoom out, centering the bouquet on the screen as it goes. When the effect is used properly, the end result is stunning and can make the viewer forget that he isn't watching live video.

To use the Ken Burns effect in iMovie, first make sure that you're in the Photo pane and then select the image that you want to apply the effect to. At the top of the Photo pane are the controls that you'll use to determine the path that the virtual camera will take, how long the resulting video clip will be, and how far in or out the virtual camera will be zoomed.

For example, I've chosen a picture of an orchid that I want to apply the effect to. I've decided that I want to start the video zoomed in on one of the flowers, and then zoom out to show several. To do this, I click the Start button, and then click and drag the image within the Ken Burns effect image well. This enables me to center where the camera will be starting when the effect is applied. Next, I adjust the Zoom level either using the slider control or by directly typing in the Zoom field. The start settings of my Ken Burns effect are shown in Figure 11.5.

To complete the effect, I need to repeat the same process for the finish point of the effect. This time, I click the Finish button, click and drag the image so that it appears as I want it in the image well, and then adjust the zoom so that I can see several of the orchid's flowers, as shown in Figure 11.6.

FIGURE 11.5

*Choose the starting
location and zoom for
the image.*

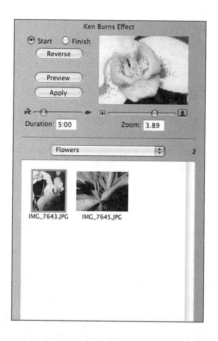

FIGURE 11.6

*Set the finish point and
zoom level to complete
the transition.*

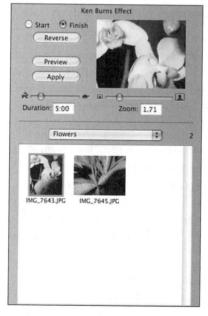

To preview the Ken Burns effect before you actually apply it to an image, click the
Preview button. To reverse the path that the virtual camera takes (effectively switching
the start and finish points), click the Reverse button. If you want the total time the

transition takes to last more (or less) than 5 seconds, adjust the duration slider or type directly into the Duration Time field. Finally, to add the image with the Ken Burns effect to the Timeline or Clip view, click the Apply button. The effect might take several minutes to apply (watch the little progress bar that appears above the image in the Clip Viewer mode).

> The settings you choose when adding the Ken Burns effect to a photograph are used as the default for subsequent images you add. Because iMovie attempts to apply the Ken Burns effect to *everything*, make sure that what it's doing is really what you want.

Adding Photos Directly

You can easily add photos directly to iMovie by dragging the image files from your desktop into the Clip Organizer pane, the Clip Viewer, or the Timeline. In all these cases, iMovie adds the image, just like a video clip, but again automatically tries to apply the Ken Burns effect using the current settings within the Photo pane. As mentioned previously, you can cancel the Ken Burns effect and use the image as a still by pressing Escape (Esc) or Command+. immediately after adding it to iMovie.

So, what if you want to add photos directly *and* use the Ken Burns effect? If the settings for the Ken Burns effect are already configured the way you want before you add your picture, you literally don't have to do *anything*. Just add your image and allow the Ken Burns effect to be applied automatically.

Task: Adding an Image with Custom Ken Burns Effect Settings

However, if you'd like to customize the effect for the image you're adding, you must follow these steps:

1. Add the image by dragging it into iMovie.
2. Cancel the automatic application of the Ken Burns effect by pressing Escape (Esc) or Command+.(period).
3. Click on the image in the Clip Viewer or the Timeline to select it.
4. Switch to the Photo panel by clicking the Photos icon on the icon bar in the lower-right portion of the iMovie window.
5. The selected image will appear in the Ken Burns Effect image well.
6. Choose the effect settings you want, and then click Apply.
7. The Ken Burns effect with your custom settings will be applied to the image you've added to iMovie directly.

11

As you can see, working with the iPhoto integration is a much more straightforward means of managing images and applying the Ken Burns effect. Hopefully, Apple will clean up this process in the future and add a preference for the automatic application of the Ken Burns effect. For now, however, you've got to make sure that iMovie doesn't start adding effects where you don't want them.

Still Images from Video

One final source for still images is a video clip itself. iMovie makes it easy to create a still image from any frame in a video file. To do this, switch to the Timeline Viewer and drag the playhead until the image that you want to use as a still appears within the main viewer. Next, choose Create Still Frame from the Edit menu. iMovie will add a still image with a 5-second duration to the available iMovie clips.

 Surprisingly, when you create a still image from a video clip, iMovie will *not* attempt to apply the Ken Burns effect!

Still Images and Duration

A point of confusion when working with still images is the duration and how the duration can be changed. A still image that does not have the Ken Burns effect applied is, by default, treated as a 5-second video clip. To change the length of time that the image will be displayed onscreen, simply double-click it within the Timeline or Clip view. The window as shown in Figure 11.7 will appear, and you can manually enter how long the clip should last.

FIGURE 11.7

Change how long a still image will be displayed.

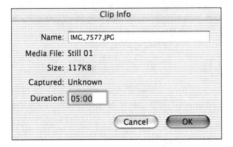

However, the same cannot be said for an image that has had the Ken Burns effect applied. Double-clicking a Ken Burns image will show a noneditable duration, as shown in Figure 11.8.

Figure 11.8

You cannot alter the duration of a Ken Burns effect image without reapplying the effect.

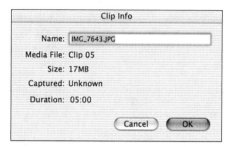

Clip Info

Name: IMG_7643.JPG
Media File: Clip 05
Size: 17MB
Captured: Unknown
Duration: 05:00

Cancel   OK

The reason for this difference is that an image that has had the Ken Burns effect applied is effectively a piece of video. It has different frames that iMovie calculated based on the settings you gave it. A "real" still image is just a single frame that iMovie understands it should display for a set length of time.

To change the duration of a Ken Burns effect image, select the image within the Timeline or Clip Viewer, and then click the Photos button to switch to the Photo pane. The selected image will be shown in the Ken Burns preview and the settings used to create the image will be loaded. Adjust the duration using the duration slider, and then click the Apply button to rerender the effect with the new duration.

Still Images, Effects, and Transitions

11

iMovie makes it simple to apply effects and transitions to images that you've added to your project. In fact, there's virtually no difference between working with still or Ken Burns effect image clips and video clips. There are two specific situations, however, when you might be prompted to do something that isn't quite clear:

Increase Clip Duration—Sometimes the length of a still image clip isn't long enough for a given transition (a wipe/fade/and so on) to be applied. In this case, iMovie will tell you that the clip must be longer. All you need to do is adjust the duration (as discussed previously).

Convert Still Clip to Regular Clips—Sometimes, when applying an effect that changes over time—like Earthquake, which makes each frame shift slightly to create a shaking appearance—iMovie will state `This effect generates different results for each frame, which will not show up on Still Clips`, as shown in Figure 11.9.

To apply the effect, iMovie must effectively change the still image into a video clip. Click the Convert button when prompted, and iMovie will render the effect. The only drawback to this is that, like an image with the Ken Burns effect added, you won't be able to change the duration as you would with a normal still image. To revert to a normal still clip, you must delete the converted clip and re-add the original image.

FIGURE 11.9

Some effects require that still clips be converted into regular clips.

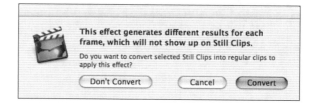

Summary

In this hour, you learned how still images can be added to iMovie presentations and how they can be made dynamic through the use of the Ken Burns effect. In iMovie, a still image behaves almost exactly like a standard video clip, and can have all the same transitions and effects applied.

In the next hour, we'll discuss adding sound to iMovies.

Workshop

The following section contains questions, answers, and exercises to help you get a better understanding of using iMovie's audio features. In the quiz, try to answer the questions *before* checking the answers. Then read the explanations, even if you get the answers right.

Q&A

Q I never plan to use the Ken Burns effect. I know I can press Cmd plus a period (.) to stop the effect from being used, but isn't there a better way to stop it from being applied at all?

A If you're an adventurous sort and want to disable the automatic application of the Ken Burns effect completely, open the file `~/Library/Preferences/com.apple.iMovie3.plist` in a text editor such as Text Editor, and then look for the line that contains the text `autoApplyPanZoomToImportedStills`. Shortly after that line you'll see the word `true`. Change the word `true` to `false`, leaving everything else the same. Restart iMovie, and the program will suddenly work just the way you would expect!

Q **You explained how to make a video into a still frame for use in iMovie, but what if I want to export a still image to use in another program or to send in email?**

A iMovie will let you save a single frame as an image in either JPEG or Pict format. Simply position your playhead at the point you want to make into a still image, and choose Save Frame As from the File menu. A dialog box will appear, and you can type a name for the image as well as choose the file format (JPEG or Pict) and where to save the image.

Quiz

1. Ken Burns is famous for which of the following?

     A. Creating award-winning documentaries.

     B. Crushing the previous world record for pole-vaulting at the 1984 Olympics.

     C. Writing the original iMovie application.

2. How do you create a still image from a frame of video?

     A. Take a picture of your monitor while that frame is visible on it.

     B. Choose File, Save Frame As.

     C. Choose Edit, Create Still Frame.

     D. All of the above.

3. Which of the following can be applied to still photos just as they can to video?

     A. Titles

     B. Transitions

     C. Effects

     D. All of the above

Quiz Answers

1. **A.** Ken Burns is an award-winning filmmaker.

2. **D.** Technically, all of these methods will work, but option C is the most efficient method. If you choose option B, you must import the still you save back into iMovie, and option A requires you to import an image of questionable quality from your camera and into iMovie.

3. **D.** You can apply titles, transitions, and effects to a still photo. However, some transitions and effects can be applied only to elements over a minimum duration or those that have been converted to video with multiple frames.

Exercises

1. Practice adding images (with and without the Ken Burns effect) to your iMovie.

2. After you've added some images, try applying titles, transitions, and effects to them. Note that some transitions and effects must be applied to elements of longer duration, so you might get messages that your effect cannot be applied. Also, if you try to apply some effects to a still photo, you might be asked whether you want to convert the still to video so that the effect can be applied.

HOUR 12

Adding Sound to iMovies

If you've added film clips to your project from your camera or from other sources, they've almost certainly had sound accompanying them. What if you decide that you don't like the sound that goes along with your movie clip? Do you have to reshoot the video just for a new audio track? No, not at all. iMovie provides you the ability to use dozens of canned sound effects, record audio from your computer's microphone (if available), use music from your iTunes library, and even take the sound from other video clips and use them with different video sequences.

In this hour, you learn

- How sound works in iMovie
- How to access the iTunes music library
- How to manipulate your audio tracks
- Where to find other iMovie audio sources

Sound in iMovie

In an iMovie project, sound often plays almost as important a part as video. Sound and music can set the stage for a romance, suspense, comedy, or thrills. It can help create pacing for the movie and smooth through otherwise troublesome video transitions. If you've been using iMovie to import and arrange movies from your camera, you've already got audio in your projects. Movie clips can contain embedded sounds, and these are usually transferred and saved along with the movie files. Although this is convenient if you want to use only the sounds you've recorded with your camera, it doesn't give you the flexibility to mix sounds or add additional sounds to your movie.

Audio Tracks

To accommodate additional sound effects, iMovie includes two sound tracks that can hold any sound, music, or audio that you'd like. Figure 12.1 shows the three available iMovie tracks: video/audio, audio track 1, and audio track 2.

FIGURE 12.1

Audio can be part of a video track or can be added to either of the two audio tracks.

There's no difference in functionality between the audio 1 and 2 tracks. You can use one track to hold sound effects, and the other for background music, or mix and match them as you choose. In addition, each track can contain overlapping audio clips, giving you almost limitless layers of audio. For example, you could have a base piece of background music in audio track 1, and then perhaps an environment sound track layered on top of it, and, finally, sound effects layered on top of that in audio track 2. Figure 12.2 shows a layering possibility much like this scenario.

FIGURE 12.2

Audio can be layered via the different audio tracks or within a single audio track.

You've probably figured this out, but you must be in Timeline mode rather than the Clip Viewer to see the available audio tracks.

Sounds that are added to either of the audio tracks can be moved to the other track by clicking and dragging between the tracks in the Timeline. No matter what type of sound you're adding, it's referred to within iMovie as an *audio clip*.

Audio Playback

However you've decided to layer your audio, iMovie will automatically composite it correctly when you play back your movie project. If you've included audio clips in all the tracks, they'll all automatically play back when you play the movie.

This can sometimes get to be a bit of a pain as you try to fine-tune your special effect sounds and don't want to hear the dialog from your video tracks or the background music you've added. To enable you to focus on a single set of audio, Apple has provided the ability to control audio playback using the three check boxes to the right of the video and audio tracks, as shown in Figure 12.3.

FIGURE 12.3

Turn audio tracks on and off to focus on a particular part of your sound editing.

You can also control the overall volume of the movie preview using the volume control slider to the right of the main playback controls.

Working with Audio

There are a number of different ways to add audio to a project, so we'll start with one of the most common (and useful), and then discuss how to work with audio clips that have been added to a timeline, and, finally, examine other means of importing audio.

Accessing the iTunes Music Library

Adding audio to an iMovie project takes place through the Audio palette, which is accessed by clicking the Audio button in the icon bar on the lower-right half of the screen. Figure 12.4 shows the iMovie window with the Audio palette active.

Your iTunes library is the default source for audio that's added to the project. You can use the pull-down menu at the top of the iTunes listing to choose between your iTunes playlists or type a few characters into the search field at the bottom of the song list to filter the songs that are shown.

12

FIGURE 12.4

Access audio import features by clicking the audio (speaker) icon in the lower-right portion of the iMovie window.

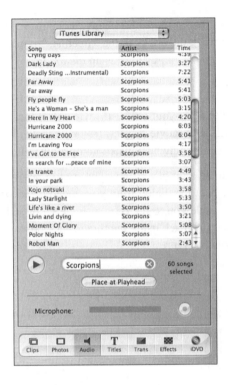

 When using the search field to find your iTunes music, you'll notice that an X appears at the end of the field after you've typed in a few characters. Clicking the X will clear out the search results and return to the full list.

If you have a library of thousands of songs and can't remember which one you're looking for, you can choose a song from the list, and then click the Play button underneath the list to listen to the song.

 Remember that using copyrighted material without permission is *against the law*. Be sure that any songs you're using in a movie are public domain or properly licensed. If you're making the movie just for yourself, you can use music you own—but if the final product will be distributed to others, you cannot use copyrighted material.

Adding iTunes Audio to the Project

After you've located the song file that you want to add to the iMovie project, position the playhead where you would like the sound to be inserted, click within the audio track that should receive the sound file, and then click the Place at Playhead button in the Audio palette. iMovie will take a few seconds (or minutes, depending on the length of the file), and the corresponding audio clip will appear in the selected audio track as a colored bar labeled with the name of the audio file, as shown in Figure 12.5.

FIGURE 12.5

iMovie has just finished adding the chosen song to the selected audio track.

In the shipping version of iMovie, there is no obvious means of telling which audio track is currently selected. The last track you clicked in is the one used for inserting audio.

If you happen to end up with audio inserted in the wrong track, simply click and drag the audio from one track to another.

Another, perhaps more elegant, way to add an audio clip to the project is to drag a name from the list in the Audio palette to the audio track where it should be inserted. As you drag the name into the Timeline, a yellow insert bar will appear to show you where the audio will be inserted when you stop dragging.

You can even extend this technique to the Finder by dragging audio files directly from your desktop into the Timeline.

12

Manipulating Audio Within the iMovie

After a piece of audio has been added to an audio track, it can easily be manipulated to match up with your video tracks or the volume can be changed to better mix with the video or other audio files.

Repositioning Audio

Sometimes you place a sound in a movie and it just doesn't fit, or doesn't sync up with the video. To move an audio clip, click and drag it horizontally within the Timeline. The audio segment will move to any position you'd like within the project. While you're dragging, the playhead will automatically track the start position of the audio, enabling you to position it perfectly within the project, as shown in Figure 12.6.

FIGURE **12.6**

Drag the audio clip to reposition it.

For extremely fine control of audio positioning, click to select the audio clip in the Timeline (it will darken in color to show that it's selected), and then use the left and right arrow keys to move the clip frame by frame along the Timeline. Holding down the Shift key will increase the movement to ten frames at a time.

If you decide that you want to remove an audio clip from the project, simply click on it and then press Delete or choose Clear from the Edit menu.

Locking Audio to a Video Clip

The act of moving audio around is often an attempt to synchronize it with a piece of video. iMovie's capability to position on a frame-by-frame basis makes this simple, but what if you decide later that you want to reposition the video clip? If you drag the video, all of your hard work synching the audio will be lost.

To lock a piece of audio to the video track, select the audio that you've positioned where you want it and then choose Lock Audio Clip at Playhead from the Advanced menu. The audio track will then be attached to the video that occurs at the same place as the audio. Moving the video track within the Timeline will move the audio as well, keeping your synchronization intact. You can tell a lock is in place because of graphical pushpins that appear on the audio and video tracks, as seen in Figure 12.7.

FIGURE 12.7

Pushpins denote an audio track that's locked to a video track.

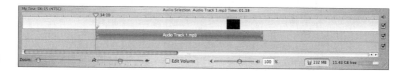

To unlock an audio clip, select it within the audio track, and then choose Unlock Audio Clip from the Advanced menu.

Locking audio to a video clip works *one way*. It does *not* lock the video to audio. If you drag the video clip, the audio will move with it, but not vice versa. Dragging the audio will simply reposition the lock to the video, potentially losing any synching work you've done.

By default, all locked audio clips are displayed with the pushpins all the time. To change the display so that the pushpins are shown only when the audio clip is selected, be sure to check the Show Locked Audio Only When Selected option within the iMovie preferences.

Using Crop Markers

Like video, audio clips also have crop markers that can be used to choose how much or how little of a clip is played. These two arrows appear at the ends of an audio clip and can be dragged with the mouse to limit audio playback to a certain part of a sound, as demonstrated in Figure 12.8.

FIGURE 12.8

Drag the crop markers to limit what parts of the song are played.

To completely crop (remove) the portions of the audio clip that aren't being played, mark off the appropriate portions with the crop markers and then choose Crop from the Edit menu.

12

Adjusting Volume

Suppose that you want soft background music in one portion of your movie, but want it to slowly build to a blaring orchestra in another? Before iMovie 3, the only way to do this was to edit the sound files in another audio program. Adjusting the volume is now as simple as clicking and dragging.

To enter the volume-editing mode, click the Edit Volume check box at the bottom of the iMovie window. Within a few seconds, all the audio clips (and the video clips that contain audio) will display little lines through them. This line represents the volume level of the clip.

To change the volume level of a clip, highlight the clip within any of the tracks (remember, even the video track's audio can be adjusted here) and then click and drag the volume adjustment at the very bottom of the iTunes window, or type a new volume level (100% being the default volume) into the field beside the volume slider. As you change the volume level, the line will raise or lower within the clip. Multiple clips can even be selected at once (Shift + mouse click) and simultaneously adjusted with this control.

"Okay, that's nice," you're thinking, "but it still doesn't get me the fine-tuned control I need to really mix different audio clips together." Don't worry; volume adjustment can be as simple (as we've seen) or as complex (as we're about to see) as you want.

To alter the volume level within a specific part of an audio or video clip, click and drag the volume line within the clip. As you drag, an adjustment handle (a big yellow dot) will appear. Dragging this dot up or down raises or lowers the volume at that point. To carry the volume change through to a different part of the clip, simply click wherever you want another volume adjustment handle to be added, and the level changes will be carried through to that point. (If you add additional adjustment handles to a clip, the inactive ones will be purple.)

Each handle that's added also carries with it a transition point that determines how the audio clip will transition to the new volume level (will it happen abruptly? smoothly?). The transition point is displayed as a small purple square to the left or right of the adjustment handle. The point can be dragged so that it's right above or below an adjustment handle, making for an immediate transition in volume, as shown in Figure 12.9.

FIGURE 12.9

Moving the transition point directly above or below the adjustment handle causes an immediate volume transition.

To smooth things out a bit, the transition point can be dragged all the way along the volume line up to another adjustment point. The transition, displayed graphically as an orange line segment, takes place between these two points. For example, Figure 12.10 shows the same volume adjustment being made as in Figure 12.9, but the transition places over a much larger span of the audio clip.

FIGURE 12.10

The transition point can be used to spread the volume transition out over a long span of the audio clip.

Volume adjustment can be used to ramp down an audio clip while ramping up another (this is called a *cross-fade*), or to create any number of other effects within your project.

Splitting Audio

If you have a sound or song that you want to play part of at one time and another part of at another time, you have two choices: You can import the audio clip twice, or you can simply split the existing clip into different pieces and use them wherever you'd like. To split an audio clip, position the playhead where you'd like the clip to break and then choose Split Audio Clip at Playhead from the Edit menu.

New crop marks will appear at the location of the split within the audio clip. You can use these markers to fine-tune the split location, as shown in Figure 12.11.

FIGURE 12.11

Using the split feature adds crop markers at the location of the Playhead.

To finish the split, you must choose Crop from the Edit menu; otherwise, the split audio segments will still be attached to one another and can't be moved separately.

Other iMovie Audio Sources

Now that you've learned how to work with audio clips in iMovie, let's take a quick look at the other sources of audio that are available for adding audio clips to your project. At the top of the Audio panel is a pop-up menu with additional choices for importing audio clips. As you've already seen, the iTunes Library and playlists are available.

iMovie Sound Effects

A great source for canned sound effects is the included iMovie sound effects library, which is accessed by choosing iMovie Sound Effects from the top of the Audio panel in iMovie. The iMovie sound effects, shown in Figure 12.12, encompass a wide range of environmental and special effect sounds. The Skywalker Sound Effects (from George Lucas's Skywalker Ranch) are extremely high-quality effects that can be used to create a very impressive soundtrack.

FIGURE 12.12

Choose from dozens of built-in sound effects.

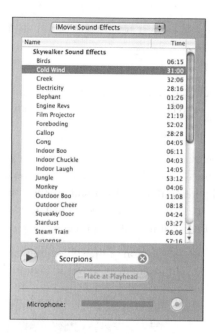

Unlike iMovie music, you cannot click the Place at Playhead button to insert a selected sound effect. (I can't imagine why not, but it doesn't work!) Instead, you must click and drag the name of an effect into your audio track. Once the effect is added, it behaves like any other audio clip.

Audio CDs

To add a sound track from an audio CD, put the CD in your computer's CD-ROM drive and then wait a few seconds. iMovie should automatically switch to Audio CD mode, query the Internet CD database to get a list of track names, and then display the contents of the CD in the Audio panel, as shown in Figure 12.13.

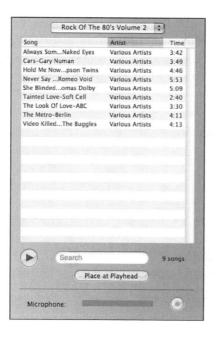

FIGURE 12.13

The contents of the audio CD will be displayed in the Audio panel.

Choose the song you want to add to one of your iMovie audio tracks and then either click the Place at Playhead button or drag the song to the Timeline to add it to the project.

Recording a Voice Track

If you'd like to narrate a portion of the video, position the playhead where you'd like to start recording from your computer's microphone and then click in the audio track that should receive the audio. Finally, click the red Record button to the right of the Microphone label at the bottom of the Audio pane. A graph of the level of sound input is shown beside the label as it records. To stop recording live audio, click the Record button again.

The new audio clips will be added to your project with the sequential labels Voice 1, Voice 2, and so on.

Extracting Audio from Video Clips

As I've already mentioned, the video track often also contains audio that accompanies a video clip. When adjusting volume, you can adjust the volume of a video clip just as you would an audio clip in an audio track.

12

Having video so closely tied to audio, however, has its disadvantages—you cannot manipulate the audio and video independent of one another. Thankfully, iMovie enables you to decouple the audio and video from one another. To do this, select a video clip with audio and then choose Extract Audio from the Advanced menu. After a few seconds, the audio from the video clip will appear in the audio track below the video clip. Figure 12.14 shows a video clip in the Timeline before audio extraction, and Figure 12.15 shows the same clip after extraction.

FIGURE 12.14

Normally, audio is embedded in the video clip...

FIGURE 12.15

...but it can be easily extracted.

After audio is extracted from a video file, it can be manipulated like any other audio clip.

In some cases, audio extraction happens automatically. For example, if you cut and paste a video clip using the Paste Over at Playhead option of the Advanced menu, iMovie automatically extracts the audio of the original clip and moves it to an audio track so it isn't replaced by the paste over. The video clip that's pasted over will be lost, but the audio will remain.

This feature can be disabled by deselecting Extract Audio in Paste Over in the iMovie preferences.

iMovie has the capability to speed up and slow down video clips as well as reverse their playback. These features do *not* work on audio clips. However, you can apply the transformations to a video clip and then extract the audio, and the changes will carry with it.

Summary

This hour demonstrated the available iMovie audio functions that are at your disposal. Although simple to use, the audio features can enable novice editors to create layered audio tracks with ease. iMovie supports a variety of audio sources for easily getting sound into your video project, and includes some of the best built-in sound effects outside of a Hollywood editing studio.

In the next hour, we'll begin our introduction to DVD basics, starting with the engrossing topic of DVD video.

Workshop

The following section contains questions, answers, and exercises to help you get a better understanding of using iMovie's audio features. In the quiz, try to answer the questions *before* checking the answers. Then read the explanations, even if you get the answers right.

Q&A

Q Can I add sound effects of my own to iMovie?

A Yes, you can, but you have to know where to store the files so that iMovie will display them in the Sound Effects pane of the Audio tab. Please note that your sound files must be in .aiff format. You can convert MP3s to aiff format using QuickTime Pro.

To add your own sound effects, open the Library folder of your user account and look for a folder called iMovie. It should contain a folder called Sound Effect. If the iMovie folder doesn't exist, create it and add a new folder inside it called Sound Effect. Create a folder inside the Sound Effect folder and name it anything you'd like. Then drag your aiff sound files into that folder.

After you restart your computer, your added sound effects will appear in the Sound Effects pane in the Standard Sound Effects list.

Quiz

1. How many audio tracks can you work with in iMovie?

    A. 1

    B. 2

    C. 3

    D. None

2. How can you edit the volume of audio tracks in iMovie?

    A. You can't—you must have an audio editing program for that.

    B. Use the volume control under the Preview window.

    C. Check the Edit Volume box at the bottom of the iMovie window and adjust the volume setting.

12

3. How do you add narration to an iMovie?

    A. You must have an audio editing program to record the voiceover.

    B. Open the Audio palette, click the button for Microphone, and speak into your computer's microphone.

    C. Give a running narration while you film your video footage.

    D. B and C.

Quiz Answers

1. **C.** Trick question! There are two separate audio tracks, but the video track can include audio as well.

2. **C.** To change the volume in a clip, you have to check the box for Edit Volume. If you drag the Volume control under the Preview window, you're adjusting the volume only for your movie preview.

3. **D.** You can record a voiceover in the Audio palette after you've filmed scenes, or you can import video that includes narration.

Exercises

Open the Sound Effects panel of the Audio palette and listen to several sound effects. Drag one into an audio track of your current project and position it at a specific point in your video. For bonus points, lock the audio to that point in the video clip.

PART III

DVD Basics

Hour

HOUR 13

Understanding DVD Video

In this lesson, we look at DVD basics by investigating the way that DVD video works as well as how iDVD works with video. The more that you learn about DVD video, the more you might appreciate how simple (and powerful) iDVD software is.

Throughout this hour, we discuss the following topics:

- How DVD video works
- Preparing DVD video
- Encoding DVD video
- Multiplexing

How DVD Video Works

DVD video is a form of *digital* video, and much like the way that digital video is stored on a computer hard drive, digital video is stored as data files on the DVD disc. When you insert a DVD disc in a player that's connected to a television, a small computer in the DVD player looks for the DVD video files and displays them on the TV screen.

When you watch or make a DVD, there are two types of video that you can experience: regular video such as a movie (as seen in Figure 13.1), and video that's contained in a motion menu.

FIGURE 13.1
Watching regular video in a DVD.

 A *motion menu* is simply any screen on a DVD from which you're making menu choices and something is moving in the background behind the DVD menu. iDVD refers to the video used in motion menus as *background video*. See Figure 13.2.

FIGURE 13.2
A DVD motion menu with background video of clouds slowly passing by, which adds an interesting touch to an otherwise motionless DVD menu.

One of the advantages of iDVD is that it enables you to incorporate motion menus in your DVDs by allowing you to choose from various customizable motion menu backgrounds. The creation of motion menus normally can be a complex process, but iDVD gives you the advantage of motion menus without all the hassle.

Working with DVD Video

There are four stages of working with DVD video: preparing, importing, encoding, and burning.

- **Preparing**—In this stage, you edit your video in iMovie before opening it iDVD. Using a program like iDVD is also known as *DVD authoring*. You'll find that you spend more time preparing the files for your DVD than you spend on any other task. After the files are ready, it's easy to put the DVD together.

- **Importing**—To use your video in iDVD, you must import it into the project you're working on.

- **Encoding**—Digital video must be encoded into the MPEG-2 format for it to work with DVD. In the field of DVD authoring, there are a number of different techniques and tools for encoding video for use in DVD. iDVD makes the encoding process simple: When you import video into iDVD, the encoding happens automatically.

Encoding can be a very involved process. DVD Studio Pro is a professional DVD-authoring program—iDVD's "older cousin"—and it uses a separate program for encoding with a number of adjustable settings. There are people in Hollywood known as *compressionists* whose primary task is to use advanced programs to encode video into MPEG-2 format; they attempt to squeeze the highest amount of quality out of the video that will fit on the DVD.

- **Burning**—When you're done creating your DVD project, you're ready to burn a DVD disc. With iDVD, you insert a blank disc and burn it using the built-in SuperDrive that came with your Mac.

If you don't have a SuperDrive-equipped Mac you can't use iDVD.

13

Preparing Digital Video for DVD

To prepare digital video for use in iDVD, you create and edit your iMovie until you're happy with it, and then open the iDVD palette, shown in Figure 13.3, and click Create iDVD Project. Alternatively, you could choose File, Export Movie, and choose the to iDVD option from the Export pop-up menu at the top of the Export Movie window. The outcome is the same either way—the iDVD interface launches with your movie.

FIGURE 13.3

You can export video from iMovie for use in iDVD in the iDVD palette.

By default, iMovie saves your iMovie to iDVD by creating a file inside the Documents folder in your home account. Even if you don't tell it to save, a file with the extension `.dvdproj` will be created there.

Importing Digital Video into iDVD

If, for some reason, you want to import only a clip from an existing iMovie into iDVD, you simply need to import it into iDVD by choosing File, Import, Video. A file browser window will open, in which you can select the video file. See Figure 13.4.

FIGURE 13.4

Importing video into iDVD.

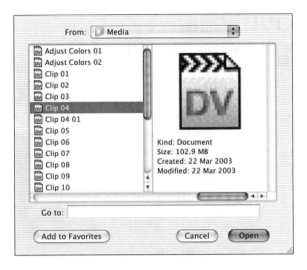

When you import a movie or a clip into iDVD, a reference to the file is made in the DVD project, but no copy is made in the `.dvdproj` file. If you move or rename the original file, iDVD won't be able to reference the file as needed when it comes time to burn your disc.

Encoding DVD Video

iDVD automatically encodes your video, so you don't need to do anything in particular —just import it. When you import a file into iDVD, it starts encoding your video automatically *in the background*, which basically means that it uses the processing power of the computer to encode with whatever free time it has to offer. See Figure 13.5.

FIGURE 13.5

The Status tab of the iDVD tray, which is accessed by clicking the Themes button in the main iDVD window. This tab shows an ongoing account of the video files that have been imported into iDVD and are being encoded in the background.

13

Burning DVD Video

When your iDVD project is done, the digital video that you're using in the project is ready to be burned to a DVD disc. When you click the Burn button in iDVD, it becomes active. See Figures 13.6 through 13.8 to see the different states of the Burn button and the progress window that appears when a DVD is being burned.

FIGURE 13.6
The Burn button in iDVD is usually covered.

FIGURE 13.7
When you click the Burn button, it becomes active.

FIGURE 13.8
Burning a DVD with readout of remaining time.

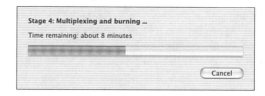

What Is Multiplexing?

When you burn a DVD disc, iDVD has to prepare the files in a process known as *multiplexing*. Multiplexing allows the files to be understood by a DVD player. Multiplexing basically means that iDVD is translating the files into a proper DVD format, which you'll see in the following task.

Task: Examining a DVD

To get a better sense of what's going on under the hood of a DVD, try taking a closer look at a DVD movie that you own or have rented using your Mac as a "DVD microscope."

> DVD Player is a program that starts automatically when you insert a DVD in your Mac.

▼   1. Insert the DVD disc in the DVD drive on your Mac.

2. Wait a few moments. If your Mac automatically launches the DVD player software, either quit out of the software entirely by pressing Command+Q or choose Quit from the DVD Player menu. If the DVD is taking up the entire screen, you can move the mouse up to the top of the screen to reveal the menu.

3. Look on your desktop for the icon that represents the DVD, and double-click to open it. See Figure 13.9.

FIGURE 13.9

The DVD icon that appears on the Mac desktop when a DVD is inserted.

4. When the window that represents the DVD opens up, you'll see a VIDEO_TS folder. This same folder is on *every* DVD that you can watch in a DVD player. If the VIDEO_TS folder isn't there, the DVD player won't understand the disc. Double-click the VIDEO_TS folder (see Figure 13.10) to open it.

FIGURE 13.10

The infamous VIDEO_TS folder is present on every DVD.

5. When the VIDEO_TS folder opens, you might want to choose View, As List to see the files better. See Figure 13.11.

FIGURE 13.11

The files within the VIDEO_TS folder, which contain everything a DVD player needs to create the interactive experience.

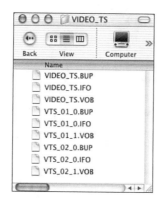

13

It isn't particularly important to understand what the individual files in a VIDEO_TS folder do, but it can be interesting to look at things from the perspective of what a DVD player does. At this point, the digital video files within a VIDEO_TS folder have been encoded into MPEG-2 and multiplexed into their final DVD-ready form.

The following list explains what the file extensions (the last three letters of the file) mean for files on a DVD:

- **IFO** (stands for *information*)—These files contain the information about the DVD menu screens that a DVD player uses to construct the interactive experience.
- **BUP** (stands for *backup*)—These files are simply copies of the IFO files.
- **VOB** (stands for *video objects*)—These files are the actual video on the DVD.

The SuperDrive DVD Burner

A discussion of DVD video basics wouldn't be complete without some mention of the DVD burner that made the independent DVD video revolution possible.

In January of 2001, Apple made history by introducing the first affordable DVD burner, integrated within the G4 desktop Power Mac line. This DVD burner, known as the SuperDrive, brought the power of DVD authoring to the masses, giving them the ability to take digital video and make it into *DVD video*. See Figure 13.12.

FIGURE 13.12

The revolutionary SuperDrive, on countless desktops around the world, with a blank DVD disc. Thanks, Apple.

DVD authoring had formerly been the domain of Hollywood, and DVD burners cost upward of $4,000—but then Apple came out with an entire computer *and* DVD burner for less than the price of what a DVD burner had cost. Apple has always been a leader in working with digital video, and it was only natural that, after the great success of iMovie and Final Cut Pro, Apple's next contribution would be iDVD and DVD Studio Pro along with the DVD drive that makes it all happen.

Although external DVD burners are available, iDVD requires the built-in SuperDrive. Other DVD development software, such as iDVD Studio Pro, will work with external drives.

Apple issued an important software update that prevents damage to some models of SuperDrive when they're used with newer high-speed DVD media. Refer to the first question in the "Q&A" section in Hour 15, "DVD Discs," for further information.

Summary

In this hour, you got your feet wet in the world of iDVD, making the transition from digital video into *DVD video*. The more you learn about the related technology, the more you might find yourself appreciating how good a job Apple has done, making it easy to use, and enjoyable, and *fun*.

In the next hour, we'll take a bird's eye view of digital video, considering DVD alongside other options you have for sharing your iMovies. Before you know it, the sun will be rising and you'll have to consider how you can fit some sleep in while you're getting your creations ready to share with the world.

Workshop

The following questions will test your knowledge of working with DVD video. Answers are provided for your reference.

Q&A

Q How much digital video can I fit on a DVD disc? The manufacturers say you can fit two hours, but iDVD says it can only fit 90 minutes' worth. What gives?

A iMovie uses a preset bit rate when it automatically encodes video for DVD, and in the current versions of iDVD, you can't adjust this bit rate. Adjusting the bit rate when encoding is how you can adjust how much video fits on a disc: If you lower the bit rate sufficiently, you can fit two or more hours of video on a DVD.

Q If I already have video in MPEG-2 format, can I import it into iDVD?

A Nope.

13

Quiz

1. What are the four stages of working with DVD video?

    A. Preparing, encoding, burning, exporting

    B. Capturing, editing, enhancing, sharing

    C. Preparing, importing, encoding, burning

2. What's a motion menu?

    A. A DVD menu with computer animation

    B. A DVD menu with digital video

    C. A menu that's being waved around impatiently in a restaurant

    D. A and B

3. How do you encode digital video after you import it into iDVD?

    A. Choose File, Encode.

    B. Choose Encode, Video.

    C. You don't need to encode the video; iDVD does it automatically.

Quiz Answers

1. **C.** Get your iMovie ready and bring it into iDVD. iDVD automatically encodes while you're putting the DVD together. When you're ready, click the Burn button! Oh wait, you're out of blank DVD discs! Go to the store and get some more.

2. **D.** Any DVD menu with some kind of motion is considered a motion menu.

3. **C.** iDVD does it automatically. To check on its progress, you can look at the status area by clicking the Themes button in the main iDVD window and then clicking the Status tab in the tray.

Exercise

Watch a DVD on your Mac using the DVD Player application. DVD Player should open automatically when you insert a finished DVD into your optical drive.

HOUR 14

DVD Features

In this hour, we look at various DVD features as a foundation for understanding what can be done in iDVD and how the program fits into the overall DVD picture. Whether you're an avid DVD collector or have never owned a DVD player but want to get into the fun, investigating how DVDs work will help you to get a sense of how iDVD will let you do things.

As we examine some of the features that DVD is capable of, you'll see how powerful iDVD is in terms of incorporating features and making them easy to add to your own DVD projects. You'll also see some advanced features that can be added using iDVD's older cousin, DVD Studio Pro.

Throughout this hour, we discuss the following:

- DVD players
- DVD menus
- Motion menus
- Slideshows
- How iDVD fits into the picture
- Subtitles and multiple camera angles

DVD Players

DVD players make the whole DVD experience possible. In the early days, as in the early days of CD players, prices were high and the availability of DVDs to rent or purchase was limited.

But more recently, sales of DVD players have exceeded sales of VCRs for the first time, even though the vast majority of them won't *record* DVD discs. It's just now that you can find DVD recorders that function like a DVD equivalent of VCRs (see Figure 14.1).

FIGURE 14.1
A typical DVD player from Pioneer.

In the present generation of DVD players and recorders, they all offer the same compatibility with DVD features. DVD manufacturers got together and agreed on what the players would support so that you could take any DVD and play it on any brand of DVD player in your region. (The world is divided into regions, so a DVD from one region will not play in another.)

DVD Menus

The defining characteristic of a DVD is that it gives you the ability to watch digital video interactively on your television. It's possible to make a DVD disc that goes directly to the video when you put it into a DVD player, but most DVDs have some kind of menu. A DVD *menu* is simply a screen that gives you several choices, with selectable buttons of some kind that lead directly to video or to other menus (see Figure 14.2).

FIGURE 14.2
A simple DVD menu with a number of choices with the currently selected choice is highlighted (Nergil, the second gerbil from the left).

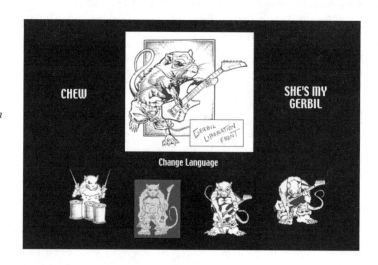

How DVD Screens Work

Much like a Web page, a DVD menu screen represents a series of interactive links, which in turn enable the viewing audience to choose what they want to see. On most DVDs, there's a main menu that appears when you insert the disc. Depending on how much *content* (video, audio, graphics) there is, there are often a number of submenus. Submenus usually have more choices, such as special features, extra scenes, and so on, serving as doors to enable you to get further into the DVD.

Figure 14.3 shows the main menu of a training DVD, where the audience can go directly to the video with the PLAY option. Users can also select the CHAPTERS option to go directly to a particular segment, or scene, of the training video.

FIGURE **14.3**

The main menu on a training DVD. The PLAY selection starts the video, whereas the CHAPTERS selection goes to a scene menu.

In Figure 14.4, you see what's known as a *scene selection menu,* from which you can choose to go directly to a desired part of the overall video. The four main choices represent the first four segments of the training video. (These scenes/segments are the chapters referred to in the previous paragraph.)

This type of DVD is often achieved through the use of *chapter markers,* where the DVD creator can use a single video clip on his DVD. The chapter markers (also known as *chapter points*) enable you to send people directly to particular spots in that clip.

You may recall from Hour 7, "Exporting iMovies," that you can add chapter markers to an iMovie that can be read by iDVD. When you export an iMovie with chapter markers to iDVD, the resulting iDVD menu will show the option to play the entire movie as well as a scene selection menu.

14

FIGURE **14.4**

The scene selection menu allows direct access to four segments of the training, 1–4, and at the bottom of the screen, other segments can be chosen.

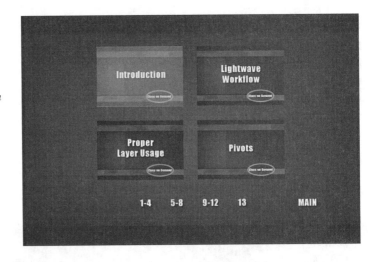

 Without chapter markers, the alternative is to break the video up into multiple files.

For example, at the bottom of the DVD screen in Figure 14.4, there's a row of DVD buttons that enable the audience to choose additional scene selection screens.

In Figure 14.5, you're looking at the next successive scene selection screen, from which you can click to go directly to segments 5 through 8 of the training video.

FIGURE **14.5**

The scene selection menu, choices 5–8.

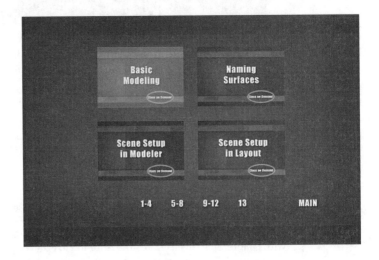

Advanced DVD Features

Even though iDVD isn't capable of achieving all the advanced features that can be put on a DVD, it does have a lot of power. In some cases (such as with motion menus), it has features that advanced DVD-authoring programs don't even have.

We'll consider DVD features that iDVD can add as well as advanced features that you often find on commercial DVD releases, which you would sometimes need a more advanced program to accomplish. But in general, as with iMovie, iDVD gives you powerful, built-in, easy-to-use capability—features that pack a lot of punch for the buck.

Motion Menus

One of the coolest features of DVD is the way you can have motion menus that can add action and excitement to spice up a plain old DVD menu. Motion menus combine the standard DVD menu choices and include some kind of movement, whether it's a video clip or animation.

In Figure 14.6, a motion menu has been created to highlight four separate music videos. A futuristic animation rotates slowly in the background, adding vibrancy and contributing to the mystique of the DVD.

FIGURE 14.6

This motion menu was created in DVD Studio Pro using an animation that was originally developed in Adobe After Effects and then combined with an Adobe Photoshop file.

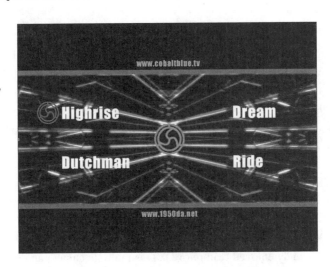

Among the menu themes available through iDVD are several motion menu options. You also have the option to add your own video to a background to make customized motion menus. We'll look at menus and customization options in Hours 18, "DVD Menus in iDVD," and 19, "Customizing DVD Menus."

14

DVD Slideshows

One of the lesser-known capabilities of DVD is its capability to make digital slideshows. Slideshows harness the power of DVD by enabling people to put a collection of digital pictures on a DVD that can then be shared and viewed with the convenience of watching on television (see Figure 14.7).

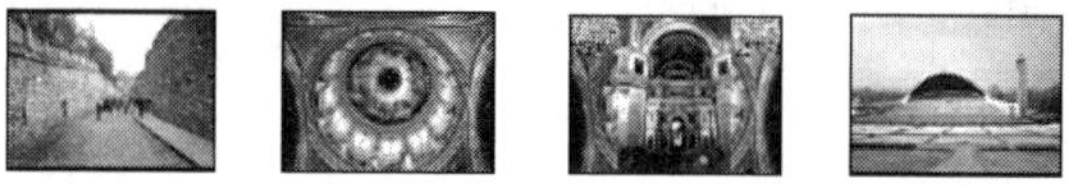

FIGURE **14.7**

Digital pictures, ready to be dropped into a DVD slideshow.

The pictures never wear out, the quality is good, and you can easily add audio to make comments. You don't have to wait for the holidays to gather everyone together to watch a slideshow—you can send it to them in the mail!

> Slideshows can be created and customized within iDVD. We'll discuss the details in Hour 20, "DVD Slideshows."

DVD Subtitles

Although not available in iDVD, subtitles are a fascinating capability of the DVD medium that will surely make the world a little bit smaller, and enable everyone from Homewood to Hollywood to distribute their creations in more than just their native language.

DVD subtitles are like closed captioning or subtitles that you might see in a foreign film, except that you can have a number of subtitles available *at the same time*, enabling the people in the audience to choose what they want to view. Subtitles also can be used to provide content for the hearing-impaired in a native language to simulate closed captioning, or in creative ways such as to display lyrics for music videos (see Figure 14.8).

Multiple Angles

Another widely enjoyed feature of DVD is multiple camera angles, which enable a DVD to be created from which the audience can choose the "camera" they're watching the action from.

Most fictional movies, documentaries, and other productions use multiple cameras to begin with. When the footage is brought back into the studio, the best from each camera is combined to put together an enjoyable experience. But there's still a lot that people never usually see, and it's fun when the audience is given the choice to choose its own angles, whether it's seeing footage that was never in the movie or seeing a concert from the perspective of the musicians onstage.

Figure 14.8

Alternative subtitles: sing-along lyrics at the bottom of the screen.

Task: Exploring a DVD—Subtitles and Camera Angles

Okay, get ready to go back to school (or to do some extra credit, if you're in school already). In this assignment, you have to find, rent, borrow, or purchase a DVD that includes subtitles and multiple camera angles, and perhaps some other special feature such as director commentary. If you already have a DVD collection, chances are that most of them have subtitles on them, and a fair number have multiple camera angles. If you don't have any DVDs and have never rented one… do it! (I know it's a big sacrifice to make, but it will help you to explore the world of DVD.)

Another interesting feature that's similar to multiple camera angles is multiple audio tracks. One of the most common uses of this feature is in the director commentary for a DVD movie where you can switch audio tracks and listen to the director commenting on the movie as you watch it. The current version of iDVD doesn't support multiple audio tracks, but you could make two different iMovies, one with the regular audio, one with the alternative audio, and export them to iDVD, to achieve a similar effect.

1. Get a DVD.
2. Start your Mac and insert the DVD (see Figure 14.9).

FIGURE 14.9
Watching a video in the DVD player software, in the Viewer window.

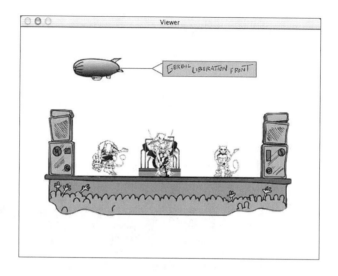

3. Choose a video segment that has subtitles and click to expand the simulated DVD remote control (see Figures 14.10 and 14.11) in the DVD Player software.

FIGURE 14.10
The Apple DVD Player software remote control.

FIGURE 14.11
The expanded remote control, allowing access to advanced features.

4. Click the Subtitle button on the remote to flip between subtitles.

5. Now go to a section of the DVD that features multiple camera angles and try clicking on the Angle button to flip between different perspectives

How iDVD Fits into the DVD Picture

Simply put, iDVD is *fun*. A case in point: A certain author who co-wrote the Macworld DVD Studio Pro Bible got into making DVDs using DVD Studio Pro, Apple's high-end DVD-authoring program. But the first time that I…I mean *a certain author*…sat down and played around with iDVD, it was refreshingly easy to put together a DVD. So, you can't do multiple camera angles or subtitles. Okay, but it's so easy and you have a DVD in no time—no muss, no fuss!

Menus: Themes and Styles

Apple, with its consistently good taste, has put together a number of built-in, customizable themes and styles in iDVD, which give you the ability to make DVDs without ever going into a separate graphic application. Of course, you can make your own styles or download ones from the Web, but you'll find that you can do some pretty cool stuff with the materials you get right in the program.

Themes and styles are graphics and video clips that you can mix and match, kind of like playing Colorforms with DVD. You click the Themes button, click on something that looks interesting, and voila! You're off to a running start on your DVD.

As you see in Figure 14.12, when you choose a theme, iDVD includes some place-holder text (GLOBAL) on the screen, which you can customize and use as a title. A number of the themes include nice-looking video clips that you can include, so now your DVD has motion in it!

Figure 14.12

The Global theme, with a globe slowly spinning in the background; the title can be changed and customized.

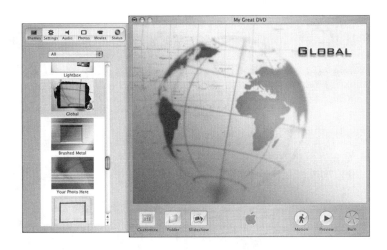

Let's say you have some music videos you shot on your camcorder. The songs have a lighter feel to them, so you might choose the Sky theme and then type in the name of a song on each DVD button (see Figure 14.13).

14

FIGURE **14.13**
A very cool theme with time-lapse clouds that move in the background—in this theme, the buttons are text buttons.

Then you think to yourself, "Gee, I wish I could include little pictures or video of the videos themselves on the menu," and you choose a different theme. The text you typed in is carried over, and you get to see things with a different look. You can either keep it or go back to the previous theme (see Figure 14.14).

FIGURE **14.14**
This theme automatically takes a bit of each video clip in your DVD and puts it into the menu, so the audience gets a taste of what's in each video. In this theme, the DVD buttons are made out of video—another form of motion menu.

Slideshows

One of the many fun things you can do with iDVD is create DVD slideshows; you can literally drag and drop digital pictures into iDVD. You can choose how long the pictures appear, play around with the order. Perhaps if you have photographic parents or relatives, you might remember them fiddling around with a slide sorter before they embarrassed you with assorted baby pictures and the like—and now you get to have fun embarrassing them (see Figure 14.15).

FIGURE 14.15
iDVD's slide sorter.

When you've put your digital pictures in the order you want them, you can easily get to the pictures with a nice DVD menu, and if you like, you can combine digital pictures with video. Can anyone say road trips, graduations, weddings, parties, or do-it-yourself documentaries? (See Figure 14.16.)

FIGURE 14.16
A simple DVD menu for accessing a DVD slideshow.

14

If you want to dig further for a fairly comprehensive list of questions, resources, and technical information, try reading Jim Taylor's excellent book *DVD Demystified*, or visiting the Web site of his equally excellent DVD FAQ (`http://www.dvddemystified.com/dvdfaq.html`) where you'll find lots of helpful information.

Summary

In this hour, we've highlighted particular DVD features, from menus to slideshows and beyond. It's pretty amazing how far iDVD goes in bringing DVD within reach of the beginner. My focus has been on things you can do in iDVD or DVD Studio Pro to whet your appetite for entering the world of DVD.

In the next hour, we take a look at DVD discs—the magic carpets that take your iMovie and iDVD projects all the way to the land of television. At first glance, DVD discs might not seem particularly noteworthy, but some odd folk do actually find DVD discs to be exciting (raises hand). When you take a closer look at a DVD, you'll see how much more capable it is than a VHS tape, and although there are more possibilities, it doesn't necessarily have to be more complex. Getting acquainted with the disc itself (your magic carpet) will enable you to have more fun (read: less frustration) as you make your way through the world of DVD.

Workshop

The Workshop consists of quiz questions and answers to help you to develop a better grasp of DVD features. First try to answer the questions, *before* you check the answers. Then read the explanations, even if you get the answers right—the explanations will contribute to your overall understanding of DVD.

Q&A

Q How do I make a motion menu of my own?

A You can import your own video clip as a background for a motion menu. Professional motion menus are generally made with a program such as Adobe After Effects, in which you can combine several layers of video, but you can use any program you like to generate animation or make the video clip. Then you import it and it becomes the backdrop of your motion menu. (Click on Customize button in iDVD, click the Settings tab, and drag your video clip onto the Background icon.)

Q **Why can't I add subtitles and multiple camera angles in iDVD? You mean I have to spend $1,000 and get DVD Studio Pro just to do those things?**

A iDVD is a very powerful program; it does motion menus and has a good amount of customizability. For the price you're paying, you do really get a lot, and keep in mind that only a short while ago, it cost five or six figures to even begin to do what you can now do so easily in iDVD. Yep, you have to get DVD Studio Pro to do those extra features, but you get a whole lot more. And as with iDVD, DVD Studio Pro represents a rather mind-blowing reduction in price over what it used to cost only a short while ago. DVD Studio Pro and iDVD really blew the lid off the DVD-authoring industry; prices will continue to go down and features will be added. Remember that it's nowhere near as easy to create motion menus in DVD Studio Pro.

Quiz

1. How is a motion menu created?

    A. By clicking a theme in iDVD

    B. By compositing animated background elements and static foreground Photoshop menu designs in a compositing program such as Adobe After Effects

    C. By shaking the television while you're watching a DVD

    D. A and B

2. How do you make a slideshow?

    A. Wait for your photographs to be developed, put all your slides in a slide sorter, arrange them, prepare an exciting monologue, and then retire to the kitchen for cookies and punch

    B. Drag your digital pictures into iDVD

    C. Drag your digital pictures into iPhoto, and then into iDVD

    D. B and C

3. If you have a main menu on a DVD, how do you get to a submenu?

    A. Click the Submenu button on the remote

    B. Click a button on the main menu that leads to the submenu

    C. Go to Subway

14

Quiz Answers

1. **D.** iDVD automates the process of motion menus and even allows some customization. In DVD Studio Pro, it's up to you—you create and combine the graphics.

2. **D.** You can adjust and arrange your digital pictures in iPhoto before bringing them into iDVD if you want, or you can create a slideshow directly in iDVD.

3. **B.** There is no Submenu button on a DVD remote control.

Exercises

1. At the end of Hour 13, "Understanding DVD Video," your homework was simply to watch a DVD on your Mac. Now, put the same DVD back in your drive and explore the menu system of the DVD. Notice how you move through the items, as well as any special features available.

2. Launch iDVD and open the Customize tray window by clicking the Customize button at the bottom of the main iDVD window. Then open the Themes tab and click through the options looking for motion menus.

HOUR 15

DVD Discs

In this hour, we take a closer look at DVD discs themselves and various types of DVD discs, including the kind that you use with iDVD and the built-in SuperDrive. We also consider options for including computer files on a DVD, which is known as DVD-ROM content.

The goal is to get a better understanding of the capabilities and limitations of DVD discs so that you can use your Mac to the fullest and have a good experience at the same time. There are many DVD formats and options out there, and the new variety of recordable disc formats could lead to some confusion when you're at a store trying to figure out which kind of blank disc to purchase. This potentially frustrating situation with DVD formats has been brought about by competition among the makers of DVD players who are pitting DVD-R against DVD+RW and so on. But a simple review of what DVD discs are, and what kind are compatible with your Mac, will prepare you to avoid the confusion and get on with having fun.

Throughout this hour, we discuss the following:

- DVD storage capacity
- Recordable DVDs (DVD-R)
- DVD-R compatibility
- Manufactured DVDs
- Rewritable DVDs (DVD-RW)
- Purchasing the right blank DVDs
- Adding DVD-ROM content

DVD Storage Capacity

Unless you plan to include computer files on your DVD as mentioned later in this hour, the best way to think of DVD storage capacity with iDVD is in terms of how many minutes of video you can fit on the disc. The amount of video you can fit on a disc is determined by how much the video is compressed. Because iDVD does the encoding automatically, the limit is about 90 minutes of video on the disc.

If you're talking about the disc in terms of bytes and megabytes, however, you might be familiar with the often-quoted measurement of 4.7 gigabytes (GB)—that is, the claim that you can store up to 4.7 gigabytes of data on a single-layer DVD disc.

This is only partially true. If you were putting data files on a DVD and had 4.7 gigabytes' worth of files on your computer, you'd find that you can fit only about 4.37GB on the DVD—this has to do with the difference between the way data is stored on a computer hard drive and the way it's stored on a DVD. Essentially, you can store 4.7 billion bytes of data on a DVD, but only about 4.37GB.

But regardless of how you look at it, DVD is an incredible medium. The CD format typically allows only 650MB of data on a disc, whereas the DVD format enables you to put up to 4,370MB on a disc! To put this in perspective, consider that many computers you see on the shelves in stores are likely to have 3.5" floppy disk drives. Each of these plastic floppies holds about 1MB of data, so a DVD disc holds the equivalent of about 4,370 floppy disks! See Figure 15.1.

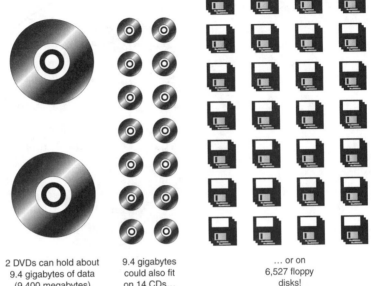

FIGURE 15.1
The relative capacities of different storage methods.

2 DVDs can hold about
9.4 gigabytes of data
(9,400 megabytes)

9.4 gigabytes
could also fit
on 14 CDs...

... or on
6,527 floppy
disks!

Recordable DVDs

Recordable DVDs (DVD-R) enable you to write data a single time to a disc. They're much like the CD-R discs that are so popular these days. Much like the phenomena of dropping prices with CD burners and recordable CDs, the price of making your own DVDs will continue to drop.

The kind of recordable DVDs that you can use with the built-in SuperDrive on your Mac are known as DVD-R media, which technically speaking, is called DVD-R General media. In most cases, when people refer to recordable discs, they don't specify DVD-R General media—they drop the word *general*. See Figure 15.2.

Recordable DVD Compatibility

DVD-R compatibility is an important factor to take into account when you're considering distribution of a DVD project on DVD-R media. Theoretically, if you make a DVD project and burn a DVD-R disc, that DVD-R disc should play in the majority of DVD players. The newer the player is, the more likely it is to be compatible with DVD-R media. And, vice versa, the older a player is, the less likely it is to accept DVD-R media.

FIGURE 15.2

Apple's DVD-R media, blank and ready to go.

There are compatibility lists online at a variety of sources, including `www.apple.com/dvd/compatibility/`, where companies and individuals have tested DVD-R media with a wide range of players. The questions to ask are what kind of project are you going to share? and what kind of audience is it?

Manufactured DVDs

The only way to guarantee 100% compatibility with all DVD players is to manufacture a DVD. This means sending the project off to be manufactured by automated machinery. There are companies like EMVUSA (`www.emvusa.com`) who are aggressively going after the do-it-yourself DVD market by offering attractive pricing and accepting DVD-R media as a master disc. Accepting DVD-R media as a master disc is a break from the tradition of requiring a DVD project to be submitted on a special format known as *DLT*, or digital linear tape.

In addition to compatibility, other things you gain are the ability to have more professional packaging and a better-looking disc. When a DVD is manufactured, a design is imprinted directly on the DVD itself, rather than a label being applied.

Some advanced DVD formats, designed primarily to allow longer movies or additional footage, have more than one side or more than one layer within the DVD, as seen in Table 15.1.

TABLE 15.1 Capacities of Various Manufactured DVD Formats

Format	Approximate Capacity	Number of Sides	Number of Layers
DVD-5	4.4 gigabytes (4.7 billion bytes)	1	1
DVD-9	7.95 gigabytes (8.5 billion bytes)	1	2
DVD-10	8.75 gigabytes (9.4 billion bytes)	2	1
DVD-18	17.5 gigabytes (18.8 billion bytes)	2	2

For inquiring minds that want to know, Appendix B, "Getting a DVD Manufactured," includes advice about getting a DVD manufactured from a master created in iDVD.

Rewritable DVDs

The development of the SuperDrive was a joint effort between Apple and Pioneer, and in addition to recording to CD-Rs, CD-RWs and DVD-Rs, the mechanism that's used in the SuperDrive has the capability to record to DVD-RW discs. See Figure 15.3.

FIGURE 15.3
Pioneer's DVD-RW discs, compatible with the SuperDrive.

You can record to a DVD-R disc only once. At the time of writing, the best price you can get for DVD-R media is $3.00 (U.S.) each, so blank DVDs are still fairly pricey. So, if you're just testing your project, and essentially use the DVD-R disc only once, you're out a few bucks.

> At the time of writing, $3.00 U.S. is a common price that can be found when doing a price search on a Web site such as cnet.com.

This makes the idea of using a DVD-RW disc even more appealing. It's a great way to back up video files and to move DVD-related files from one place to another. DVD-RW discs are twice as expensive, but you can use them over and over again.

Apple doesn't emphasize the fact that the SuperDrive can burn DVD-RW discs, and perhaps for good reason. DVD-RW discs are compatible with only about 70% of DVD players out there, compared with DVD-R discs, which are compatible with closer to 90%.

Purchasing the Right Blank DVD Discs

The easiest thing to do when you need to purchase blank discs is to get them directly from Apple, which ensures compatibility and has always had good pricing.

But if you want to get blank DVDS on your own, make sure that you're purchasing DVD-R General media. If the product packaging or salesperson says that the disc is DVD-R but there's no indication of whether or not it's General, chances are that you're fine. You'll occasionally come across DVD-R Authoring media, which won't work in the SuperDrive.

Another thing to look out for if you're shopping for blank discs is that you're purchasing DVD-R (minus R) media and not DVD+R (plus R) or DVD+RW (plus RW) discs. The plus discs are designed for other kinds of DVD burners.

To get a better sense of things, glance through Table 15.2, which gives a good indication of the situation consumers face as a result of the Format Wars. (It's sort of like the VHS versus Betamax competition when VCRs first came out. But, in a nutshell, DVD-R is better and more compatible with DVD players, and that's what you have in the Mac, so get DVD-R media.)

TABLE 15.2   DVD Recordable Media

Format	Features	Compatibility with SuperDrive
DVD-R (General)	Can be recorded to once	Yes
DVD-R (Authoring)	Designed for older DVD burners; easy to confuse with DVD-R General media	No
DVD-RW	Can be recorded to many times (up to 1,000 times)	Yes (Note: Projects burned to DVD-RW discs are compatible with only about 70% of DVD players)
DVD+R (plus R)	Similar to DVD-R	No
DVD+RW (plus RW)	Similar to DVD-RW	No

DVD-ROM Content—Adding Computer Files on a DVD

DVD is a flexible medium for creating and sharing interactive presentations, but the possibilities aren't limited to what you can view on a television. Thanks to the nature of the DVD disc, you can also include files on a DVD that people can access using their computers. This feature is known as DVD-ROM.

DVD-ROM is essentially the equivalent to CD-ROM. ROM stands for *read-only memory*, which means that you can put data on the disc that can be read by a person with the appropriate drive in his computer. The most typical use for CD-ROM is the discs you use to install software on your computer. Software manufacturers haven't completely switched over to DVD-ROM discs yet, but DVD-ROM drives are becoming much more common in computers, so it's just a matter of time before DVD-ROM drives and discs become as popular as CD-ROMs.

Software that currently comes on several CDs could fit on a single DVD. If you used iLife to install iDVD3, that software is delivered on a DVD-ROM.

With Hollywood DVDs, the typical use of the DVD-ROM possibilities of DVD is WebDVD, which is sometimes referred to as *Web-connected DVD*. For example, you might have inserted a rented or purchased DVD in your computer and looked at special features of the DVD that are available only when looking at the disc through the computer. This could include things such as the opportunity to look at the screenplay of the movie, or games and other programs that aren't possible to view on a DVD player. See Figure 15.4.

The great thing about DVD is that you can put your video on the DVD and someone can view it on his DVD player connected to a television, but you can also put data files that he can access on his computer. It could be that you want to include Web links, documentation, pictures, or any other kind of computer file.

For example, when you make your DVD, you start by creating an iMovie. Then, in iDVD, you can also use the slideshow feature to add pictures that can be viewed on the television. But let's say you want to pass a number of digital pictures along as files so that your colleagues can use the pictures on their Web pages. You might ask yourself, "Do I have to burn them on a CD?" With the DVD-ROM feature in iDVD, you can put the pictures right on the disc.

FIGURE **15.4**

Example of DVD-ROM content, from the DVD that comes with the MacWorld DVD Studio Pro Bible. *The disc features the* VIDEO_TS *folder that contains the standard encoded video for a DVD player, as well as the DVD-ROM content, a series of folders including tutorial files, a PDF version of the book, and so on.*

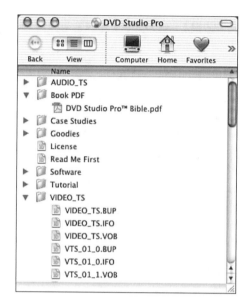

Or, let's say you have a number of stories or a screenplay that you've written in a word processing program such as AppleWorks or Microsoft Word. Now, if you want to, you could include the files on the DVD disc. So, you could make a DVD with the video that can be watched on the television, and if the recipient wants to, she could put the DVD in her computer and look at the original screenplay by opening the file as she would with any other kind of disc she inserts in her computer.

DVD-ROM content isn't anything that you have to do—it's just a great thing to have the flexibility to add computer files to your DVD.

- Consideration Number One—Does the person have a DVD-ROM drive? Many computers these days have DVD-ROM drives, but not all of them. If the person you want to share files with doesn't have a DVD-ROM drive, you might be better off using your SuperDrive to burn them to a CD.

The purpose of the DVD-ROM feature in iDVD is to add extra material to video DVDs. It isn't recommended as a way to back up your data files. Instead, use the Burn Disc option available in the Finder's File menu to burn a data DVD.

- Consideration Number Two—Is the person on Mac or Windows? If you're burning files to a DVD and you want a person on Windows to be able to use them, be sure to include the appropriate file extensions on the end of your files

15

> Microsoft Windows relies on the file extension to recognize which application is needed to open a file. For example, JPEG files need a `.jpg` at the end for a Windows machine to launch a program capable of displaying JPEGs. These days, many Mac programs automatically put on a file extension, but be sure to use them if you're sending your DVD to Windows users.

Task: Adding Computer Files to a DVD

TASK

You can easily add computer files to your DVD using iDVD:

1. Launch iDVD and open your project. See Figure 15.5.

FIGURE 15.5
The main iDVD window.

2. Click the Customize button in the lower-left corner of the iDVD window.
3. Click the Status tab, which will initially give you a running report of how any background encoding is going. (this is the automatic encoding of video that's being done while you're working on your project). See Figure 15.6.

FIGURE 15.6

The Status tab of the tray in iDVD, which slides out from to the left when you click the Customize button in the main window in iDVD.

4. Click the Status pop-up menu and switch from Encoder Status to DVD-ROM Contents as shown in Figure 15.7.

FIGURE 15.7

The DVD-ROM Contents option.

5. Drag files and folders into the DVD-ROM Contents area. In Figure 15.8, the Stuff for DVD folder has been dragged directly into iDVD, containing a manual in PDF format, some digital pictures, a Microsoft Word document, and a QuickTime movie. iDVD may also add a file called .DS_Store.

As you drag large media files in as DVD-ROM content, remember to keep an eye on the size of your project. (Conveniently, this information appears at the top of the Status tab.)

Technically speaking, the .DS Store file is created by the Finder. Per Apple: "Each directory in the file system can contain a hidden object, `.DS_Store`, containing data which includes a list of files stored there. This object is created when a local user views a given directory using the Finder." The .DS_Store file isn't necessary for burning, but you can simply ignore it.

15

FIGURE 15.8

Dragging files from the hard drive into the DVD-ROM Contents area in iDVD.

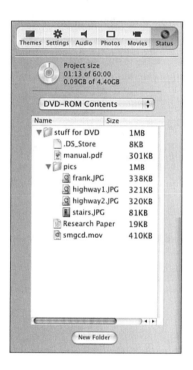

iDVD doesn't move the files or make duplicates of you add as DVD-ROM content . Instead, it creates a reference to the file on your system. If you delete a file or move a file after you've added it to the DVD-ROM list, its name appears in red to tell you that something's wrong. If you try to burn the disc anyway, a File Not Found error message will appear.

To delete a file from the DVD-ROM Contents list, select it and press Delete.

Summary

In this hour, you were immersed in DVD discs—the final goal of every iDVD project. DVD-R discs are becoming cheaper all the time, and it might be wise to stock up on them because you'll probably soon find yourself wanting to share your projects with anyone who has a DVD player. Keep in mind that the DVDs you burn will play in 90% of the players out there, but if you *must* have 100% compatibility, you need to send your project off to be manufactured. You also learned how to add computer files to your DVD as DVD-ROM content.

In the next hour, we'll learn about the basics of iDVD by going through a simple example as well as the steps for burning a DVD.

Workshop

In the following section, we'll take a look at a few things that you may find yourself wondering about at some point, and we'll ask you a few questions. Answers are provided for your convenience.

Q&A

Q I heard that the SuperDrive can burn at 2x and 4x speeds; how do I get it to do that?

A To get the SuperDrive to burn at 2x, you have to have the right kind of blank DVD disc.

Burning at 4x is also a matter of purchasing the right discs. However, use of 4x media might require you to update the software for your SuperDrive. (If your SuperDrive isn't compatible with 4x media, trying to use it might cause serious damage to your computer!)

To find out whether your SuperDrive needs to be updated, follow these steps:

1. Open the Apple System Profiler application, which can be found in the Utilities folder in the Applications folder.

2. Open the Devices and Volumes tab.

3. Expand the CD-RW/DVD-R item by clicking the disclosure triangle.

4. Examine the information given. If Pioneer is the vendor, you might need the update. To find out for sure, look at the product identification code. For drives with the product identification DVR-104, no update is required if the device revision number is A227 or higher. For drives with the product identification DVR-103, no update is required if the device revision number is 1.90 or higher.

15

5. If your drive comes from Pioneer and doesn't have the upgrade in place, go to the Apple Web site (www.apple.com), search for *SuperDrive update*, and then download and install it.

> To get media that can burn at 2x or 4x, you need to read the label carefully.

Q If I need to burn a lot of discs, at what point is it better to send them off for manufacturing?

A The answer to this question might also involve compatibility: If you need 100% compatibility, have the discs manufactured. If copied DVD-R discs are okay, there are a number of places that will take your DVD-R and make 1 to 100 or more copies for you, sparing you the time and wear on your DVD burner. In certain cases, the manufacturer can make pretty nice-looking labels and other improvements. If it's purely a financial matter, you probably need to get into the several-hundred-to-1,000 disc range before it's cheaper per disc to manufacture.

> Having someone copy a DVD just means duplicated in the same way that you could do at home, as opposed to *manufactured*, which is often called *pressing* a disc.

Quiz

1. What kind of disc does the SuperDrive use?

    A. DVD-R

    B. DVD-R General

    C. DVD-R Authoring

    D. A and B

2. How do I add DVD-ROM content to a DVD-R?

    A. Click the Customize button at the bottom of the iDVD main window, click the Status tab, choose DVD-ROM Content in the pop-up menu, and drag my files into the window.

    B. Insert a blank DVD and drag the files to the disc from the Finder.

    C. A and B

3. What percentage of DVD players will my DVDs work on?

    A. 90%

    B. 80%

    C. 70%

    D. A and B

    E. A and C

Quiz Answers

1. **D.** iDVD uses DVD-R General media, but it's becoming common to refer to DVD-R General media simply as DVD-R.

2. **C.** Trick question. You can add DVD-ROM content to a blank DVD disc using the method in A, but if you don't need to make a DVD with video, you can just burn computer files to a DVD disc using the method in B. (By the way, the method explained in option B is the recommended method of backing up large files from your computer hard drive.)

3. **E.** Sorry, another trick question. If the question were, "What percentage of DVD players will my DVD-Rs work on?", the answer would be 90% because you'd be using DVD-R discs. But *DVDs* could mean either DVD-Rs or DVD-RWs, and DVD-RWs are compatible with 70% of the players out there.

> If you're shopping for a DVD player, many players now list whether they play DVD-R and/or DVD-RW media. In general, Pioneer DVD players play the discs. Otherwise, even if a DVD player doesn't list DVD discs, if it lists the capability to play CDs, it probably plays DVDs. To be certain, get a Pioneer player or one with an explicit label for DVD-R or DVD-RW media.

Exercises

1. Follow the steps outlined in the first question of the Q&A section to find out whether your SuperDrive requires a software update. If it does, download and install the update as directed before going any further. Better safe than sorry!

2. To test your SuperDrive, create a DVD backup of any important files on your hard drive from the Finder. To do this, place a DVD-R disc in the drive, give the disc a name when prompted, and then drag the files you want to back up into the disc icon that appears on your hard drive. After you've added all the files you want to backup, select File, Burn Disc from the Finder's menu bar. If you change your mind, you can eject the DVD before burning by pressing the Eject key on your keyboard or by choosing Eject from the File menu.

PART IV

Learning iDVD

Hour

Hour 16

Introducing iDVD

In this hour, we take a look at iDVD, Apple's revolutionary, easy-to-use DVD-authoring software. Anyone who has a Mac with a SuperDrive can now make her own DVD productions using inexpensive hardware and software that only used to be within the reach of Hollywood studios.

iDVD has been instrumental in making DVD creation both affordable, user friendly, and fun. You'll find that you can dive right in and make your own DVDs with a minimum of confusion and hassle.

Throughout this hour, we discuss the following:

- The DVD creation revolution
- iDVD themes
- iDVD slideshows
- iDVD video encoding
- iDVD disc burning
- iDVD capabilities

The DVD Creation Revolution

iDVD is a part of history because before Apple introduced it in early 2001, the only tools available for people who wanted to make their own DVDs were prohibitively expensive.

Not only was the software complex and pricey, but the DVD burners themselves cost more than many computer systems. For example, before iDVD came out, the only available DVD burner cost about $4,000, the Pioneer DVR-S201, shown in Figure 16.1.

FIGURE 16.1

Pioneer DVR-S201 DVD burner.

Basically, Apple got together with a few different companies including Pioneer, and made some deals that benefited the digital video–making public. The result was that Apple was able to introduce a desktop G4 Power Mac model that included a new DVD burner, as well as iDVD software, for the same price that just a DVD burner alone cost at the time.

Since Apple took this first step in 2001, the prices of both DVD burners and blank discs have gone down, and a host of other companies have joined in the fun. So, part of the fun in working with iDVD is realizing how revolutionary it really is, in keeping with Apple's spirit of innovation.

Basic Features

It used to be that putting together a DVD project was a very complex process, requiring the DVD author to perform a great number of steps and have a significant amount of knowledge about the underlying technology. iDVD simplifies the process of DVD authoring—it's as easy as dragging and dropping files into the iDVD window.

The other great thing about iDVD is that it's not only a DVD-authoring program, but it also includes built-in DVD menu design, which basically means that you can make your DVD screens inside the program. This is another area in which DVD authors used to have to spend a lot of time outside the DVD-authoring program creating graphics and designing backgrounds. iDVD includes a number of customizable designs, called themes, that are ready to go.

Themes

Themes are like costumes for a DVD screen. They include different background and button designs that enable you to express yourself and create a unique space to drop your iMovies into.

iDVD includes a central window, as shown in Figure 16.2, where you can easily try out different themes.

16

Click on a theme in the list to add it to your project

FIGURE 16.2

Choosing a theme in iDVD.

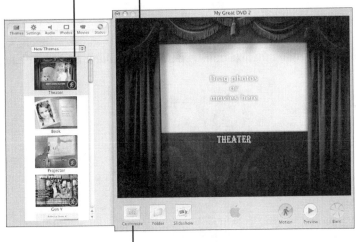

Click on the Customize button to expand the window and
open the Themes tab to get the list of available themes

By default, the Apple logo is shown in the lower-right corner of all the themes. To remove it, open the iDVD preferences and uncheck the Show Apple Logo Watermark box.

Some of the available themes actually have video clips as backgrounds, and some also include sound. These themes enable you to include what's known as a *motion menu* on your DVD. You might discover (if you haven't already) that sometimes when you're working on a DVD project, you want to turn off the motion. This is accomplished simply by clicking the Motion button, as shown in Figure 16.3.

FIGURE 16.3

The Motion button to turn motion menus on or off.

You can use the Motion button to turn a motion menu on to see how it looks and then turn the video or sound off while you continue working on your project. (Just remember to turn motion back on before burning your final version!)

When you want to go beyond the automatic colors that are chosen for text, you can select custom colors for text from a convenient pop-up menu (see Figure 16.4).

FIGURE 16.4

iDVD gives you the ability to choose your own color for text.

Another great feature of iDVD is that it enables you to choose different styles of button shapes for your DVD screens (see Figure 16.5). In essence, you don't have to be a graphic designer to have good-looking DVD screens, but iDVD makes it easy to experiment and play with different options if you want to.

When you choose to customize your DVD, and if you like what you've done, you can save the settings for later use in a Favorites list. A customized theme can be saved so that you can access it later for other projects, as shown in Figure 16.6.

FIGURE 16.5

iDVD enables you to choose custom buttons.

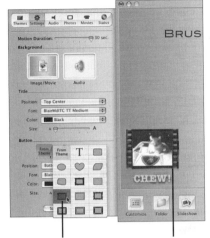

You can choose a different shape for your buttons, such as a "film" look

FIGURE 16.6

A customized theme in the Favorites list.

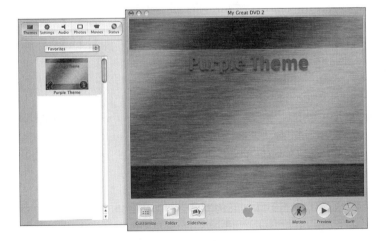

iMedia Browsers—The Audio, Photos, and Movies Tabs

You can insert a variety of content, including music, still photos, and movies, into your iDVD project. To make this easier, version 3 and later of iDVD integrates with recent versions of iTunes and iPhoto so that you can easily access files stored in their libraries.

The Audio palette, shown in Figure 16.7, integrates with your iTunes library to enable you to add background music to your chosen DVD theme.

FIGURE 16.7

Select songs from your iTunes library.

Besides integrating with your iTunes library, iDVD connects directly to your iPhoto library. From the Photos palette, shown in Figure 16.8, you can drag and drop photos to create slideshows, which we'll look at in Hour 20, "DVD Slideshows," or to customize themes that contain drop zones. (Refer to Figure 16.8 for an example of a theme containing a drop zone; we'll discuss their use further in Hour 19, "Customizing DVD Menus.")

> Be sure that you've upgraded your version of iPhoto to at least version 2 and your version of iTunes to at least version 3 before trying to use the Audio and Photos tabs in iDVD. Also, make sure that you've launched iPhoto and iTunes at least once so they can perform file system changes that are compatible with iDVD.

The Movies tab differs slightly from the other two iMedia browsers in iDVD. iMovie automatically creates clips that are compatible with iDVD, and there is no iMovie library on your hard drive to correspond with the iTunes and iPhoto libraries. The Movies tab lists all the movies stored in the current user's Movies folder, which the default location for iMovie to store your projects.

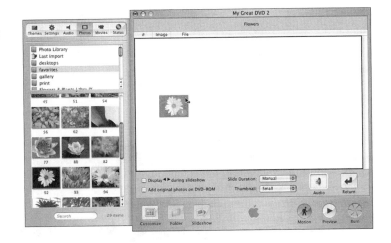

FIGURE 16.8

Drag and drop photos from your iPhoto library.

We'll discuss the use of the iMedia browsers further in the next hour, "Making a Sample DVD."

Slideshows

DVD slideshows can be a nice way to share digital pictures, so that people who watch your DVD can see the pictures on their televisions. Just as when you're working with video clips in iDVD, a slideshow is as easy as dragging and dropping digital pictures into the iDVD window (see Figure 16.9).

FIGURE 16.9

Slideshow editing window with individual images.

When you drag digital pictures into the editing window, you can easily rearrange them and preview the show, just as you might have done with a traditional slide projector and the infamous slide sorter.

There's also an option for iDVD to draw arrows on the screen so when a person views your DVD, there's a visual reminder to press the arrow keys on the remote to select which slide he wants to see. See Figure 16.10 for an example.

FIGURE 16.10
Slideshow preview showing arrows that indicate there are additional slides to view.

Refer to Hour 20 for a detailed explanation of this feature and its use.

> Although you can add individual elements (such as movies and slideshows) to your DVD main window, you can also create folders in the menu to add a secondary menu, or *submenu*, in which you can add even more elements. Simply click the Folder button at the bottom of the iDVD window. Double-clicking a folder opens it so that you can add content and even apply a completely different theme!

Status of Video Encoding

When you make your own DVDs, at some point in the process the computer system has to *encode* the video into a special format (MPEG-2) so that a DVD player can play it properly.

It used to be that you had to use a separate program and adjust a variety of advanced settings to prepare video for DVD. In iDVD, you simply drag your iMovie into the program, and iDVD automatically encodes the video for you as you work on your project.

And if you want to check in on how things are going, iDVD can give you an update on how the encoding is coming along, when you click on the Status tab of the Customize tray window, as shown in Figure 16.11.

FIGURE 16.11

Taking a look at how encoding is going.

As you learned in Hour 15, "DVD Discs," you can also use the Status tab to add DVD-ROM content to your DVD and to organize that bonus material into folders.

Disc Burning

When you've finished your DVD project, you probably want to preview it first by clicking the Preview button, and then you're ready to burn a DVD disc. You simply click the Burn button to activate it (see Figure 16.12), and then click it again.

> Before burning a DVD, be sure to read the first question in the Q&A section of Hour 15 to see whether your SuperDrive requires a software update.

When you click the Burn button a second time, the SuperDrive opens. You can insert your DVD disc (see Figure 16.13), and you're off!

FIGURE **16.12**
Clicking the Burn
button.

Before   After

FIGURE **16.13**
Clicking Burn causes
the SuperDrive to
open, and you can
insert a blank DVD.

Look ahead to Hour 17, "Creating a Sample DVD," for a more detailed discussion of burning a DVD.

iDVD Capabilities

When you're just starting out with a few video clips and DVD screens, you might not need to think much about exceeding iDVD's capabilities. But at some point you'll probably be curious about how many minutes of video you can fit on a DVD, how many menu screens you can have, and so on.

- **Items on a menu = 6**—When you create a DVD, the buttons on the menu screen can lead to movies, slideshows, or other menus. iDVD enables you to have up to six buttons on each screen.

- **Images in a slideshow = 99**—You can add up to 99 digital pictures to each slideshow that you have on your DVD.

- **Movies/slideshows on a DVD = 99**—You can add a total of 99 movies and or slideshows to a DVD project, assuming that the total amount of video used in the movie portion of your DVD does not exceed 90 minutes. Because digital pictures take up a relatively small amount of space, you don't have to be concerned about how many pictures you add.

- **Motion menus in a DVD = 30**—Because motion menus use short video clips, you're limited to using 30 of them on a DVD project, whether you are using a motion menu from a built-in theme or importing your own.

- **Minutes of video in a DVD = 90**—The total number of minutes of video you can fit on a DVD is 90 minutes, or one and a half hours.

- **Encoding for 60 minutes or less = high quality**—If you use less than an hour of video, iDVD encodes your movies at the highest quality setting.

  Technically speaking, iDVD automatically encodes your video at a particular *bit rate*, a setting that essentially determines the quality of your video.

  When computers encode video, the higher the bit rate that's used, the higher quality video you get. And when you have a higher bit rate, the video takes up more space on the disc.

  So, when you have less than one hour of video in a DVD project, iDVD encodes the video at a bit rate of 8 megabits per second (8 Mbps).

- **Encoding for 90 minutes or less = good quality**—When you have between 60 and 90 minutes of video, iDVD uses a lower bit rate so that it can fit more video on the disc. In this situation, iDVD encodes video at 5 megabits per second (5 Mbps).

System Requirements

When you purchase a Mac that includes iDVD software, it comes with everything you need to run iDVD, so you don't really need to be concerned about the system requirements. But if you're curious, the system requirements for iDVD are Power Mac G4 with SuperDrive, 256MB of RAM, and Mac OS X v10.1.

The only thing that you might want to consider is getting additional hard drive space at some time because working with iMovies can use up a fair amount of space. Also, even though your Mac comes with enough RAM memory to run iDVD, it never hurts to have more RAM when working with digital video.

Summary

In this hour, you became acquainted with iDVD and the various options it provides for making a variety of DVD projects that can include a combination of movies and digital pictures. As you saw, iDVD makes it easy to put together a good-looking DVD that you can burn yourself.

In the next hour, we'll make a sample DVD project that will help you to become more familiar with what's involved in making (and burning) a DVD. You'll see how backgrounds, buttons, and video can be combined to enable viewers to experience your DVD through menus from which they select certain buttons that lead to the movies on the DVD. You'll also see how you can create additional menu screens so that you can have a main screen that leads to additional screens with more movies or slideshows.

16

Workshop

The Workshop consists of quiz questions and answers to help you to check and increase your familiarity with iDVD. First, try to answer the questions *before* checking the answers. Then read the explanations, even if you get the answers right—the explanations will help you to see how the iDVD clock ticks.

Q&A

Q Is there any way that I can adjust the quality of the video encoding in iDVD?

A No, not really. To keep things simple, iDVD uses a preset bit-rate of 8 megabits per second (8 Mbps) when you're working with less than one hour of video, and 5 megabits per second (5 Mbps) when working with 90 minutes or less. 5Mbps is still fairly good quality. If you want to get into encoding your own video and other advanced DVD tasks, you'll probably want to take a look at DVD Studio Pro (see Hour 24, "Going Beyond iMovie and iDVD").

Q Can I add sound to a menu or slideshow?

A Yes. Later you'll see how you can just drag a sound file into a slideshow or motion menu so that you can use your own sound, such as music or maybe a narration that you have recorded using the Voiceover feature in iMovie.

Q Do I have to use a single theme for the whole DVD?

A No, you can actually choose a different theme for each screen in your DVD if you like.

Quiz

1. How many menus can you add to a DVD?

    A. 9.

    B. 99.

    C. You can't add menus to a DVD.

2. How many minutes of video can you add to a DVD?

    A. 90 minutes

    B. 60 minutes

    C. *60 Minutes*

    D. *Nightline*

    E. A and B

3. How can you use digital pictures in a DVD?

    A. In a DVD slideshow

    B. As a background image

    C. As a button image

    D. All of the above

Quiz Answers

1. **B.** You can have a total of 99 individual menu screens on your DVD. Menu screens are any screen in which you have buttons leading to a movie, a slideshow, or another menu screen.

2. **E.** When you have 60 minutes or less of video, you get the highest quality encoding. When you have between 60 and 90 minutes of video, you get good quality encoding.

3. **D.** Trick question. You can use digital images as pictures in a slideshow, and you can also use them as a background image for a menu screen or for a button image.

Exercises

1. If you haven't already explored the iDVD interface, give it a try. Open all the tabs in the Customize tray window and see what options are available.

2. If you want to use elements from your iTunes or iPhoto libraries in you iDVD projects, check their version numbers against the most recent versions available for download from Apple's Web site (`www.apple.com`). Install any updates so that you'll be ready to work when the time comes. (You'll find software version information under the About option of the iTunes and iPhoto menus that are visible in the menu bar while each application is active.)

16

HOUR 17

Making a Sample DVD

In this hour, we go through the process of making a sample DVD project in iDVD. It's entirely okay to get distracted by things you want to try doing differently from the way we do it in the example. For example, the sample might have ample examples of sample settings, but you might want to sample other settings and thereby trample the example.

But seriously, the idea is that if you want to follow along, because there's no disc with the book, you must have a few video files to work with. Video clips that you've imported using iMovie are automatically in the proper format. You can also add most video files supported by QuickTime, which will end in the file extension .mov.

The great thing about iDVD is that, outside of video clips, you don't necessarily need to have any additional files—you can type in your text for DVD screens and choose a built-in theme. But as you'll see, if you want to, you can add digital images to your DVD to enhance what you're sharing.

Throughout this hour, we discuss the following:

- Preparing a DVD project
- Importing files

- Customizing a DVD menu
- Adding a new screen to a DVD
- Moving buttons and titles

Preparing the DVD Project

To begin, we start a new project in iDVD, adjust a few settings, and generally get things off the ground. There are no particular rules about what you have to do first, but in general it's a good idea to get in the habit of saving your project frequently. As you work on your project, you can get in the habit of choosing File, Save at regular intervals so that you don't lose your work if lightning happens to strike or your Mac freezes up for some reason.

Task: Preparing the DVD Project

TASK

To prepare for this project, we get a few things in order to set the stage for importing video into the DVD project:

1. Launch iDVD and create a new project. You will be prompted to name and save your project automatically.

> The name you give your project is the name that will be automatically applied to the DVD disc when you burn your completed project. However, you can change the original project name to a different one by choosing Project, Project Info from the menu at the top of your screen. In the window that opens, simply type a new disc name and click OK.

2. Choose iDVD, Preferences to bring up the Preferences dialog box (see Figure 17.1).

FIGURE 17.1

The iDVD Preferences dialog box.

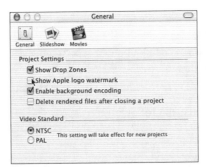

3. In the Preferences dialog box, click to uncheck the Show Apple Logo Watermark option. This removes the Apple logo from the lower-right corner of the DVD production. Of course, you can leave it in if you want.

4. In the main iDVD window, click the Theme button in the lower-left corner, click the Themes tab if necessary, and click to select a theme (see Figures 17.2 and 17.3). (Using the pop-up menu in the Themes tab, you can choose to view Old Themes, New Themes, or All. You can also view a subset of themes you've customized and saved as Favorites.)

FIGURE 17.2

You can use the iDVD Themes menu to select a background for your iDVD project. In our example, we use the Sky theme.

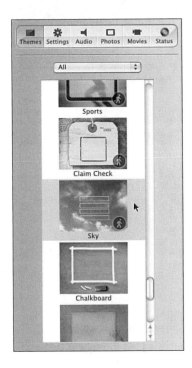

5. To customize the title, click the text so that it's selected (as shown in Figure 17.4) and you can start typing.

FIGURE 17.3
The iDVD background with the placeholder text "Sky."

FIGURE 17.4
The placeholder text "Sky" can be replaced with your own text.

Importing Files

You learned in Hour 7, "Exporting iMovies," that you can create an iDVD project directly from iMovie if you'd like. That would open your iMovie directly into iDVD, including any chapter markers you've added to make it easier for viewers to skip to specific scenes.

If you wanted to add clips rather than your entire iMovie, there are three methods for importing video: select File, Import, Video; open the Movies tab in the Customize tray window; or drag the file directly into the DVD from a Finder window.

Remember that video clips imported with iMovie have automatically been encoded in the appropriate format for them to be compatible with iDVD. iDVD supports only QuickTime movies with linear video tracks. Other formats, such as QuickTime VR, MPEG, Flash, streaming or encrypted movies, and QuickTime spanned movies, cannot be added to your iDVD project.

If you try to import a file that isn't compatible with iDVD, an Unsupported File Type message appears.

Using the Movies Tab and the other iMedia Browsers

A moment ago, you read that you can add video to your iDVD project by dragging movies files in from the Movie tab in the iDVD Customize drawer, but you might be wondering how that works. Quite simply, the integration between the applications that Apple calls iLife (iTunes, iPhoto, iMovie, and iDVD) allows them to recognize and display each other's files.

The Movie, Audio, and Photos tabs in iDVD, which are collectively called *iMedia browsers*, link directly to the respective folders on your hard drive that contain your iTunes library, your iPhoto library, and the default location for storing iMovie projects. These tabs give you direct access to these elements so that you can incorporate them into your DVD projects without having to leave the comfort of the iDVD interface.

However, for these tabs to function, you must make sure that you're using compatible, recent versions of each of the i-applications. Specifically, you must be using at least version 2 of iPhoto, and version 3 of both iTunes and iMovie. Also, to use the Audio and Photos browser tabs, you must have opened iTunes and iPhoto at least once after they've been updated to compatible versions so that your media libraries can be cataloged in a format that iDVD understands.

To add a video clip from the Movies tab, you only have to open the tab, select a file, and drag it into the iDVD main window.

By default, the Movies tab shows only the movie files stored in the Movie folder of your home account. If you tend to store your movies in other places, you can add search paths to those places in the Movies settings of the iDVD preference panel. Click the Add button to navigate to a folder that contains movie files. Now, when you open the Movies tab, those files will also appear.

If you delete a folder for which you've added a search path, simply open the Movie preference settings, highlight the out-of-date path, and click the Remove button.

17

Task: Importing Files from the Hard Drive

▼TASK

When you choose a theme for your DVD in iDVD, the DVD buttons consist of either small images that represent the video or text buttons. One of the nice things about iDVD is that if you've chosen a theme that uses buttons with text, the filename of the video clip that you're importing into iDVD automatically appears on the DVD buttons. You can always change it, but it's often close to what you want anyway.

1. Open the folder containing your video clips and drag one directly from the Finder into the iDVD window (see Figure 17.5). If you're still looking at the tray that extends from the left edge of the window, you can click the Customize button to retract the tray so that you have more room to work.

FIGURE 17.5

You can drag QuickTime movies (at the left) directly into the iDVD window, and the filename becomes the DVD button name.

2. Continue dragging the remaining clips into the project, until you end up with something like Figure 17.6.

3. At this point, you could click the Preview button in the main iDVD window to preview the project, which is always a good way of seeing whether things turned out the way you wanted them to. (If you're satisfied with the project you've created, skip ahead to the section on burning your DVD.)

As you add files to your project, it's wise to keep an eye on the size of your files. (DVDs hold a lot of information, but video takes up a lot of space!) You can monitor the size of your project in the Status tab, as seen in Figure 17.7.

Remember, you might need to click the Customize button to get to the Status tab.

FIGURE 17.6
iDVD automatically creates titles from the filenames of the imported QuickTime movies.

FIGURE 17.7
Encoder status: iDVD encodes your video clips while you work on your project.

17

Burning Your DVD

Burning a DVD is really as simple as clicking a button and waiting for your masterpiece to be created. There are, however, several steps you should take to be sure that your DVD turns out well: previewing your project, burning the DVD, and testing the finished DVD. We'll cover these steps in detail now.

Task: Previewing Your Project

Before you burn your finished DVD to disc, you should preview it to make sure that everything is exactly as you want it. Although it's tempting to skip this step when your project is so close to being completed, if you made any mistakes, you'll have to burn the project all over again and end up waiting twice as long to view it.

1. To preview your project, click the Preview button.

2. In the remote control that appears on your screen, click the arrow buttons to select a menu button, as shown in Figure 17.8. When you press Enter, the content linked to the selected button will play.

FIGURE 17.8

In Preview mode, iDVD displays a remote control so you can navigate through the menus of your project.

3. Repeat step 2 until you've tried all the elements in your project, even those in sub-menus, to make sure that you finished all the portions of your project.

4. When you've tested everything, click the Preview button or click the Exit button on the remote control to return to edit mode.

While previewing your project, make sure that you have motion activated so you can see any motion effects in the menus or menu buttons. You'll know motion is activated if the Motion button is green.

To make sure that things go smoothly while your computer burns a DVD, there are a couple of steps you should take:

Quit out of any other applications you have running, such as iMovie or an email program. Burning DVDs is a resource-intensive process, and it's best to let your computer focus all of its processing power on iDVD.

Next, you will want to make sure that your Mac doesn't go to sleep in the middle of burning. (This doesn't seem to affect all Macs, but it's better to be safe than to waste a DVD-R.) To do this, go to the Apple menu at the upper left and open the System Preferences panel. Choose Energy Saver from the Hardware section, and set the slider that controls the length of inactivity before the computer sleeps to Never (see Figure 17.9).

FIGURE 17.9

Open the Energy Saver pane of the System Preferences to ensure that your computer doesn't sleep during disc burning.

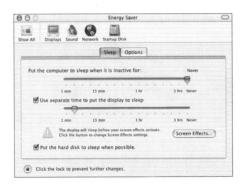

Task: Burning Your DVD

After you've tested your project and prepared your computer, burning the actual disc is quite simple. Just make sure that there's nothing else you want to add to your project. Remember, once you burn a DVD-R, it can't be reused.

Apple has issued an important software update that applies to using high-speed DVD-R discs in some SuperDrives. Before burning a DVD, read the first question in the Q&A of Hour 15, "DVD Discs," to see whether your SuperDrive is one that requires the update.

As you learned in Hour 15, there are many kinds of DVD media. Make sure that you're using 2.0 General DVD-R discs. Also, some brands of disc—even the right kind—don't seem to work in iDVD. For that reason, it's best to test a single disc before buying DVDs in bulk from one manufacturer.

▼ 1. Click the Burn button. When clicked, the gray button will retract to reveal a pulsing button in its place.

2. Click the pulsing button to confirm that you're ready to burn your project to DVD.

 If you have turned motion off in the iDVD interface, iDVD will ask whether you want to burn a DVD without motion menus. You can click Cancel to back out of the burning process you've initiated and turn motion on, or you can click Proceed to burn your disc with motion disabled.

3. You'll be prompted to insert a blank DVD-R disc into the drive, as shown in Figure 17.10.

FIGURE 17.10
iDVD prompts you to insert a blank disc.

Disc Insertion...
Please insert a blank DVD-R disc.

Cancel

▲ 4. Insert your disc and wait for iDVD to do its thing.

 Be careful not to press the Eject key while burning is in progress. Doing so might interrupt burning and result in an unusable disc.

It'll take a while for your computer to create the disc. Exactly how much time depends on your computer's processor and how much content is on the disc. Generally, it'll take two to three times the length of the video on the disc for that video to be encoded and written.

Task: Testing Your DVD

After your DVD has been written, there's one step yet remaining—to make sure that the disc works! To find out whether the disc has been created correctly, the best option is to try it in the computer that wrote it. If the DVD works in your computer, chances are good that it will play in most newer DVD players and DVD-drive equipped computers. (See www.apple.com/dvd/compatibility/ for a list of compatible players.)

1. To test your DVD, insert it into your computer's drive.

2. The DVD Player application should open automatically with your DVD main menu visible.
▼

3. Using the remote control that appears on your screen, click the arrows to select a button and click Enter to watch that segment of your DVD.

Customizing the DVD Project

iDVD gives you a variety of ways to go beyond the automatic settings that it chooses for you. In general, the automated settings work fairly well. For example, when you type in text for a title on your DVD screen, the automatic setting is for the text to be centered on the screen. Similarly, the vertical position of the text on the screen starts out being situated toward the top. But if you want to change the way things are arranged, there are a few simple steps to follow.

Task: Customizing the DVD Project

In this example, we're going to adjust the position of the text on the DVD screen, as well as change its size, so that we can fit more on the screen. To customize the project:

1. Open your DVD project and click the Customize button in the lower-left corner of the iDVD window

2. When the tray opens, click the Settings tab.

   The Settings tab, shown in Figure 17.11, contains a number of options that you can play with to affect the way the way that the DVD screen looks. We're going to adjust the Title and Button settings.

3. In the Title area, click the Position pop-up menu and switch the setting from Top Center to Custom. This enables you to click on the title in the DVD screen and move it to the desired position (see Figure 17.11).

4. In the Button area, click the Free Position radio button to free up the buttons so that they can be moved (see Figure 17.12). The original setting, Snap to Grid, aligns the buttons automatically for the selected theme.

5. If you haven't already, click each button and the title on your DVD screen and drag them to your desired positions. Your screen might look something like Figure 17.13.

If you choose to use Free Position for your buttons, be careful not to position them in ways that your audience will find difficult to use! You might even want to turn on the TV Safe Area feature under the Advanced menu. This puts a border around the region of your menu that's most likely to be visible across different models of television. In case you are wondering, the preset button positions that are used with Snap to Grid fall well inside the TV Safe Area.

TASK

17

▼

FIGURE 17.11

The options in the Settings tab can be used to change the features of the title and buttons in your iDVD menu.

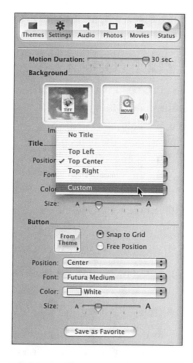

FIGURE 17.12

Changing from Snap to Grid to Free Position enables you to reposition buttons.

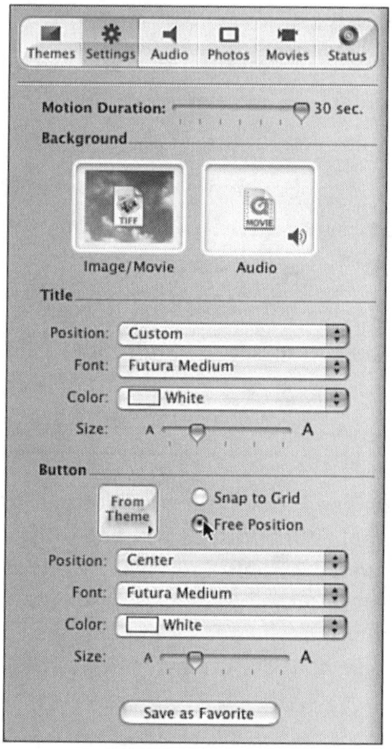

▼

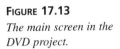

FIGURE 17.13

The main screen in the DVD project.

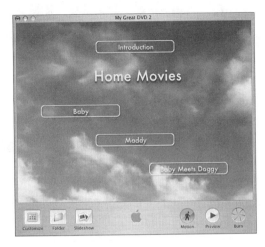

17

Now we're going to adjust the size of the text.

6. At the bottom of the Title area of the Settings window, click on the blue Size selection button. Hold the mouse button down and drag it to the left or to the right to adjust the size of the title text (see Figure 17.14).

FIGURE 17.14

Changing the size of the title text.

If you look at Figure 17.15, you'll see that we wanted to include more information on the DVD screen. In this case, we had to change the size of the title text just to fit it on the screen.

FIGURE 17.15

To fit the line of text on the screen, the size of the text was adjusted.

Limitations: In iDVD, you can't have multiple lines of text on the screen and you can't have a title that spans more than one line. This can present challenges depending on what you want to say or include on a DVD screen. For example, even though we were able to include a Web address in the screen shown in Figure 17.15, it's a little cramped.

Adding More Screens

In this section, we look at a way to get around this limitation. We move the Web site address in our example to a separate page by adding a picture that we created in the image-editing program Adobe Photoshop.

Task: Adding a New Screen

To provide a graphic for our DVD example, we've gone into Photoshop and prepared a graphic that is 640 pixels wide by 480 pixels tall (see Figure 17.16), which is the size for iDVD background images that Apple recommends. For a review of pixels and other related concepts, see Hour 13, "Understanding DVD Video."

If you've never worked with digital images, you might want to look into how to work with images in a program such as Photoshop. You can also get a very functional but much less expensive starter version of Photoshop from Adobe called Photoshop Elements. Try downloading a trial version of Photoshop from www.adobe.com.

FIGURE 17.16

Creating the screen image in Photoshop, 640 pixels wide by 480 pixels tall, with the screen grab image positioned in the middle and a red background.

The goal with this image was to make a simple screen in iDVD that would make use of a *screen grab*, which is a snapshot of something on the computer screen. I wanted to include a picture of the Web page on the DVD screen, so I pressed Cmd+Shift+3 to get the screen grab and loaded the image into Photoshop. In Photoshop, I made a solid background and positioned the image from the screen grab so that it appeared in the center, still leaving room for text. The reason I gave the picture a background is because I didn't want the image to fill up the entire screen.

When you perform a screen grab, the picture file appears on your desktop in PDF format.

When you use the Folder option, iDVD creates a new screen where you can either add video, or in this case, a graphic. To add a new screen to your DVD:

1. In the main iDVD window, click the Folder button (see Figure 17.17).

FIGURE 17.17

The Folder button in the main iDVD window.

▼   2. Click the newly created button (My Folder) that appears on the screen and drag it
      to the desired position (see Figure 17.18). If you have Snap to Grid set, the other
      buttons will move aside to let you place the select button where you want it.

FIGURE 17.18

iDVD creates the button and you can then reposition it and type in new text.

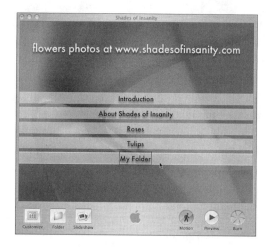

   3. Double-click this new button to get to the new screen, which you see in Figure
      17.19, with the temporary title for the theme inherited from the previous screen.

FIGURE 17.19

When you double-click your new button, you can see the new screen iDVD makes for you. The little arrow graphic is to enable people to get back to the main screen.

▼

▼   4. To import the Photoshop graphic into the new DVD screen, choose File, Import,
        Image and locate your graphic (see Figure 17.20). If you don't have a created
        graphic, a digital photograph will work just as well. The new graphic will cover the
        default background of the theme.

FIGURE 17.20
Importing a file.

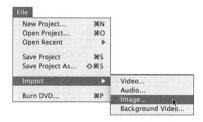

▲   5. Continue to customize the title text as desired, and you'll end up with something
        like the screen in Figure 17.21.

FIGURE 17.21
The finished screen with imported image.

The main DVD screen should now look something like the one shown in Figure 17.22,
where the Web Site button leads to the next screen, providing a nice way to add some
extra information.

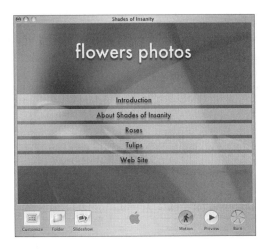

FIGURE 17.22

The finished screen. Four buttons lead to video clips and the last button leads to a separate screen.

Summary

In this hour, we took a look at how simple it is to do an iDVD project. As you've seen, your projects can look just fine without adjusting any additional settings, but if you want to, there are ways to customize the way the DVD works and looks. In the next hour, we'll be getting into the nitty-gritty of DVD menus in iDVD, where you give the audience their choice of how to experience your DVD project.

Workshop

The Workshop consists of quiz questions and answers to help you to develop a better grasp of DVD creation. First, try to answer the questions, *before* checking the answers. Then you'll want to read the explanations, even if you get the answers right—the explanations will contribute in a small way to your overall understanding of DVD.

Q&A

Q How do I add more than one line of text on an iDVD screen?

A There's no way in the current versions of iDVD to add multiple lines of text. The text capability is designed for working with titles, but not really for adding anything else. The example at the end of this hour shows how you can get around this kind of limitation by making your own screen image and importing it as a background. To add multiple lines of text, you would simply make an image containing text and import it into iDVD, thereby bypassing the text limitation.

Q **What's the best way to get the position of buttons to look aligned when I'm moving them around on the screen using the Free Position feature?**

A In the current version of iDVD, you can't use arrow keys to move the buttons (maybe in a new version?), so you have to click and drag them. Really the best way to do this is to use your best judgment. And you can always switch things back to the Snap to Grid option in the Customize window.

Quiz

1. Where's the Free Position setting for moving buttons located?

   A. In the main iDVD window

   B. In the Settings tab

   C. In the Button area of the Settings tab

   D. B and C

2. What size would an image have to be to import it for use as a background image?

   A. 64×38 pixels

   B. 640×380 pixels

   C. 400×300 pixels

   D. Any of the above

3. When a video clip is added to a DVD project, how do you change the automatically generated text on the DVD button?

   A. Choose Edit, Change Text

   B. Click the text in the button and type in the new text

   C. Take a felt-tip marker and write the text directly on the screen

Quiz Answers

1. **D.** The Button area is located in the Customize tab of the iDVD tray, which is accessed by clicking the Themes button in the main iDVD window.

2. **B.** Apple recommends images be sized to 640×480. (However, technically speaking, any image with the aspect ratio of 4×3 will work because iDVD imports graphics and resizes them for you.)

3. **B.** B is the best option, but if you choose option C, make sure that you don't use permanent ink!

17

Exercises

1. Practice adding clips to a project from the Finder or the Movies tab. Then try to add a clip using the File, Import, Video method.

2. Change the disc name of a project you have in progress to something you'd want to appear as the title of the finished disc. Pick something descriptive so that you'll know what to expect from the title.

HOUR 18

DVD Menus in iDVD

In this hour, we take a look at how to work with menus in iDVD. The menu is the central part of any DVD project, and it's the gateway for your audience to experience your DVD.

In iDVD, you can choose your favorite background from the list of built-in themes and then begin to make your DVD. As you'll see, this is a simple and enjoyable process. Throughout this hour, we discuss the following:

- DVD menus
- Choosing a background
- DVD titles
- DVD buttons
- Entering text
- DVD folders (multiple screens)

DVD Menus

In general, DVD menus consist of a background and a series of buttons that lead to other parts of the DVD. In iDVD, the first thing you do is choose your background from the list of available themes. A screen comes up that automatically gives you a title that you can customize, as shown in Figure 18.1.

FIGURE 18.1

A fresh new DVD screen with sample text that you replace with your own text.

To create DVD buttons, all you need to do is drag a video clip onto the background, as shown in Figure 18.2.

FIGURE 18.2

Dragging a video clip directly into iDVD is one way of adding it to a project; choosing File, Import, Video is another.

Throughout this hour, we take a look at some individual tasks that you end up doing as you work on your DVD menus.

Themes

iDVD makes it easy to choose a background theme for your DVD project. You can simply scroll through the list of options in the Themes tab. There are three basic categories of themes:

- Static background themes display a regular, non-video image. An example is Chalkboard.
- Motion themes display a short videos repeats. An example is Global.
- Drop Zone themes include areas where you can add your own slideshows, movies, or still images. An example of a Drop Zone theme is Theater, where the stage curtain opens and closes over a space in which you can add your own scene. We'll talk more about working with themes containing drop zones in Hour 19, "Customizing DVD Menus."

Different types of themes suit different purposes, but switching between them isn't difficult. You can always click on a different theme when you're working on your project—iDVD enables you to play and experiment as much as you want. All the elements in your DVD and the titles you've given them will carry over between themes.

18

When choosing, look for the one that best suits the mood you're trying to achieve. You can change the type of buttons—text or video—in any theme, so it doesn't matter whether a theme is preset to use text or video buttons. We'll find out how in the next hour.

Task: Choosing a Background

▼ TASK

iDVD makes it easy to choose a background for your DVD project. After you've started a new project:

1. Click the Customize button in the lower-left corner of the main iDVD window to display the Themes list. If the Themes list doesn't appear, you might need to click the Themes tab.

2. Click on a desired theme in the Themes list, and it automatically displays a theme in the main iDVD window (see Figure 18.3).

▲

You can always click on a different theme when you're working on your project—iDVD enables you to play and experiment as much as you want (see Figure 18.4). All the elements in your DVD and the titles you've given them will carry over between themes.

FIGURE 18.3

Selecting the Brushed Metal theme from the Themes list.

FIGURE 18.4

The Claim Check theme—an example of a theme that doesn't move, but has audio.

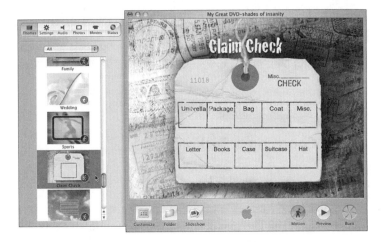

If you choose a theme that has sound or motion (indicated by a small circular walking man symbol) or displays previews of the project clips as video buttons, you might want to temporarily disable the sound or motion. You can do so by clicking the Motion button (see Figure 18.5) at the bottom of the main iDVD window.

FIGURE 18.5

Click the Motion button to turn motion on and off in iDVD. This option applies only to themes that have motion menus or video buttons.

DVD Titles

In iDVD, titles are simply the text that appears at the top of your DVD screen. When you choose a theme, the title initially appears as sample text and then you can type in your own text.

One approach to working with menus in iDVD is to type in your title text and then switch between various themes—iDVD automatically carries the text you typed into the other themes you're trying. For example, Figures 18.6—18.8 show title text (Travel DVD) that was typed in using the Brushed Metal theme, the Theater theme, and then the Chalkboard theme, respectively.

FIGURE 18.6

Looking at title text in the Brushed Metal theme.

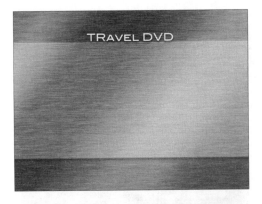

FIGURE 18.7

Looking at title text in the Theater theme.

FIGURE **18.8**
*Looking at title text in
the Chalkboard theme.*

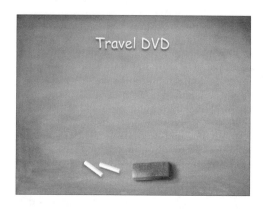

Task: Making a Title

After you've chosen a theme, making a title for your DVD is as simple as clicking and
typing:

1. Click once on the sample text that appears when you initially select a theme. It will
   be selected as shown in Figure 18.9.

FIGURE **18.9**
*Clicking on text to
select it; you can just
start typing and the
original text is
replaced.*

2. Type in the text that you want. It automatically replaces the sample text, as shown
   in Figure 18.10.

FIGURE **18.10**
*The new text is typed
in and the selection
rectangle is still there.*

3. Press the Return key on your keyboard and the selection rectangle disappears, leaving your new text on the screen, which you can always go back and change (see
   Figure 18.11).

Figure 18.11
The new text appearing at the top of the screen.

DVD Buttons—Video and Text

In iDVD, you can have two different kinds of buttons, depending on the theme that you choose. In some themes, there are text buttons, which contain only letters (see Figure 18.12).

Figure 18.12
A text button.

In other themes there are video buttons, which include letters and a preview of the video clip or slideshow you're linking to (see Figure 18.13).

Task: Making a Text Button

The process of making a text button is as simple as choosing a theme, choosing a clip, and typing:

1. Choose a theme (such as Sky) from the Themes list.

2. Drag your video clip directly into the iDVD window or choose File, Import Video (see Figure 18.14). Remember: You must use a clip that is in a format compatible with iDVD, as discussed in Hour 17, "Making a Sample DVD."

▼ **TASK**

▼

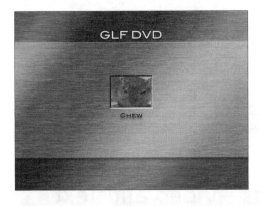

FIGURE 18.13

A video button with a preview of the clip.

FIGURE 18.14

Adding a video clip.

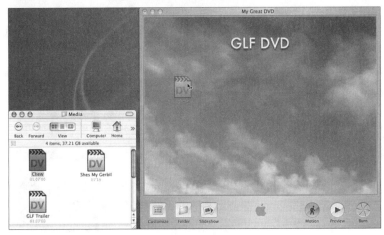

3. The text button is automatically named according to the filename of the clip that's imported, but you can always click on the text in the button to change it if you want.

Task: Making a Video Button

Making a video button is as easy as making a text button. In fact, a video button is basically a text button that also includes video.

1. Choose a theme (such as Brushed Metal) from the Themes list.

2. Drag your video clip directly into the iDVD window or choose File, Import, Video (see Figure 18.15).

FIGURE 18.15
Adding a video clip.

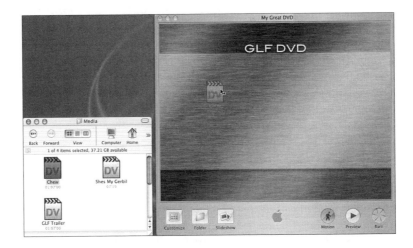

3. If you want, you can click on the text in the video button to change it. The video button is automatically named according to the filename of the clip that was imported (see Figure 18.16).

FIGURE 18.16
The video button with a preview of the underlying clip.

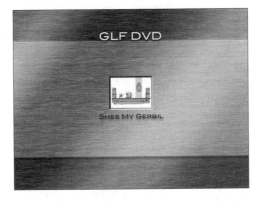

18

Task: Adjusting a Video Button

iDVD gives you a number of ways to make simple adjustments to a video button right in the main iDVD window. The automatic setting is for the button to start playing the movie from the beginning, but you can change where the video displayed on the button starts or simply have a picture appear instead of the video.

1. Click a video button to get the adjustment controls, as shown in Figure 18.17.

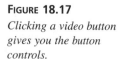

FIGURE **18.17**

Clicking a video button gives you the button controls.

2. Click the slider and drag it to the desired position within the mini-movie to change where the mini-movie starts (see Figure 18.18).

FIGURE **18.18**

The slider in the button controls enables you to choose where you want the preview to begin.

3. If you don't want the video button to be in motion, uncheck the Movie option and use the slider to choose the nonmoving image from the mini-movie, as shown in Figure 18.19.

FIGURE **18.19**

Unchecking the Movie option gives you a picture preview instead of a video preview.

▲

4. When you're done adjusting, click on the video button again and you'll see the button (see Figure 18.20).

FIGURE 18.20
The adjusted video button with a motion-less picture.

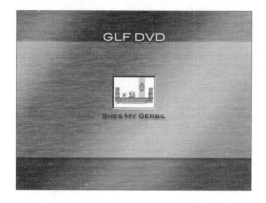

> When working with video buttons, remember that they're in motion as you're working on them only if you have motion in iDVD turned on. If the Motion button at the bottom of the main iDVD window is green, motion is activated. Similarly, unless you specifically uncheck the Movie option as described earlier, your video buttons will move.

18

DVD Folders (Adding Multiple Screens)

In Hour 16, you learned that iDVD enables you to add up to six menu items per screen. But sooner or later, you'll probably want to add more than six items to your DVD. To do this, you'll need to add additional screens, or submenus, to your DVD project. Each submenu can contain an additional six items, until you hit the limit of 99 movies and slideshows or 30 motion menus.

iDVD represents submenus with the metaphor of folders. Think of DVD folders just like you have folders on your hard drive. You can put multiple items in a folder, and to get to the contents, you click on the folder. Similarly, in iDVD, the folder provides the audience with a way to get to another screen.

Task: Adding a DVD Folder

When you add a DVD folder, you always add the first folder to the main menu, and then you can add additional folders to the main menu or within other folders to create many layers of menus.

When you import a movie with chapter markers made in iMovie as discussed in Hour 7, "Exporting iMovies," iDVD creates a button with the title of the movie (so that the viewer can play the entire movie) and a Scene Selection button that links to a scene submenu (so the viewer can select which scenes to watch and in what order). If you'd like, however, you can set your iDVD preferences so that scene submenus are never created or so that iDVD asks what you'd like on each imported movie.

You can add a folder to a theme that includes text buttons or video buttons. Our example uses the Brushed Metal theme, which includes video buttons.

Follow these steps to get a sense of how things work:

1. Drag an iDVD-compatible video clip directly into the iDVD window or choose File, Import, Video (see Figure 18.21).

FIGURE 18.21

Adding a clip and then clicking on the Folder button.

2. Click the Folder button in the main iDVD window to add a folder (see Figure 18.21). iDVD automatically adds a button that looks like a video button with an icon that looks like a folder. (If your theme supports text buttons, your folder will be added as a button labeled "My Folder.")

3. Double-click the new folder button in your menu to get to the new folder screen you have just added (see Figure 18.22).

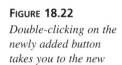

FIGURE 18.22

Double-clicking on the newly added button takes you to the new folder screen.

One thing that you might not realize is that you aren't limited to using a single theme throughout your entire DVD. For instance, if you use the Portfolio B&W theme for the main menu in a DVD, you could choose a different theme (such as Sky) for another screen or submenu on the DVD.

4. Drag additional video clips into the new screen (see Figure 18.23). If desired, customize the buttons using the techniques you learned earlier this hour. Then click on the small arrow in the lower-left corner of your folder screen to get back to the main screen.

FIGURE 18.23

Adding clips to the new folder screen.

5. Single-click on the folder button in the main screen to active the button controls.
6. Use the slider in the button controls to choose which button from your folder screen you want to feature. The changes that you make to the video buttons on your folder screen are carried over to this preview (see Figure 18.24).

18

FIGURE 18.24

Adjusting the preview on the new folder button.

When you're done, your main screen should look something like Figure 18.25, where you have a video clip that you can access directly from your main screen and a video button that leads to an additional screen.

FIGURE 18.25

The completed project with a clip and a folder button leading to another screen.

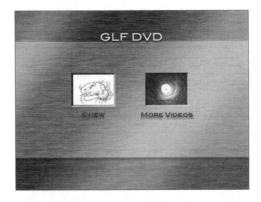

Summary

In this hour, we examined how DVD menus are put together, using a combination of backgrounds and buttons (and don't forget the movie clips!). Chances are that iDVD will set things up automatically so that your DVD comes out looking nice, but you can always go in and tweak things as much as you want.

In the next hour, you'll learn how to further customize DVD menus in iDVD by changing themes and by adjusting text sizes, colors, and other settings that you can access in the Settings tab in the Customize tray window.

Workshop

The Workshop consists of quiz questions and answers to help you to develop a better grasp of DVD menus. First, try to answer the questions *before* checking the answers. Then read the explanations, even if you get the answers right—the explanations will contribute to your overall understanding of DVD.

Q&A

Q **I want to make a video button and I dragged the clip into iDVD, but all I see in the button is a solid black color. What happened?**

A You might need to turn motion on in iDVD by clicking the Motion button at the bottom of the main iDVD screen. But if you just want a motionless image from your video clip, you probably need to use the technique of clicking on the DVD button and choosing the right frame of the movie to use as a still clip so that you don't see black.

Q **If I want to use a video button, but want to use a different video clip for the preview, how do I do it?**

A Read on, read on! Hour 19, "Customizing DVD Menus," will tell you how.

Quiz

1. Text can be adjusted on what kind of button?

    A. A text button

    B. A video button

    C. Both text and video buttons

2. How can you add a new folder to a DVD?

    A. By selecting a folder in the Themes window

    B. Clicking the Add Folder button

    C. By dragging a folder containing multiple video clips into iDVD

    D. B and C

3. How do you change a video button so that it will sit still when you burn your DVD and give it to someone?

    A. Click the button and uncheck the Movie option in the button controls

    B. Click the Motion button in the main iDVD window to turn off motion in iDVD

    C. A and B

18

Quiz Answers

1. **C.** Text buttons have only text, whereas video buttons also include video, but you can adjust the text on either.

2. **D.** Trick question; option C is a treat for those hardy souls who are actually going through the quiz—it's nice to know you can drag an entire folder of video clips directly into iDVD.

3. **C.** To make only a given video button motionless, uncheck the Movie option in the button controls. Turning off motion in iDVD will make all of your video buttons as well as you motion menus motionless in the burned DVD of your project.

Exercises

1. Open an existing project that contains video clips, or start a new project and add a few clips. Try applying various themes. Note which themes contain only music, which contain motion backgrounds and/or drop zones, and which display text or video buttons.

2. Open a project containing video clips and apply a theme that contains video buttons. Turn off motion for a single button only and make it show a frame of the movie it represents.

HOUR 19

Customizing DVD Menus

In this hour, we look at how you can customize your menus in iDVD if you want to go beyond the built-in settings. iDVD often makes your DVD look perfectly fine without having to customize anything. But it can be fun to try making things look different, and sometimes you'll run into situations in which the built-in settings limit the way that you want things to look.

Throughout this hour, we discuss the following:

- Working with drop zones
- Customizing backgrounds
- Customizing buttons
- Customizing titles

Customizing Drop Zone Themes

In the last hour, you learned that some of iDVD's themes include *drop zones*, or areas that you can customize by adding slideshows, movies, and still images. Drop zone themes offer a simple way to personalize your menus.

To add a movie or image to a theme containing a drop zone, select the media file and drag it on top of the drop zone, as shown in Figure 19.1. We're using Theater, a motion menu theme in which stage curtains open and close across the drop zone.

FIGURE 19.1

The borders of the drop zone change when you drag a file on top of it.

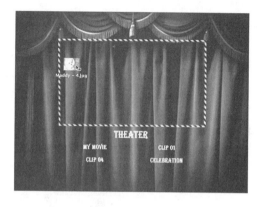

If you're using a drop zone–enabled theme and you want to add a movie as content to your project, drag it to an area of the screen outside the drop zone, or your content will show up in the drop zone region instead of as a button.

Also, by default, the buttons in themes with drop zones are text buttons. If you'd like, you can change them to picture buttons in the Settings pane of the Customize window. We'll talk more about customizing buttons later in the hour.

When your file is added, it will fit inside the drop zone, as shown in Figure 19.2.

FIGURE 19.2

The drop zone now displays the file you added.

The aspect ratio of the image you insert will be preserved, with the image scaled to fit against either the top and bottom or left and right edges of the region. If the best part of the image doesn't fall in the center of the visible area, you can reposition it. Simply drag the image inside the drop zone to choose which portion of the image is visible in the drop zone.

When you drag a movie to a drop zone in a DVD menu, the movie you added is played over and over again when the menu is onscreen. You can set the duration of the movies using the Motion Duration slider in the Settings pane of the Customize tray window. You can choose the number of seconds you want the movies to loop, up to 30 seconds.

To add a slideshow that plays inside a drop zone, simply drag a folder of images into the drop zone. The speed of the slideshow is controlled by the number of images it includes.

To remove files from the drop zone, drag the image within the drop zone out of the iDVD window. Be sure that you're dragging it outside the window, or else you will only move the image, not delete it!

If you choose a drop-zone theme that has background sound or motion (indicated by a small circular walking man symbol) or displays previews of the project clips as video buttons, you might want to temporarily disable the sound or motion if it becomes distracting or seems to slow your computer's reaction time. You can do so by clicking the Motion button, which shows an icon of a walking person, at the bottom of the main iDVD window. Remember, however, to turn motion back on before burning your project to DVD, or the motion won't be included.

19

Customizing Backgrounds

Although drop zones add a lot of opportunity to make a theme your own, customizing a menu by adding your own overall background or theme music is something you might want to do.

Figure 19.3 shows a sample DVD project in which the Customize button has been clicked to display the tray, and the Settings tab has been selected to reveal all the different options. This is the area that we'll discuss for the rest of the hour.

Task: Customizing a Background

To add a new background image to a DVD project, you must have an image prepared that you want to drag in. It could be something like a digital picture you have taken, an image you have downloaded from the Web, or an image that you've prepared in a program such as Adobe Photoshop Elements (or its professional equivalent, Photoshop). Apple suggests you make sure that your image is sized to 640×480 in order to fit the screen exactly.

 You can get as complicated as your imagination allows when working with digital images for a DVD, but you can also keep it fairly simple and do just fine.

You can drag elements into two wells in the Background section of the Settings tab in iDVD. See Figure 19.4.

FIGURE 19.4

The Image/Movie and Audio wells in the Background section of iDVD's Settings tab.

To import a new background image:

1. Open a Finder window containing the file that you want to be the new background and position it next to iDVD.

> You can add an image from your iPhoto library by opening the Photos tab, selecting the image, and dragging it to the Settings tab button. This switches you to the Settings tab, where you can drop the image into the Image/Movie well.
>
> Likewise, if you want to create a motion menu, you can drop a movie from the Movies tab in the same way.

2. Click and drag the file into the Image/Movie well in the Background section as shown in Figure 19.5.

FIGURE 19.5

Importing a new background image in iDVD.

The new background file becomes the new image you see in your DVD screen (see Figure 19.6).

> If you want to create your own images in a program such as Photoshop, Figure 19.7 shows some sample measurements that you can enter into Photoshop when you're creating your new images.

19

FIGURE 19.6

The new blue background image that was dragged into iDVD.

FIGURE 19.7

Sample measurements in Photoshop. Note the width and height measurements.

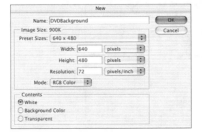

Task: Adding a Sound to a DVD Menu

If you want to add a sound to your DVD menu, you can drag it into the Audio well in the Background area of the Settings tab:

1. Open your iDVD project. In the main iDVD window, click the Customize button to get the expanding window.

2. Click the Settings tab in the tray window.

3. Drag a sound file into the Audio well in the Background section of the Settings tab. See Figure 19.8.

The icon in the Audio well changes to reflect the type of file that you're dragging in. For example, compare the icon in with the icon of the file that's being added in Figure 19.8.

Notice in Figure 19.9 that there's a Motion Duration slider. The automatic setting is for 30 seconds, which is the time that the sound/music plays before repeating. This also holds true for the video portion of a motion menu.

FIGURE 19.8

Dragging a sound file into iDVD.

FIGURE 19.9

The Motion Duration slider in iDVD sets the time that the sound file plays. Note the automatic setting of 30 seconds.

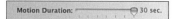

19

If you decide that you no longer want the sound that you've added to a project, drag the sound file icon from the Audio well to any point outside your iDVD window, and it will disintegrate into a puff of smoke on your monitor. When no audio file is set as the menu's background, the audio well will appear with a speaker icon instead of a file icon, as in Figure 19.10.

If you want to temporarily silence a menu to keep it from playing over and over again as you work, you can click the speaker icon in the lower right of the audio well to mute it. However, remember to unmute it before you burn the DVD or it won't be heard in the finished version.

FIGURE 19.10

*This motion menu is
not accompanied by
sound.*

Customizing Titles

The Title area of the Settings tab enables you to change various settings to customize the title text that appears on your DVD screens. iDVD automatically chooses a certain size for title text when you make your DVD, and the size is usually a good match for many DVD projects—large enough to read on the TV, but small enough so that you can type a reasonable number of letters. You'll probably want to change text at some point; the following list corresponds to the options shown in Figure 19.11.

FIGURE 19.11

*Options for changing
the Title text in iDVD.*

- **Position:** Enables you to choose a preset position or free position
- **Font:** Enables you to choose a different style of text

- **Color:** Enables you to choose a color for your title text
- **Size:** Enables you to make the text bigger or smaller

Task: Customizing a Title

In this section, we walk through making changes to titles:

1. To change the position of a title, click the pop-up menu and choose one of the options. The Custom option enables you to fine-tune the position of a title. See Figure 19.12.

FIGURE 19.12

Different positions that a title can be moved to in iDVD.

2. To change the font, click the pop-up menu and select one of the available fonts. The fonts that you have available will depend on your system, but every Mac comes with an abundance of built-in fonts. See Figure 19.13.

3. To change the color, click the pop-up menu and choose from the list of built-in colors. See Figure 19.14.

4. To change the size of a title, drag the Size slider as shown in Figure 19.15.

19

FIGURE 19.13
Click the Title Font choice menu in iDVD.

FIGURE 19.14
Title color choices in iDVD.

FIGURE 19.15
Changing the size of a title in iDVD.

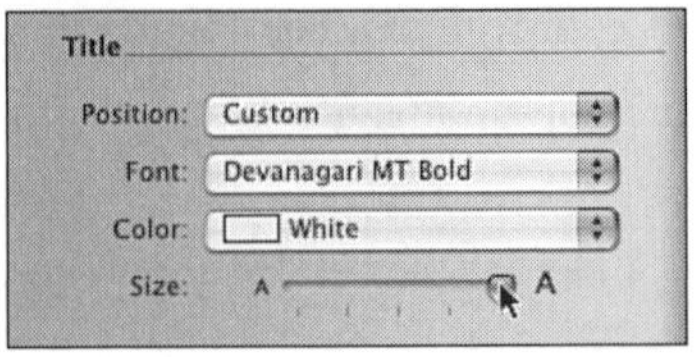

When you're done, you'll have something that looks approximately like Figure 19.16.

FIGURE **19.16**
A sample iDVD project
with the changed title.

Customizing Buttons

The Button area gives you the ability to choose from a variety of different options to add a nice touch to the way that buttons look in your DVD project. It also enables you to adjust things if the automatic settings don't suit your taste. See Figure 19.17.

FIGURE 19.17
Options for changing
button features in
iDVD.

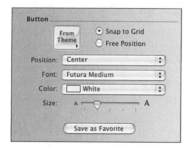

19

The adjustments you can make include the following:

- **From Theme**—Enables you to choose a different button shape to choose between text-only and video buttons.

- **Snap to Grid/Free Position**—Determines whether buttons on the screen start out being automatically aligned to each other (Snap to Grid) or not aligned (Free Position).

- **Position**—Affects the position of the button text in relation to the button.

- **Font**—Affects the style of text.

- **Color**—The same colors are available here that were available in the Title area mentioned previously.
- **Size**—Affects the size of the button text.

Task: Customizing a Button

Although the built-in button shape settings have been automatically chosen to go well with the built-in themes in iDVD, it can be fun to choose a different button shape and customize the new button:

1. Click the From Theme pop-up menu and select a new button shape, such as the movie button shape shown in Figure 19.18. (Adjust your video buttons to show the full video or a flattering still frame as you learned in the previous hour.)

FIGURE 19.18

Button shapes you can choose in iDVD.

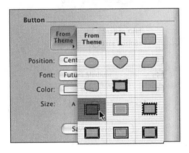

> Depending on the theme you started out with, you might have to rearrange your buttons so that they don't overlap, as shown in Figure 19.19. To do this, click the radio button for Free Position and drag the buttons where you want them.

2. Click the Font pop-up menu and select a new font.
3. Click the Color pop-up menu and choose a color for your button labels, as shown in Figure 19.20.
4. Drag the Size slider to choose a different text size, as shown in Figure 19.21.

FIGURE 19.19

In some themes, changing button styles will result in overlapping buttons. You'll have to reposition them or apply a new theme and try your button style again.

FIGURE 19.20

Color choices for button text in iDVD.

FIGURE 19.21

Changing the text size in buttons in iDVD.

19

When you're done, you should have something that looks approximately like Figure 19.22.

FIGURE 19.22

Your finished buttons in iDVD. Well done!

Task: Saving a Custom Theme

If you like the changes that you've made in customizing your DVD project, you can save this customized theme in the Favorites list of iDVD:

1. Click the Save as Favorite button at the bottom of the Settings tab that you've been working in. See Figure 19.23.

FIGURE 19.23

Opening a dialog box where you can give the current theme a name.

 2. Type in a name for your new theme and click OK. See Figure 19.24.

FIGURE 19.24

Naming the customized theme in iDVD.

When you want to choose your special theme, you can access it in the same Themes list where you normally choose a built-in theme by clicking the pop-up menu and selecting Favorites as shown in Figure 19.25.

The Favorites list displays any custom designs that you've made, and enables you to choose your customized theme for use with any screen in a DVD project that you want (see Figure 19.26). The main value of this Favorites option is that it saves you from having to manually adjust things on every screen in a custom DVD project.

FIGURE 19.25
Accessing the customized theme in iDVD.

If you make a change to one menu that you want to appear in other menus, you can easily update them using the Apply to Project and Apply to Folders options in the Advanced menu. Apply to Project makes all menus match the one visible in the iDVD main window, whereas Apply to Folders makes all the subfolders of the current menu match it.

19

FIGURE 19.26
Customized designs or themes in iDVD.

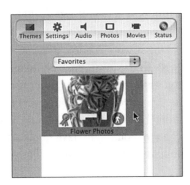

Summary

In this hour, you learned about how to customize the way that your DVD looks by using themes with drop zones and the Customize features in the Settings tab of iDVD. Although the built-in automatic options in iDVD look good, things can look even better when you take the time to play with these settings.

In the next hour, we'll take a look at another exciting feature of working with iDVD: slideshows. Slideshows enable you to share your still photos elegantly and easily.

Workshop

In the following section, we'll consider several issues related to customizing your menus that you may find yourself wondering about at some point, and we'll ask you a few questions to test your knowledge.

Q&A

Q I added a folder of images to a drop zone to create a slideshow in a menu, but some of the images seem distorted. What did I do wrong?

A iDVD seems to get confused when a slideshow contains images that are set to different aspect ratios. In the case in which a mix of portrait and landscape images are used, this problem is especially apparent! To keep photos from being distorted, you must make sure that they're all sized to the same dimensions or least to sizes that are proportionally the same. By that, I mean that you could have an image that's 640×480 together with one sized 320×240 or 1,280×960—all of which are in the aspect ratio 4×3.

Q Can I create my own background with drop zone by setting an existing drop-zone theme and then dragging a new background image into the Image/Movie well of the Settings tab?

A Yes, but there's a trick to making it work. Let me explain. When you drag an image into the Image/Movie well with a drop zone–enabled theme visible in the main iDVD window, the image you apply becomes the entire background and the drop zone disappears. However, if you select Apply Theme to Project from the Advanced menus, the drop zone becomes active again, as long as there's more than one screen affected by the change. You might have to click to another menu and back again for the drop zone to reappear.

Q **I want to put more than one line of text for a title in my DVD. How do I do it?**

A iDVD only allows for one line of text in the title, but if you prepare your own background graphic (640×480) in a program such as Photoshop Elements, you can incorporate the title text spanning multiple lines into the background image itself.

Quiz

1. How do you turn off the sound in a motion menu in iDVD?

   A. Unplug your Mac

   B. Click the Motion button in the main iDVD window

   C. Set the Motion Duration to Off

   D. B and C

2. How do I change the color of text?

   A. In the Text menu

   B. In the Color pop-up menu

   C. A and B

   D. Putting on colored glasses

   E. B and D

3. How many different styles of text can you use?

   A. 42

   B. 23

   C. It depends on the fonts that you have installed on your system

   D. 4,127

Quiz Answers

1. **D.** You can turn off the sound either way. Keep in mind, however, the shutting off sound using the Motion button also turns off the menu's motion effects.

2. **E.** Trick question. Normally you'd change the color of text in a DVD by choosing the Color pop-up menu in either the Title or Button area, but you could also provide your audience with inexpensive colored glasses.

3. **C.** Your computer comes with built-in fonts, but you can always add more to the system and they'll become available in iDVD.

19

Exercises

1. Open a project and apply a theme that contains a drop zone. Add a still photo to the drop zone. Practice positioning your photo in the visible space. Notice that portrait and landscape drop zones exist in different themes, which work better or worse with different photographs.

2. Open a iDVD project containing several menu items and turn on the TV Safe Area under the Advanced menu. Click through several default themes. You'll notice how none of the important elements of the menu appears within the shaded region near an edge of the screen.

3. Add your own background image to your current project using either graphics file, still image, or movie. If you don't like the result, you can delete the background by dragging it from the Images/Movie well out of the iDVD window. For bonus points, read the second question in the "Q&A" section, and try adding your own background while maintaining a drop zone.

HOUR **20**

DVD Slideshows

In this hour, we examine how to work with DVD slideshows in iDVD. DVD slideshows are a nice way to enhance a DVD production; they enable you to add digital pictures to a DVD project that also has video in it. Or, you could make a DVD project that's nothing more than a slideshow. There's no reason why you necessarily must have video on a DVD. The great thing about DVD slideshows is that your friends and family can view the slideshow conveniently on their television.

Throughout this hour, we discuss the following:

- Creating a slideshow
- Slideshow options
- Rearranging slides
- Getting images for a slideshow from the Web

Understanding Slideshows

Using iDVD to create a slideshow is as simple as using other parts of the program; it's a simple matter of dragging your files directly into the iDVD window. After adding your pictures to the slideshow in your DVD project, you can make a number of adjustments if you like.

> If you've already assembled a slideshow in iPhoto, and are using at least iPhoto version 2, you can export it directly to iDVD 3 using the iDVD option of the Organize mode. Your slideshow will appear as a menu item in iDVD under the name of the iPhoto album from which it was created. The music you've set in iPhoto will also carry over. iDVD enables you to adjust this slideshow just as you could a slideshow created inside iDVD.
>
> Note that slideshows exported from iPhoto will be added to the top level of the DVD project.

Task: Creating a Slideshow

Before you can create a slideshow, you must open a new iDVD project or reopen a DVD project that you've been working on that you'd like to add a slideshow to.

1. Open your DVD project.
2. Click the Slideshow button (see Figure 20.1) to create a slideshow.

FIGURE 20.1
The Slideshow button in iDVD.

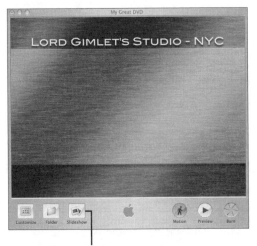

Click the Slideshow button to make
a new Slideshow in your DVD

3. To customize the name of your slideshow, click the text underneath the button that appears. Work through the task "Changing the Slideshow Icon Image" later in this

▼ hour to customize the thumbnail image of the button and change it from the image of slides that appears as shown in Figure 20.2.

FIGURE 20.2
When you click on the Slideshow button at the bottom of your iDVD window a new slide-shaped button appears.

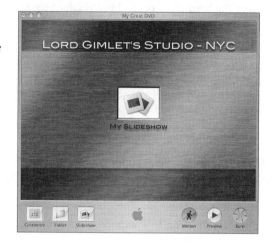

4. To get into the slideshow, double-click on the My Slideshow button that appears on ▲ your main DVD screen.

When you double-click the My Slideshow icon, the slideshow editor opens. From there, you can add slides and make adjustments to your slideshow (see Figure 20.3).

FIGURE 20.3
The slideshow editor will appear in iDVD's main window.

20

Task: Adding Slides

 Adding slides to an iDVD slideshow is as easy as dragging and dropping the files into the iDVD window from the hard drive or the Photos tab of the Customize tray window. You can also use the File, Import, Image option.

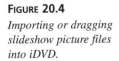 In order for iPhoto and iDVD to integrate, you must be using iPhoto version 2 or later. Also, you must have opened that version of iPhoto at least once for your photo library to be encoded in a format that iDVD can work with.

1. Open your iDVD project and click on the Slideshow button in the main iDVD window to reveal the Slideshow editor.

2. Locate the picture files you want to import.

3. Click on one of the files, and while holding the mouse button down, drag the file into the Slideshow editor (see Figure 20.4).

FIGURE 20.4

Importing or dragging slideshow picture files into iDVD.

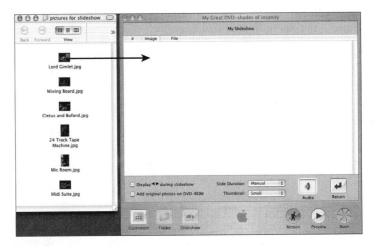

You can also drag multiple files at once into the Slideshow window. To accomplish this, place the mouse pointer near one of the file icons, click and hold the mouse button down, and drag upward and over all the icons you want to select. Then click directly on one of the selected icons and you can drag them all over at once, as shown in Figure 20.5.

The slides appear and can be repositioned and adjusted according to your taste (see Figure 20.6).

FIGURE 20.5

Dragging multiple files into the Slideshow window in iDVD.

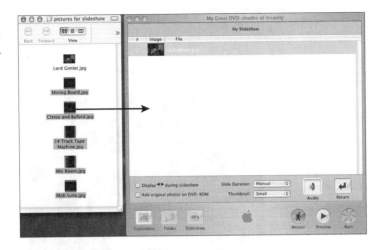

FIGURE 20.6

Picture files in the iDVD Slideshow window.

Slideshow Options

20

The Slideshow window has a variety of options that you can use to adjust both the order of slides and how the slides behave.

Display Arrows During Slideshow

The Display Arrows During Slideshow option causes arrows to be displayed on your slideshow screens that are a reminder that there are previous or remaining slides (see Figures 20.7 and 20.8).

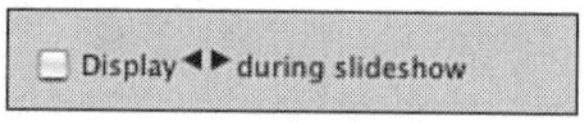

FIGURE 20.7

This option puts arrows on the screen in your DVD.

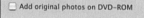

FIGURE 20.8

Display arrows in a sample iDVD project. They represent how a person can use the arrow keys on his DVD remote to go through slides.

Adding Picture Files to DVD-ROM

When you add photos to a DVD as a part of a slideshow, the images are encoded as part of the DVD. If someone wanted to work with the image as a file to print it out or send it in email, she wouldn't be able to do so. However, the Add to DVD-ROM option enables you to add the individual slides to your DVD as graphics files—a nice option for enabling people to watch the slideshow on television as well as being able to put the DVD in their computer to have the pictures available for sending via email and other activities (see Figure 20.9).

FIGURE 20.9

Click the Add to DVD-ROM check box if you want to have the files accessible on the DVD disc.

When you burn your final DVD with this option checked, the slides in your slideshow are converted into a series of individual files. They're saved on the DVD disc along with the normal DVD project and are accessible by any computer with a DVD-ROM drive. (Refer to Hour 15, "DVD Discs," for more information about adding DVD-ROM files to your project.)

When adding DVD-ROM files, remember that only people with DVD-ROM drives on their computers will be able to read them. Although the files are encoded in typical computer file formats, they're written to a DVD!

Setting Slide Duration

The Slide Duration option enables you to set the time that a slide displays on a screen (see Figure 20.10).

FIGURE 20.10

The Slide Duration pop-up menu controls how long a slide appears.

The Manual setting basically means that the user presses the right or left arrow on her DVD remote control to advance to the next slide or go back to a previous slide. But if you want a slideshow to run on its own, you can adjust the duration. To adjust the duration of a slide, simply click the Slide Duration pop-up menu and choose a duration, as shown in Figure 20.11.

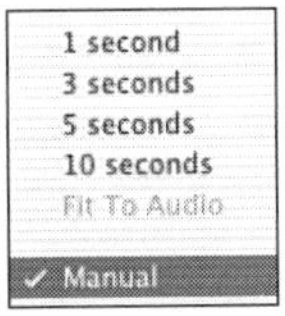

FIGURE 20.11

You can set the amount of time that the slide appears on the screen by choosing different options in this menu.

The Fit to Audio option on Slide Duration menu is available only after you've added background music to your slideshow. Also, after you've added an audio file, the default setting becomes Fit to Audio and the Manual option is no longer available.

20

Thumbnail Size

The Thumbnail option determines the size that the mini-preview of each slide appears in the slideshow window in iDVD (see Figure 20.12).

The Thumbnail setting affects only the Slideshow window that you see while you're working in iDVD—it has nothing to do with the slideshow on the finished DVD.

FIGURE 20.12
The Thumbnail option in the Slideshow window.

There are two options for thumbnail size. The Large setting works better to see a preview of the individual slides, whereas the Small setting works better when you need to see more slides in the window at a time, such as when you're adjusting the order of slides (see Figure 20.13).

FIGURE 20.13
Setting the thumbnail size in the Thumbnail pop-up menu.

In Figure 20.14, you see a slideshow with larger thumbnails; compare this view with the one you saw in Figure 20.6.

FIGURE 20.14
Slideshow window with the larger thumbnail option.

Audio

The Audio option enables you to add a sound file to a slideshow. It works the same as adding audio to a motion menu—you simply drag a file into the well (see Figure 20.15). Refer to Hour 19, "Customizing DVD Menus," for more information.

FIGURE 20.15

The Audio well.

Working with Slides

One of the most common tasks you'll undertake when working with slideshows is rearranging slides so that they appear in a different order. It's really easy to do this and can be fun to play around with as you develop your slideshow. Remember, at any time, you can click on the Preview button at the bottom of the iDVD window to preview your slideshow. Just remember that to get out of the preview mode back into the slideshow editor, you have to either close the miniature remote control by clicking Enter or click the Preview button.

Task: Rearranging Slides

Rearranging slides is as simple as clicking and dragging:

1. Click on a slide, and while holding the mouse button down, begin to move the slide toward the position you want it to be in (see Figure 20.16). As you move the slide, its new position will be outlined in black.

FIGURE 20.16

Moving slide number 1, Lord Gimlet, to a new position in the slideshow window.

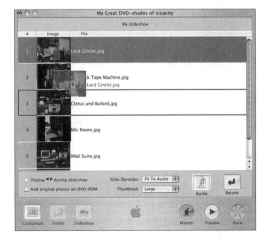

20

▲   2. Put your slide into position and let go of the mouse button.

The slide snaps into position (see Figure 20.17) and you can continue to make adjustments to your slideshow or add new slides. Figure 20.18 illustrates the completed slideshow lineup.

FIGURE 20.17
The Lord Gimlet slide snapping into its new position in the Slideshow window.

FIGURE 20.18
The finished slideshow. Different slides now occupy positions 1 and 2, and the Lord Gimlet slide occupies position 3.

Task: Adding Sound

To add a sound to a slideshow, you again have multiple options. You can drag files in from any folder on your hard drive or from the Audio tab, which links to your iTunes library. You can also use the File, Import, Audio option.

For iTunes and iDVD to integrate, you must be using iTunes version 3 or later. Also, you must have opened that version of iTunes at least once for your music library to be organized in a format that's compatible with iDVD.

1. Open your iDVD project and click on the Slideshow button in the main iDVD window to reveal the Slideshow window.

2. If you're importing a sound file from your iTunes library, open the Audio tab. If you're importing a sound file from somewhere else on your hard drive, position the Finder window with the sound file to the right of the main iDVD window.

3. Click the desired sound file and drag it directly into the Sound well (see Figure 20.19).

FIGURE 20.19

Dragging a sound file into the slideshow window.

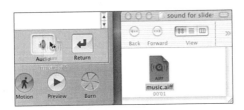

4. If you want the audio to determine the length of the slideshow, choose the Fit To Audio option (see Figure 20.20). This option divides the slideshow according to how many slides there are and plays them for an equal amount of time, based on how long the audio clip is.

FIGURE 20.20

The Slide Duration menu has a Fit To Audio option.

20

Deleting the audio from a slideshow is just like deleting the audio from a menu—click the audio file icon in the Audio well and drag it to the trash can in the dock. A cloud of smoke will appear on your screen to let you know that the background music is history!

Task: Getting Images for a Slideshow from the Web

One source of images for your slideshow might be a Web page where you already have some pictures available. In many cases, you can simply save such pictures to your hard drive and then drag them directly into a slideshow. Keep in mind that if a picture's *pixel size* is less than 640×480, iDVD will scale the picture up to fit the screen, so if you have a picture that's smaller than 640×480, it might look bad in iDVD. A work-around for this problem is to make a simple background screen that adds a margin around the picture so that the picture isn't resized.

> Images on Web sites are copyrighted material, so be careful how you use them. Don't create a DVD slideshow of another person's work and then try to sell it! Also, for projects you create for your own use, it's considered polite to acknowledge the source of photos you borrow.

1. Find your image on the Web.

2. Hold down the Ctrl key on your keyboard and click on the image, choosing the Download Image to Disk/Save Image command (see Figure 20.21).

FIGURE 20.21

A digital picture, convenient source material from your Web page for a slideshow.

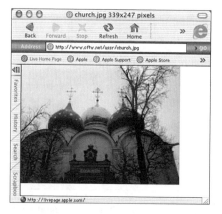

3. Save your image in a convenient location.

4. Open your iDVD project, click on the Slideshow button in the main iDVD window, and drag the image into your slideshow (see Figure 20.22).

Figure 20.22

The downloaded image imported into an iDVD slideshow.

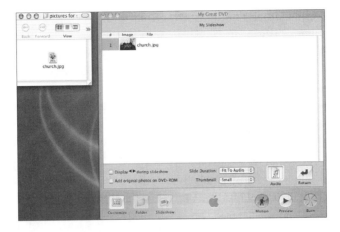

Task: Changing the Slideshow Icon Image

One of the nice things about the way that iDVD enables you to customize DVD menus is apparent when you're working with slideshows. After you've added slides to your slideshow, the image on the button that leads to your slideshow can be changed.

1. After adding slides to your slideshow, come back to the menu containing the button that leads to your slideshow and click it once (see Figure 20.23).

> To come back to the menu that leads to your slideshow, click the button labeled Return, which displays a bent arrow, at the lower right of the slideshow editing window.

Figure 20.23

Clicking on the button that leads to a slideshow gives you a slider that enables you to choose pictures.

20

▼   2. Move the slider to choose the picture you want to appear on the DVD button (see
         Figure 20.24).

Click and drag slider to choose a picture
from the slideshow to be the thumbnail image

FIGURE 20.24

Selecting a thumbnail image.

3. Click somewhere on the menu screen outside the button you have selected to dese-
▲   lect it (see Figure 20.25).

FIGURE 20.25

No more boring generic icons: The DVD button for the slideshow with a new image in place. Great!

Remember, iDVD also enables you to customize buttons representing folders and submenus in a similar way.

Summary

In this hour, you learned how to put together a digital slideshow that you can use to
enhance your DVD project. Slideshows can be a nice way to share digital pictures with

the convenience of seeing them through a television set. In fact, because of the relatively small amount of space that digital pictures take up, you could fit thousands of them on a DVD.

In the next hour, we'll work through a sample project containing submenus for multiple screens.

Workshop

The Workshop consists of quiz questions and answers to help you to develop a better grasp of DVD slideshows. First, try to answer the questions *before* checking the answers. Then read the explanations, even if you get the answers right—the explanations will contribute to your overall understanding of DVD.

Q&A

Q I have a number of pictures that are old-style prints (not digital pictures) that I'd like to add to my DVD slideshow. How do I do it?

A The most convenient way to digitize prints is to find the negatives that came with the prints and order a picture CD, which can be made when you send in the negatives and pay a fee to have them converted. What you end up with is a CD that you can insert in the computer and copy the digitized pictures to your hard drive (see www.kodak.com). Another option, which gives you more control and flexibility, is to purchase an inexpensive scanner and scan the prints yourself.

Q When I export a slideshow from iPhoto into iDVD, it appears on the project's main menu, but I wanted it to go on a submenu. Is there anything I can do to change this?

A You have to let iPhoto place the slideshow on the main menu, which can be a problem if you already have six menu items inserted. You can then select and copy the slideshow button and paste it to a new location within your iDVD project. This creates a duplicate of the slideshow where you want it to be. Finish up by deleting the instance of the slideshow that's in the wrong place, and you're ready to continue.

Quiz

1. How do you add a new picture to a slideshow in iDVD?

    A. Double-click on the image

    B. Drag the image into the slideshow window

    C. None of the above

2. How do you set the duration of a slide?

    A. Choose Duration, Set

    B. Choose Set, Duration

    C. None of the above

    D. Choose a value from the Slide Duration pop-up menu

3. How many different ways can people view the images from your DVD slideshow?

    A. Through a DVD player only

    B. Through a DVD player or from a DVD-ROM drive

    C. Through DVD, DVD-ROM, or CD-ROM

Quiz Answers

1. **B.** It's as easy as drag and drop! You can also use File, Import.

2. **D.** Choose a duration that fits with the pictures. Five seconds is a nice duration if you want to move at a good pace. Opting for the Manual option enables people to choose their own pace, and is probably the best option so that people can stay on particular slides as long or as little as they want.

3. **B.** DVD slideshows are a great way to share digital pictures and enable the audience to experience them on television or on a computer with a DVD-ROM drive. Don't forget that if you check the Add to DVD-ROM option in the slideshow window, in addition to being able to watch the DVD on a computer using DVD player software, when a person inserts the DVD, she can drag the individual digital pictures onto her hard drive. For example, you might want to make the pictures in your slideshow available to the audience as files on the DVD-ROM so that they can email to friends or use them as desktop background pictures.

Exercises

1. Open a new project and create a slideshow using any digital photographs you have on your computer's hard drive. Practice adding and moving slides and then change the slideshow settings to experience what they do.

2. If you plan to create slideshows in iPhoto for export to iDVD, verify that you're using at least version 2 of iPhoto. You'll find this information by opening iPhoto, and then choosing iPhoto, About iPhoto from the menu at the top of your screen. If you're using an older version of iPhoto, you must download the new version from Apple's Web site (www.apple.com) and install it as directed before iPhoto and iDVD can work together.

Hour **21**

Example Project— Multiple Screens

In this hour, we create a DVD project that's a bit more advanced than the sample project in Hour 17, "Making a Sample iDVD." This project will help you get a better understanding of the concept of working with multiple DVD screens when you have more material than can fit on one screen.

Throughout this hour, we discuss the following:

- Multiple screens
- Project setup
- Menu creation
- Slideshows
- Customizing icons

Considering Multiple Screens

In Hour 16, "Introducing iDVD," you learned that you could have a total of six items on an individual menu. For example, if you had seven movies, you could drag six of them into iDVD onto a single screen, but then there would be no place to put the seventh movie.

So, you might want to put five movies on the main screen (five out of the six allowable items), and have one button from the main screen (the sixth allowable item) that leads to another screen with your remaining two movies (see Figure 21.1).

FIGURE **21.1**

An example of how multiple menus enable you to use more than six movies.

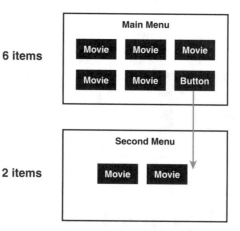

In our sample project in this hour, we'll create a main screen that leads to several additional screens that contain both slideshows and movies.

Setting Up the Project

You don't necessarily have to organize your files and folders as they appear in the example, but you'll want to organize them in some way that makes sense. Although you could drag a video file into iDVD from one location on your hard drive and drag an image from a completely different location, it can be helpful to gather all your files in one place so that you can find them easily (see Figure 21.2).

Also, if you want to save the project that you're using to make your DVD, it's nice to have everything in one place in case you want to move it later. Putting everything in one place also prevents certain complications, such as someone else accidentally deleting a digital picture somewhere else in your hard drive that you were using for a DVD project.

If you want to follow along with your own files, you might want to look ahead at the kind of digital images and movies that are used in this project and find some of your own files to use in their place.

FIGURE 21.2

Organizing files for a DVD.

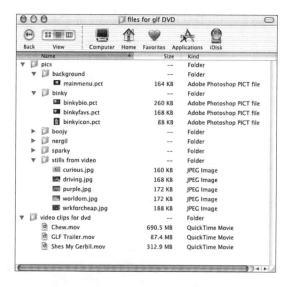

Task: Setting Up the Main Menu

This project (see Figure 21.3) ultimately involves having four buttons on the main screen and using a background image that was prepared in Photoshop.

FIGURE 21.3

Looking at the final menu screen in a sample project; four buttons lead to movies and additional screens.

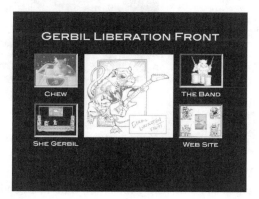

- **Button 1/Chew**—This button is a folder and leads to another screen that contains a movie and a slideshow.

- **Button 2/She Gerbil**—This button is a simple button and leads directly to a movie.

21

▼
- **Button 3/The Band**—This button is a folder that leads to a screen that enables you to view four different slideshows.

- **Button 4/Web Site**—This is a folder button that leads to a simple screen with a movie and text that shows a Web address.

To set up the project:

1. Open iDVD and create a new project, selecting the Brushed Metal theme.

2. Open the Finder window containing the files that you want to use in your DVD project and position it next to the iDVD window. This sets things up so that you can easily drag files into the iDVD window as they're needed.

3. Click on the sample text that iDVD creates for your title and type in your own. See Figure 21.4.

FIGURE 21.4

Importing image files into the main iDVD window is as easy as dragging and dropping.

4. Turn off the Apple logo in the main iDVD window if it isn't already by choosing iDVD, Preferences and unchecking the Show Watermark option (see Figure 21.5).

5. Click the Customize button to display the iDVD tray, and drag the background image into the Image well in the Background section of the Settings area.

6. Click the Folder button in the main iDVD window to add a folder to the menu.

7. Click the text that appears underneath the new folder icon and type in your own text (The Band). See Figure 21.6.

8. Add two more folders (Chew and Web Site) to the main screen. For the fourth button, drag a movie clip directly into the main iDVD window and name it (She

▲   Gerbil).

FIGURE 21.5
Preferences dialog box in iDVD.

Drag the background image onto the Image/Movie icon

FIGURE 21.6
Setting up a background image and adding a folder.

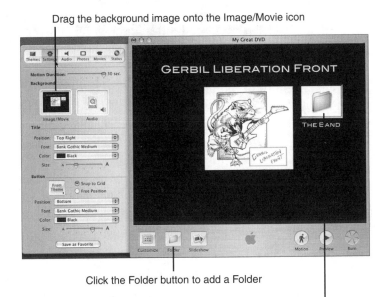

Click the Folder button to add a Folder

Click the text underneath the Folder icon and type in new text

Task: Setting Up the Slideshow

In this section of the DVD project, we add four slideshows to the additional screen that you get as the result of adding a folder:

1. In the main iDVD window, double-click the first folder icon that you created (The Band) to get to the additional screen.

2. Open the Customize tray and click the Brushed Metal theme to reapply the theme—we don't want the same image that we used for background on the main screen. If you use your own background image (as we did on the main screen), the custom image is automatically carried over when you create new folders.

21

▼ 3. Customize the title text (Meet The Band) and click the Slideshow button to add four slideshows.

4. Name the four slideshows by clicking the text beneath the generic slideshow icons and replacing the text with your own (see Figure 21.7).

FIGURE 21.7

Reapplying the Brushed Metal theme to a new screen and adding slideshows.

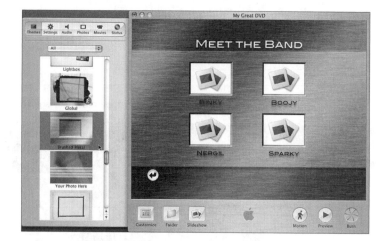

5. Double-click on one of the slideshow icons to open up a slideshow, and position the Finder window containing the digital images so that you can drag them into the slideshow window.

6. Drag the desired images into the slideshow.

7. Click the Slide Duration pop-up menu and select the Manual option.

8. Repeat steps for the remaining slideshows. When you're in the Slideshow window, ▲ you can back out of the window by clicking the Return button.

Task: Customizing the Slideshow Button Icons

▼ TASK

After you're done creating the slideshows, it's time to customize the buttons that lead to them:

1. If you're still in the Slideshow window, click the Return button to get back to your screen.

2. Click once on one of the slideshow icons, as shown in Figure 21.8, and use the slider to select one of the images from the slideshow to be a new button image.

3. Repeat steps 1 and 2 for the remaining slideshow buttons so that you end up with a ▲ screen looking something like Figure 21.9.

FIGURE 21.8

Choosing an image for the button.

FIGURE 21.9

The four slideshow buttons first seen in Figure 21.7, now with custom images that come from slides that have been added to the respective slideshows.

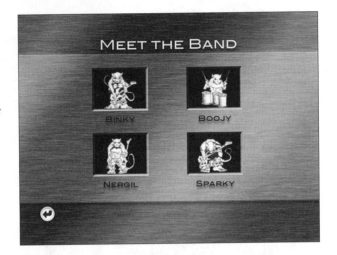

Task: Setting Up the Combination Movie/Slideshow

▼ TASK

In this section, we set up the section of the DVD project where we're adding a movie and a slideshow to the same screen:

1. From the main DVD screen (refer to Figure 21.3), double-click on the Chew generic folder icon to edit the Chew screen.

2. Drag the Chew movie directly into the screen.

3. If you like, click once on the icon for the movie and use the slider as shown in Figure 21.10 to select an image from the movie for this icon. You might also want to uncheck the Movie option if you don't want the button to use motion.

4. Click the Slideshow button at the bottom of the main iDVD window to add a slideshow, and name it as desired (Stills). See Figure 21.11.

5. Double-click the Stills slideshow icon to open the slideshow, set the Duration to Manual, and drag the desired images into the Slideshow window as shown in Figure 21.12.

▼

21

FIGURE 21.10
Unchecking the Movie option and selecting an image from a movie for a button.

FIGURE 21.11
Clicking the Slideshow button adds another slideshow; then you can click the button text and customize it (Stills).

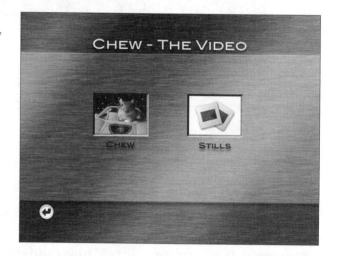

FIGURE 21.12
Images that have been added to the slideshow.

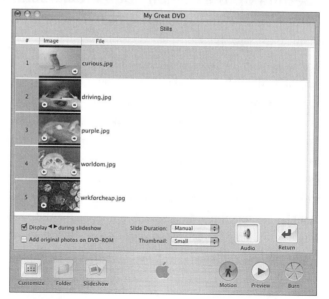

6. Click the Slideshow button and choose an image for the slideshow for the icon, as shown in Figure 21.13.

FIGURE 21.13

Choosing an image from the slideshow.

Your combination movie/slideshow screen should look something like Figure 21.14.

FIGURE 21.14

The custom screen. The button on the left goes to the movie; the button on the right goes to the slideshow.

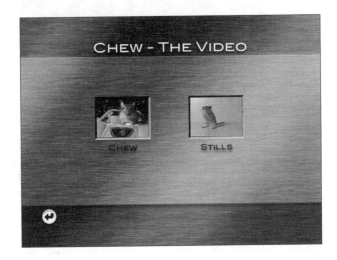

You're now in a position where you can select an image for the button on the main screen that leads to this screen (see Figure 21.15).

FIGURE 21.15

Selecting an image for the button on the main screen.

21

Task: Adding a Web Site Screen

In this section, we add a screen that's designed to promote a Web site. Because iDVD doesn't have the capability to add much text to a screen beyond a title, we're using a folder so that a person can click to find the Web site address on this screen:

1. From the main screen of the DVD project, double-click the Web Site button to get into the folder.

2. Reapply the Brushed Metal theme to the Web Site screen.

3. Drag a movie into the folder screen as shown in Figure 21.16, and adjust the title text to reflect the Web site address.

FIGURE 21.16

The movie placed into the new screen.

4. Click the button for the movie you added to this screen and select an image from the movie if you like (see Figure 21.17).

5. Click the Web Site folder icon and select an image.

FIGURE 21.17

Choosing an image for the button on the main screen.

Adding Final Details and Testing

After you've done most of the work in putting together a DVD project, often there are a few final details to cover and some additional adjustments to make. In this section, we go over a few final details. Figure 21.18 reflects what the main DVD screen should look like.

FIGURE **21.18**

The final screen should look something like this.

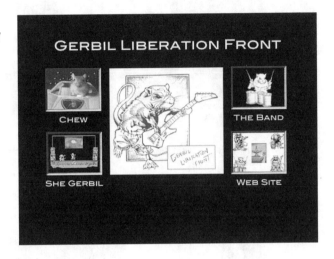

• **TV Safe Area**—Choose Advanced, Show TV Safe Area to display the TV Safe indicator (see Figure 21.19).

FIGURE **21.19**

The Advanced menu.

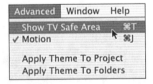

A rectangle will appear on the screen (see Figure 21.20) to give an approximation of where some TVs will sometimes cut off the outer edges of a video signal. This is a helpful tool that enables you to make some adjustments to your DVD screens so that nothing important is cut off.

• **Preview**—Click the Preview button in the main iDVD window to preview the project. Test the buttons that lead from screen to screen using the simulated DVD remote control as seen in Figure 21.21. Remember that you have to click on the little exit button on the remote to get out of the Preview mode.

21

FIGURE 21.20

The Show TV Safe Area option draws a rectangle on the screen.

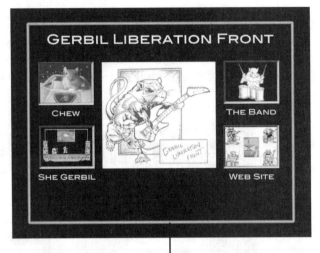

Anything outside the rectangle may not show up on a television

FIGURE 21.21

Click the Preview button, and iDVD gives you a miniature DVD remote control so that you can try your project out as if you were watching it on a television.

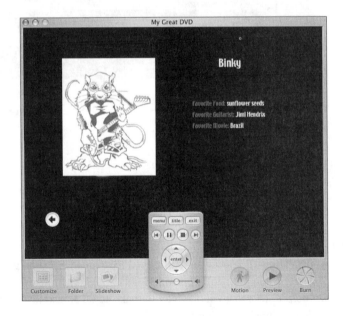

- **Encoding**—To check to see how the encoding process is going for the movie clips you're using in the DVD project, you can click the Customize button in the main iDVD window and choose the Status button shown in Figure 21.22.

FIGURE 21.22

The Status area in the tray gives you a play-by-play account of how things are going with the preparation of your video.

Summary

In this hour, you learned about a variety of ways that folders enable you to add more material to your DVD by providing more screens that you can add movies and slideshows to. Taking the time to figure out how to add custom images to the DVD buttons in your project can give it that extra special *oomph*.

In the next hour, we take a look at a different situation, a sample project in which the idea is to take a live event that you edited using iMovie and turn it into a DVD.

Workshop

The Workshop consists of quiz questions and answers to help you to develop a better grasp of the process of creating DVDs with multiple screens. First, try to answer the questions *before* checking the answers. Then read the explanations, even if you get the answers right—the explanations will contribute to your understanding of DVD.

21

Q&A

Q **I'm getting a little confused. What's the difference between folders, screens, and menus?**

A When Apple created iDVD, it tried to make the program as intuitive as possible and decided to make iDVD work somewhat like the computer itself does. Basically, when you add a new folder to a DVD project, that folder can contain more items, just like a folder on your hard drive. Technically speaking, the folder button leads to a new menu screen on your DVD. That is, when someone selects the button as they're watching your DVD project, they get a new screen in which the items appear that were added to that folder, such as a movie. So, in the world of iDVD, the words *folder*, *screen*, and *menu* can be used interchangeably, depending on what makes sense to *you*. Just playing with them will help you understand. It'll be like riding a bike, but you can't fall off!

Q **I don't have any files to play with yet. Where can I download the files for this hour?**

A Digital video files are huge, even when you encode them for DVD. It was decided that because not everyone would want to pay extra for a disc containing sample files, a disc was not included to help keep the price of the book down.

Quiz

1. How do you add a new folder to your DVD?

    A. Choose File, New Folder

    B. Click the Folder button

    C. A and B

2. How do you get back to the main screen of a DVD when you're working on a slideshow?

    A. Click the Return button

    B. Click on the little curly arrow in the lower-left corner of the DVD screen

    C. Choose Screen, Return

    D. A and B

    E. A, B, and C

    F. A, B, C, and D

3. How many folders can be added to an iDVD project?

    A. 9

    B. 99

    C. 999

    D. Unlimited

Quiz Answers

1. **B.** Clicking the Folder button in the main iDVD window gives you a new folder/screen where you can add movies, slideshows, or more folders.

2. **D.** Trick question. If you're in the slideshow editor window, there's a Return button. If you're on a slideshow screen looking at a slide, there's a little curly arrow. If you chose answer F, you might want to go to `www.joltcola.com` and order a case or two.

3. **B.** Aha! And you thought that the information would be in this hour, but no one said that there couldn't be a question about an earlier hour! Well, at any rate, you can add 99 folders.

21

Hour 22

Example Project—Event DVD

In this hour, we take a look at making a DVD based on some footage that was shot at a live event—in this case, a concert. It could just as easily be a party, ceremony, or spontaneous gathering of some kind.

iMovie and iDVD are so much fun (takes deep breath)! Okay, but to be able to have fun, it helps to experiment and play so that you know the kinds of things you can do.

Throughout this hour, we discuss the following:

- Multiple screens
- Project setup
- Menu creation
- Slideshows

Considering Event DVDs

You might decide that iMovie and iDVD could be a way to pick up some extra money by taping events for other people and making DVDs for them. (Hint: This could be a way to fund that craving you have for one of Apple's Cinema Displays.)

The process of shooting live events is known as *event videography*, and people all around the world do it every day for business and pleasure. Now, with the advent of more affordable DVD authoring, we've reached a stage when there are increasing numbers of people who engage in event DVD-ography. (Okay, I guess that word doesn't work, but you can't blame an author for trying, right?) I guess the best way to say it would be *event authoring* or *DVD event authoring*. I'll let the reviewers decide.

The thing about making a DVD is that it isn't necessarily just a by-product of video editing. As you learn about DVDs, considering what you can do with them might actually have a significant impact on how you develop and shoot the video in the first place! For example, as you learn about motion menus, you might film a friend's concert and instead of going right home to get sleep after the show as you should, you stand across the street from the venue with a tripod for a long time to shoot some video that you can use for a motion menu.

So, yes, there are weddings and other ceremonies galore, but we'll take a look at a concert of an up-and-coming performer from Chicago.

Setting Up the Project

In Figure 22.1, you see how the files in a project like this are organized—the types of files are divided into different folders, such as background images, movie clips, and so on. Whether you use the visual method of importing files, which involves dragging files directly from a window such as the one in Figure 22.1, or you use the File, Import Video command, organizing your files *before* you start a project helps in the long run. It's just like cleaning your room: If you put stuff in a place where you can find it easily, you'll thank yourself later on.

If you want to follow along with your own files, you might want to look ahead at the kind of digital images and movies that are used in this project and find some of your own files to use in their place.

FIGURE 22.1

Looking at the files for a DVD project, nice and clear, with the View mode set to display the files as a list and the disclosure triangles clicked to reveal folder contents.

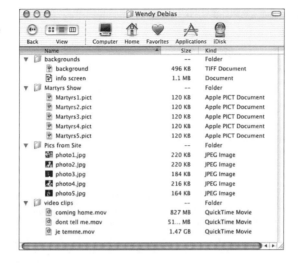

Task: Setting Up the Main Menu

This project is fairly straightforward, consisting of a main menu with three submenus:

1. Create a new project (and save it!).
2. Click the Customize button in the main iDVD window to display the tray.
3. Select the Your Photo Here theme. See Figure 22.2.

FIGURE 22.2

The Your Photo Here theme, with the sample title text "Your Photo Here" that you can replace by typing in your own title.

▼ 4. Drag your background image directly into the Image/Movie well in the Settings area of the tray.

5. Click the Free Position radio button so that you can move the sample text that appears on the screen.

6. Click the sample text and type in your new title (Wendy Debias in this example). See Figure 22.3.

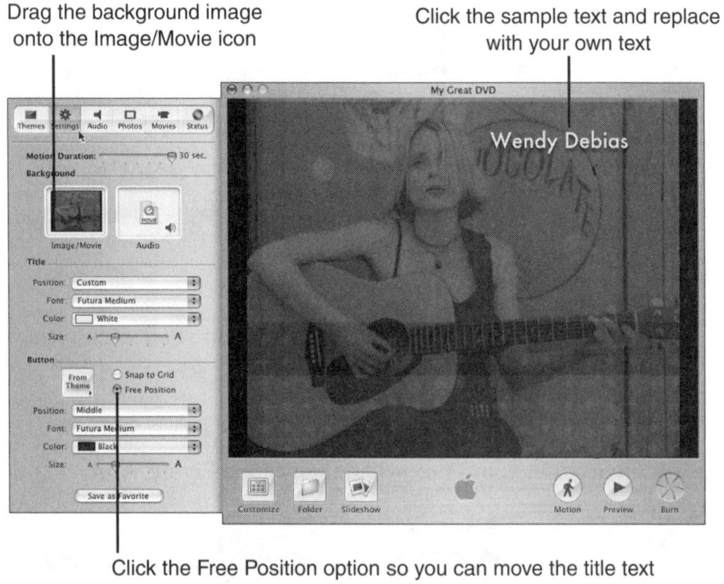

Drag the background image
onto the Image/Movie icon

Click the sample text and replace
with your own text

FIGURE 22.3
Setting up a menu screen.

Click the Free Position option so you can move the title text

7. Click the Folder button three times to add three folders to this menu, and name them according to the screens they lead to (Videos, Pictures, Web Site). See ▲ Figure 22.4.

FIGURE 22.4
These folder buttons from the Your Photo Here theme are a nice option for DVDs, even when using your own background image.

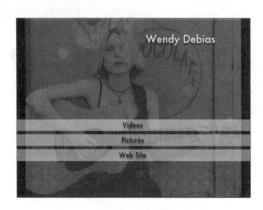

Task: Setting Up the Videos Menu

In this section, we create a Videos menu that contains three different movies.

22

> If it isn't already clear, the way you get back and forth between screens while you're working on an iDVD project is a matter of clicking and double-clicking. When you're on the main screen of your DVD, you can double-click a folder or slideshow that you've added to get into that part of the DVD. When you're working on a slideshow or on a folder, you can get back out to your main screen by clicking the curly arrow.

1. In the main screen of your DVD, double-click the folder you want to work on (Videos) to open its menu screen.

2. Select the sample title text and replace it with your own text (Videos; see Figure 22.5.).

3. If you want to reposition your title text, click the Free Position radio button in the Settings area of the tray.

FIGURE 22.5

Setting up a screen and positioning the text so that it looks nice and doesn't cover up the subject of the background image (thus resulting in a hug and a kiss on the cheek rather than an angry call from the artist).

4. Drag the movie files you want to use directly into the main iDVD window from the Finder to add them to this folder/screen (see Figure 22.6).

> Look at the filenames of the movie clips in Figure 22.1 and compare them to the names of the automatic buttons in Figure 22.6. The names of the buttons are generated automatically when the movie clips are dragged into iDVD. Notice how it's possible to name your movie clips so that you have the right name on the button without even having to type anything in. Apple rocks.

FIGURE 22.6

The buttons that result when you drag iMovies into iDVD in the Your Photo Here theme.

Task: Setting Up the Pictures Menu

TASK ▼

In this section of the DVD, the Pictures menu screen includes two different slideshows:

1. From the main screen for this DVD project, double-click the folder you created (Pictures) so that you can add something to it (see Figure 22.7).

2. Click the Slideshow button and add two slideshows to this menu. Change the text to reflect the slideshows that the buttons lead to (From Show at Martyrs-Chicago, IL and Assorted).

FIGURE 22.7

The buttons that lead to two slideshows.

3. Click the sample title text and replace it with your own text (Pictures). Remember that to position the text, the Free Position radio button must be selected.

4. Double-click one of the slideshows, and drag your digital pictures directly into the slideshow window.

5. Set the Duration option to Manual (see Figure 22.8).

FIGURE 22.8
Adding pictures to a slideshow.

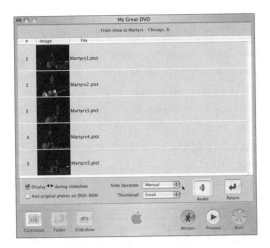

6. Click the Return button in the slideshow window when you're done making adjustments to get back out of the slideshow.

7. Double-click the other slideshow to open it so that you can start editing it.

8. Drag your digital picture files into the slideshow window from the Finder, make adjustments in the order of the slides as necessary, and be sure to set the Duration option to Manual.

9. If desired, uncheck the Display (arrows) During Slideshow option if you don't want arrows to be drawn over your pictures when someone is watching the slideshow.

Task: Adding a Web Site Screen (Extra Credit)

In this section we take a look at another approach to adding a screen to a DVD, which can mention a Web site. In this case, the same background screen is used as elsewhere in the DVD, and the DVD button itself contains the Web site URL. iDVD is designed to enable you to add title text, but it's not really designed to add extensive information to a DVD—however, it can be fooled and cajoled into some fun things.

For example, you could use the title text on a screen to display a Web site address, but that's not your only option. In this example, the title text of the Web site screen (Web Site) reflects the text on the button that leads to it (Web Site), and some would say that makes for better consistency. But what to do with the Web site address?

▼   Well, you can put the address on a button. But then what do you put in the folder? You
don't want to have anything empty if someone clicks on it. Well, you can always have
something waiting for the person—your own background image.

1. Double-click the folder icon from the main screen of your DVD to get into the
   folder you created for the Web site screen.

2. Click the sample title text and replace it with your own text (Web Site; see Figure
   22.9). Remember that to reposition the text, the Free Position option must be
   selected.

3. Click the Folder button in the main iDVD window to add a folder to your new
   screen, and enter your Web site address to name this folder
   (www.wendydebias.com).

FIGURE 22.9

*An ingenious and
world-renowned tech-
nique for including a
Web site address in an
iDVD project that
should warrant a
Nobel Prize in DVD
authoring.*

4. To get the folder you just created, double-click it.

▲   5. Drag your background image with more information about the Web site directly
        into the screen (see Figure 22.10).

In essence, what we've done is sneaked even more text into an iDVD project.

The best way to create background screens is to use a program such as Photoshop
Elements (about $100 U.S.) or the full-on, full-featured Photoshop (about $600 U.S.).
But there are other ways to do it.

For example, you could actually use AppleWorks, which comes automatically on iMacs
these days. Size the page in AppleWorks to 640×480 pixels and use the paint and text
features to add text. Save the file and then import it into iDVD; the results are shown in
Figure 22.11. This approach represents a way to create backgrounds without having to
get Photoshop. Photoshop is better and a bit easier to work with and make changes, but
the same result can be achieved in AppleWorks.

FIGURE 22.10

If someone actually selects the button with the Web site address, she gets a secret treat: whatever you put on the background screen.

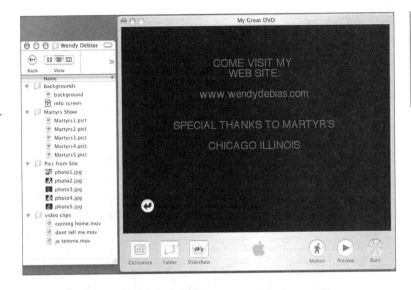

FIGURE 22.11

Using AppleWorks to make a background screen.

If you already have a Web site, another interesting technique is to lift digital images from the Web site itself. In this hour, I went to Wendy's Web site at www.wendydebias.com and did a screen grab of a portion of the screen by pressing Shift+Command+4. I dragged to the size I wanted, and then imported the resulting file into Photoshop and made it fit into a 640×480 space. The automatic screen grab feature places a numbered picture file, Picture 1, Picture 2, and so forth, on the hard drive with the highest number being the most recently grabbed screenshot.

Summary

In this hour, you learned how iDVD can be used to capture and share movies from an event such as a concert or ceremony of some kind. The DVD can be enhanced with digital pictures such as stills exported from iMovie using the video from the show (Choose File, Save Frame As). You can top it off with a nice Web page.

In the next hour, we'll take a look at a kind of showcase DVD project featuring a variety of different short clips, and an overall clip. It's something like the Hollywood DVDs on which you have your overall movie and a scene selection menu that enables you to go directly to a scene. We've been getting into things that are pushing the boundary of iDVD, and if you end up needing to go beyond its capability, that's okay. These lessons are like a booster rocket to get you into lower atmosphere. For the final thrust sequence in breaking out of earth orbit, read on to Hour 24, "Going Beyond iMovie and iDVD," which covers Final Cut Pro and DVD Studio Pro. Then sit down, take a deep breath, and look at how much those programs cost.

You might want to start thinking about picking up a legitimate used copy of Final Cut Pro or DVD Studio Pro if you want to conserve cash. As a last resort, you might want to reread this entire book, come up with some ideas for doing iDVDs and iMovies for friends and family, and think of a few projects you can do to earn some money. If you want to pick up one of the advanced programs such as DVD Studio Pro or Final Cut Pro, the newest versions cost $999 U.S. However, even if you don't want to make iDVDs for a business, let's say you did 10 projects for friends and charged only $100.00 apiece for the editing and authoring (and let them pay for the blank DVDs). They'd be getting a sweet deal and you'd have enough money for the programs! Beautiful, isn't it?

Workshop

The Workshop consists of quiz questions and answers to help you to develop a better grasp of the process of creating event DVDs. First, try to answer the questions *before* checking the answers. Then read the explanations, even if you get the answers right—the explanations will contribute in a small way to your overall understanding of DVD.

Q&A

Q Can I make my DVD so that it connects to the Web?

A No, this isn't really possible with iDVD. But if you do some research and learn how to make an HTML Web file, you could include it as DVD-ROM content That way, when a person inserts your DVD in her computer, she could click on the Web file, which could have a link to your Web site. You'd probably also want to tell the user to actually open the DVD like a disk because her computer might automatically launch a DVD player program thinking she wants to watch the video portion of the DVD. If the user is using Windows, she can right-click the DVD icon in My Computer and choose Explore. On a Mac, she just double-clicks the DVD icon on the desktop. Note that a file can be included as DVD-ROM content only with version 2.1 or higher of iDVD. Also be aware that DVD Studio Pro *can* actually have a launchable Web link (called a DVD@CCESS link) from within a DVD.

Q   I want to film a live event and want to use multiple camera angles on the DVD. How do I do that?

A   iDVD doesn't support multiple camera angles. However, if the event is short enough, you could set up two cameras and put the clips on the DVD so that people could access them as separate clips. This assumes that the event is short enough so that the entire versions from each camera would fit, or that you edit things down so they fit on your DVD. You could name them `Angle 1`, `Angle 2`, and so on. Because of the way DVD players work, you actually might be able to use the Track button on a DVD remote control player to switch between these different clips, although when you do this, the DVD player will go to the beginning of the other clip instead of to the equivalent point in the other clip. Another option to get the multiple-angle feature is to capture footage from more than one camera, and then edit a piece in iMovie so that the individual clips use footage from more than one camera—in essence, switching angles for the audience. Then you can have a version of your movie on the iDVD and name it the Multiple-Angle version to lend some of that good multiple-angle DVD feeling to your project and come across as all professional and whatnot.

Quiz

1. How do you add a screen to your DVD that includes a slideshow and a video clip?

   A. Add a folder, double-click the folder button, drag a video clip into the window, and then click the Slideshow button to add a slideshow.

   B. I've fallen and I can't get up.

   C. Choose File, Add New Screen, drag a video clip into the window, and then click the Slideshow button to add a slideshow.

2. Which program do I use for making a background screen?

   A. Photoshop

   B. Petshop Elements

   C. AppleWorks

   D. A and/or C

3. How do you get back to a main screen when you're working on a slideshow or menu?

   A. Choose Menu, Return

   B. Click the Return button

   C. Click the curly arrow

   D. B and C

   E. Just B

Quiz Answers

1. **A.** It's truly amazing how easy iDVD has made the process of DVD authoring. Apple won an Emmy award for inventing the FireWire interface that enables us to easily capture video, and methinks they should win an Oscar for iDVD.

2. **D.** Photoshop and the less-expensive Photoshop Elements are best for making background images, enabling you to easily go back and edit and so forth. But yes, Virginia, it can be done in AppleWorks.

3. **D.** Knowing how to get around is essential, whether you're on the road in a rock 'n' roll band backstage in a huge venue trying to find your way from the dressing room to the stage, or working on an iDVD project. In a slideshow, the Return button is your friend; on most other screens, the little circular arrow is your friend. At some venues, you might need a GPS positioning device or a friendly security person to show you around.

Hour 23

Example Project—Short Movie

In this hour, we take a look at making a DVD project based entirely around movie clips. There's one main movie and a series of smaller clips featuring individual characters from the movie.

Throughout this hour, we discuss the following:

- Multiple movies
- Project setup
- Menu creation
- Customizing icon images

Considering Short Movie DVDs

Typical Hollywood DVDs often have a feature movie, and some extra material such as movie trailers, which are excerpts of the movie that are used to advertise it. In addition, Hollywood DVDs often have a way to go directly to individual scenes in the movie, which is one of the nice features about DVD. With a VHS tape, you have to fast-forward and rewind everything. Including these types of features on a DVD often involves advanced DVD authoring, but there are ways of giving the same feel to your iDVD project with a creative use of folders.

Folders in iDVD are basically a built-in way in which you can have multiple menus in your DVD, so that when you have the need to include extra clips and scenes on a DVD project, you can use your imagination to organize your menu screens so that the DVD has the look and feel you want.

Let's say your short movie is 45 minutes long. You decide that you want to make a scene selection menu like Hollywood DVDs often have, where you give your audience the ability to jump to a particular scene in a movie.

This scene selection menu is normally accomplished in DVD authoring by using chapter points, where you set points in your movie in a program such as Final Cut Pro. Then, in a program such as DVD Studio Pro, you structure the DVD so that a person can select a certain button and jump directly to the scenes that you've set up beforehand. Unfortunately, the only way to accomplish this in iDVD is by exporting chapters from iMovie (see Hour 7). Although you can't set chapter points per se in iDVD, you can do what we've done with the sample project and make use of the extra space you have on your DVD. In essence, you can include a series of smaller movie clips that feature your favorite parts of the movie, or as in this project, you can feature individual characters.

Setting Up the Project

This project has a main menu and a series of submenus, which enable a person either to see the main movie or to meet the characters in the movie. In some ways, this lesson is an exercise and a sample of how you can connect one screen to another. In addition, we also touch on the use of sound clips to make the menus more interesting. These sound clips (see Figure 23.1) were prepared using the Voiceover tool in iMovie, which provides an easy way to record sound.

If you want to follow along with your own files, you might want to look ahead at the kind of digital images and movies that are used in this project and find some of your own files to use in their place.

Planning the DVD

iDVD makes it so simple to make your DVD that you probably won't need to plan much; you can simply drag clips into the program and adjust them as you like. But, if you're going to use folders to create additional screens for extra material, you might want to at least consider ahead of time how the DVD project will work. It might even be helpful to consider this issue before you finish editing your iMovie because you could decide to make excerpts of your movie and export them for use in iDVD, so that you can do something like we're doing with this project.

FIGURE 23.1

Looking at the files for a DVD project, with the main movie, extra clips, and sound files.

23

Figures 23.2 and 23.3 represent a map for this sample DVD project, which you might find it helpful to refer to throughout this hour. In Figure 23.2, the rectangles represent the screens of the DVD project, and each button that leads to a movie or another screen is represented.

FIGURE 23.2

A simple map of the sample project.

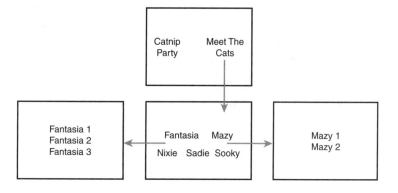

Figure 23.3 shows a map of movies and buttons. For example, you can see that on the main menu, Catnip Party is a movie clip, whereas Meet The Cats is actually a button that leads to another screen in the DVD project.

FIGURE **23.3**

The same project as in Figure 23.2, showing which are movies and which are folder buttons that lead to another screen with movies.

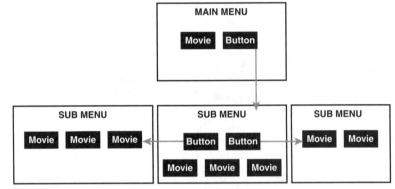

The difference between a link button and a movie button in our diagram is simply that when you click a movie button you see the movie, whereas clicking a link button leads to another screen.

Task: Setting Up the Main Menu

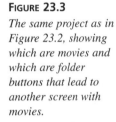

To set up the main menu (see Figure 23.4), we simply drag a clip (our main movie) into the menu, and then add a folder, which is our connection to the additional screens. You might want to review Figures 22.2 and 22.3 and then try to create the main menu simply by looking at the diagrams to put things together. You might want to create the project based on looking only at the diagrams, and comparing the map and the screenshots of how the DVD looks.

1. Create a new iDVD project and select a theme (Brushed Metal).

2. Select the sample title text and replace it with your own text (Alunniland in this example).

3. Position the Finder window that contains the files you want to use in your project so that you can drag them into the iDVD window.

4. Drag your main movie into the iDVD window.

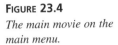

FIGURE 23.4

The main movie on the main menu.

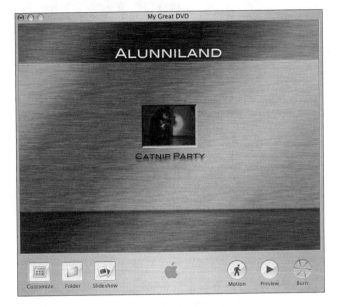

5. Click once on the movie you dragged into iDVD, and uncheck the Movie option so that you get a still image on the button rather than a movie clip.

6. Click and drag the blue slider to select a frame from the movie for the thumbnail image, as shown in Figure 23.5.

FIGURE 23.5

Choosing the featured frame.

7. Click the Folder button in the main iDVD window to add a folder to the main screen, as shown in Figure 23.6.

FIGURE 23.6

*Adding a folder to the
main menu that leads
to the first submenu,
Meet the Cats.*

Task: Setting Up the Submenus

▲ TASK

Now that the main menu is set up, we can set up the additional screens. One of the fun things about iDVD is that if you think ahead about how you're going to name your movie files when you export them from iMovie, the names come in automatically when you drag the movies into iDVD. Then the only things you must actually name are the folders that you add to the project.

We'll set up a Meet The Cats screen as well as Fantasia and Mazy screens:

1. In the main DVD screen, the main menu, double-click the folder you added to open it.

2. Click the sample title text and replace it with your own text (Meet the Cats).

3. Click the Folder button in the main iDVD window twice to add two folders to this screen (see Figure 23.7). These two folders will be named Fantasia and Mazy. We'll add three movies to the screen, corresponding to the way things are portrayed in Figures 22.2 and 22.3.

4. Click the sample text beneath each generic folder icon and replace the sample text with your own text (Fantasia and Mazy).

5. Double-click the Fantasia folder to open it as shown in Figure 23.8.

6. Drag the movie clips for this screen into iDVD (Fantasia1.mov, Fantasia2.mov, Fantasia3.mov).

▼

FIGURE 23.7

Adding the first two buttons to the sub-menu. These are folder buttons that lead to additional screens.

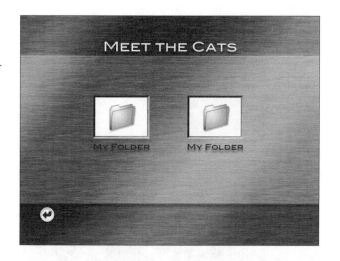

23

FIGURE 23.8

Getting ready to drag the movies into one of the submenus.

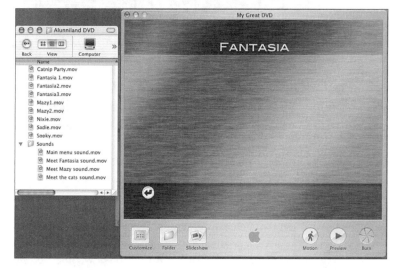

7. If you like, click each clip individually, disable the motion (uncheck the Movie option), and select a frame to feature from the movie by clicking and dragging the blue slider, as shown in Figure 23.9.

8. Click the curly arrow in the lower-left corner of the screen to back out of this folder, and click once to select the folder.

9. Repeat the steps you performed for the Fantasia movies to add the Mazy movies to the other folder on the Meet The Cats screen. When you're done, things should look something like Figure 23.10.

FIGURE 23.9

Choosing the featured frame for `Fantasia1.mov`.

FIGURE 23.10

The completed folder sections—Fantasia and Mazy—of the Meet The Cats submenu. Both have several video clips in them.

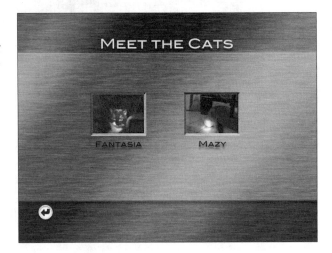

10. When you finish setting up the folders, drag the remaining movies (`Nixie.mov`, `Sadie.mov`, `Sooky.mov`) directly into the Meet The Cats screen, and set the movie button images as in step 7 if you like.

It's a matter of preference as to whether you let iDVD automatically use a portion of your clips in the button or whether you stop the motion and pick a single frame to feature. One thing that can happen if you go for the motion approach is that things can get very busy on the screen. If you want to go with the motion buttons but they aren't moving and you don't know why, you might have the overall motion turned off in iDVD, which you can turn back on by clicking the Motion button in the main iDVD window.

Task: Adding Sounds to Menus

As you see in Figure 23.11, the sounds that you export might end up having a `.mov` file-name extension. This could seem confusing if you're used to sounds with a `.wav`, `.aiff`, or another extension. But don't be concerned. Your `.mov` sounds can be imported into iDVD like any other sound; this is simply one way of exporting sound from iMovie.

FIGURE 23.11

Pondering whether or not to add sound to a menu. Will it be annoying or amusing?

1. Position the Finder window containing your sounds next to the iDVD window.

2. Click the Customize button in the main iDVD window to open the tray, and click the Settings button.

3. Select the appropriate menu in the iDVD project without going into Preview mode.

You can move around your iDVD project without having to preview it: You simply double-click the buttons as if you were previewing, and iDVD enables you to navigate from screen to screen so that you can make changes to particular screens.

▼   4. Drag your sound into the Audio well in the Background area of the Customize tab
        (see Figure 23.12).

FIGURE 23.12

*Dragging the sound
files into the Audio
well.*

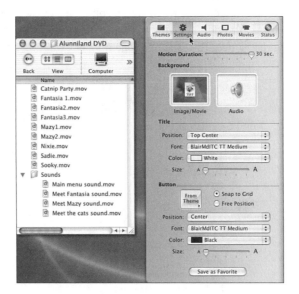

      5. Be prepared to use the Motion button in the main iDVD window to turn sound on
         and off if you have a friend, family member, or colleague who is trying to sleep or
▲   get other important business done.

Reviewing and Previewing

Let's take another look at the map of our project (see Figure 23.13). One reason why
making a similar diagram could be a good idea is simply that it might help you to keep
track of the clips that you want to use in your project. It might also help you to make
sure that you're including everything that you want to.

FIGURE 23.13

Recapping the map.

```
          ┌─────────────────────┐
          │   Catnip    Meet The│
          │   Party       Cats  │
          └─────────────────────┘
                        │
                        ▼
┌──────────────┐  ┌──────────────────┐  ┌──────────────┐
│ Fantasia 1   │  │ Fantasia   Mazy  │  │  Mazy 1      │
│ Fantasia 2   │◄─│                  │─►│  Mazy 2      │
│ Fantasia 3   │  │ Nixie  Sadie Sooky│  │              │
└──────────────┘  └──────────────────┘  └──────────────┘
```

Figure 23.14 represents how the main screen for this type of project could/should look; both images look the same, but one leads to a movie whereas the other leads to additional screens (our submenus).

FIGURE 23.14

The finished main menu.

Figure 23.15 is similar. Everything looks consistent, yet two options lead to additional screens and the rest are movies.

FIGURE 23.15

The Meet The Cats submenu.

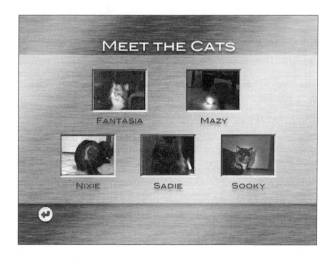

Finally, you might want to take a peek at how the encoding is going by clicking the Customize button in the main iDVD window and selecting the Status area (see Figure 23.16). Depending on how much you've added to your project, it might be a while before the encoding is done, so you might want to consider taking a walk or going skydiving for a while.

FIGURE 23.16
Checking in on the encoding.

Summary

In this hour, you learned how to build a DVD project that contains a main movie and a number of additional supporting clips. One thing that hasn't been mentioned is that if you happen to be working with humans, sometime before you completely edit your movie, you might want to make an informal DVD so that people can give you input. It's a bit hard to do this when working with cats, but if they give you any trouble, you can usually appease them by providing compensatory treats.

In the next hour, we take a look at options for going beyond iDVD and iMovie by taking a quick tour of their professional cousins, Final Cut Pro and DVD Studio Pro.

Some people can do everything they need to do in iMovie and iDVD, and they can do so quickly with little hassle. Both of these introductory tools do pack a lot of power and are easy to use. But at some point you might need to go beyond their capabilities, and taking a look at the advanced tools will help you to know if and when that time has come.

Workshop

The Workshop consists of quiz questions and answers to help you to develop a better grasp of short movie creation. First, try to answer the questions *before* checking the answers. Then read the explanations, even if you get the answers right—the explanations will contribute in a small way to your overall understanding of DVD.

Q&A

Q **Is there any way that I can add an introductory animation to my iDVD project?**

A Yes, in a way. You can't have an introductory movie play before you see your first DVD screen, but what you could do is create a 30-second or less clip and use it as a background video clip for a regular menu. Then you could have a simple button on that screen, something like Enter, so that you have an entry screen. This is much like many Web pages that have a Flash animation entry page when you enter the site. To be able to have a video clip play without a person clicking a button would require DVD Studio Pro, but you can get around by using the button/intro technique.

Quiz

1. In iDVD, how do you feature a frame from a movie on the button that leads to that movie?
   A. Click once on the movie, uncheck the Frame option, and use the slider to select a frame from the movie
   B. Click once on the movie, uncheck the Motion option, and use the slider to select a frame from the movie
   C. Click once on the movie, uncheck the Movie option, and use the slider to select a frame from the movie

2. How do you change the text that appears on a button in your DVD menus?
   A. Click on the sample text and type in new text
   B. Name a movie file what you want to appear as the button text and drag it into iDVD
   C. A and B
   D. You can't change text after it appears

3. How do you add sound to a DVD menu?

   A. Choose DVD Menu, Activate Sound

   B. Click the Motion button in the main iDVD window

   C. Drag the sound into the Sound well in the Background area of the Settings tab in the tray

   D. Drag the sound into the Audio well in the Background area of the Settings tab in the tray

Quiz Answers

1. **C.** You can also do something silly such as figure out how to make a video clip motionless by repeating the same frame for 15 seconds. Then you can use a moving image as a background so that when a person first hits a screen, it's standing still, but if the person waits, the image starts moving. (Try setting up a 15-second iMovie, exporting the first frame, importing that same frame and setting the duration for 15 seconds, and then exporting the movie for iDVD and using it as a motion menu background.) In this case, the button that leads to this menu would theoretically remain still for a bit and then start moving.

2. **C.** I don't know why I find the automatic button naming so amusing, I just like it. It's beautiful.

3. **D.** But if you're using a video clip as a motion menu background, you won't need to drag any sounds if the video clip you're using already has sound in it.

HOUR 24

Going Beyond iMovie and iDVD

In this hour, we look beyond iMovie and iDVD. We'll start with a discussion of Final Cut Pro, a program that's been taking over the world of digital video by leaps and bounds. It's the most extreme example of any software that Apple has released in terms of combining ease of use and intuitiveness with hardcore, world-class professional capability. The reason that Final Cut Pro is successful is simple: It's a great product. Unquestionably great. Insanely great. Just like iMovie. Then, we'll take a brief look at Apple's DVD Studio Pro, an excellent and powerful DVD-authoring program that still has a familiar, intuitive interface known as the Graphical View.

Throughout the hour, we discuss the following:

- iMovie and Final Cut Pro—similarities and differences
- An approach to learning digital video
- iMovie/Final Cut Pro for fun and profit
- Differences between iDVD and DVD Studio Pro
- Putting together a DVD in DVD Studio Pro

iMovie and Final Cut Pro—Similarities and Differences

It could be said that the similarities between iMovie and Final Cut Pro consist primarily of how they enable you to utilize your creativity to interact with video. Functioning somewhat like the equivalent of a word processor for video, these programs enable you to do almost anything you want.

In that sense, the goals of someone who uses iMovie would likely be very similar to the Final Cut Pro user. Both programs enable the user to

- Capture video from a camcorder
- Choose how to view the video and the interface
- Import video files from a hard drive
- Edit video in a timeline
- Add effects, titles, transitions, and audio
- Preview video and render it for a final product

Final Cut Pro does exceed iMovie in flexibility and power, but its features still tend to fall into the same categories as those of iMovie. For example, iMovie has a basic set of transitions available, while Final Cut Pro adds a large number of transitions and effects, and a variety of dedicated tools that enable you to create your own effects.

One of the main differences of Final Cut Pro is the sense that it's scalable: It can support anything from the simplest home video all the way to the most demanding broadcast or movie-related situation. So, Final Cut Pro and iMovie might have the same types of features, but Final Cut Pro's features are often based around the needs and techniques of the professional community, whereas iMovie is oriented toward consumers.

Overview

The Final Cut Pro workspace consists of several areas that are designed to enable you to instantly access the data you need by making a choice from a host of options. Many of the interface elements have equivalents in iMovie, such as the Monitor, but they're customizable and more flexible (see Figure 24.1).

Views

Figure 24.2 shows an example of the relative level of capability in Final Cut Pro—the View menu and some of its options.

FIGURE 24.1

The Final Cut Pro workspace.

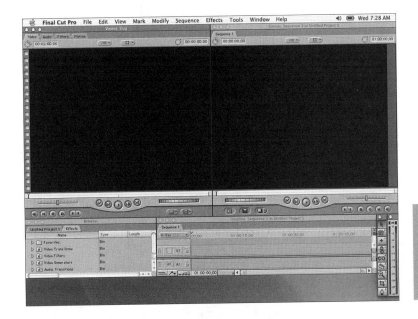

A student of Final Cut Pro or a budding independent video maker might initially feel a bit of intimidation when presented with so many options. But by trying to learn a few of the basic techniques (such as from the Final Cut Pro tutorials), and then coming up with project ideas that will help determine which options are actually used, a new user can become well versed in the program.

For example, when you first start using Final Cut Pro, you might not need any of the View menu functions that provide anything more than what you have in iMovie—that is, without changing anything, the simple ability to see the interface.

But as your projects grow in complexity, you end up needing some of the tools that live in the View menu, such as video signal evaluation tools like the Range Checker, general information like Timecode Overlays (which help keep track of where you are in a video down to a single frame), and straightforward Zoom In and Zoom Out tools.

Import/Export

Import/export capability in Final Cut Pro is another area in which you can extend and build on the knowledge gained from working in iMovie. When you have a basic understanding of how to work with digital video files, even if all you're doing is exporting from iMovie into iDVD or for the Web, you're building a reservoir of experience without even realizing it. For example, instead of thinking of video as a QuickTime file for iDVD, you begin to see it in Final Cut Pro as a 720×480 DV-NTSC stream running at 29.97 frames per second with 48KHz audio and lower fields first (see Figure 24.3).

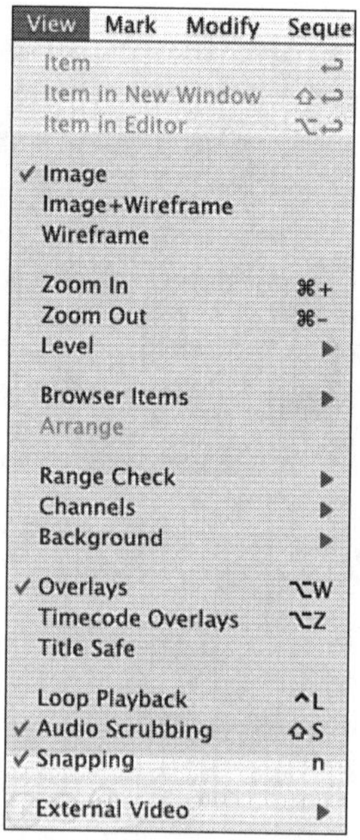

FIGURE 24.2

The View menu with a host of options to fit every conceivable situation.

View	Mark	Modify	Seque
Item			↵
Item in New Window			⇧↵
Item in Editor			⌥↵
✓ Image			
Image+Wireframe			
Wireframe			
Zoom In			⌘+
Zoom Out			⌘-
Level			▶
Browser Items			▶
Arrange			
Range Check			▶
Channels			▶
Background			▶
✓ Overlays			⌥W
Timecode Overlays			⌥Z
Title Safe			
Loop Playback			^L
✓ Audio Scrubbing			⇧S
✓ Snapping			n
External Video			▶

FIGURE 24.3

Import/export and media management options.

File	Edit	View	Mark	M
New Project				⌘E
New				▶
Open...				⌘O
Close Window				⌘W
Close Tab				^W
Close Project				
Save Project				⌘S
Save Project As...				⇧⌘S
Save All				⌥⌘S
Revert Project				
Restore Project...				
Import				▶
Export				▶
Batch Export				
Set Logging Bin				
Log and Capture...				⌘8
Media Manager...				
Reconnect Media...				
Batch Capture...				^C
Print to Video...				^M
Edit to Tape...				

When using Final Cut Pro, you might get to the point at which you need to develop the ability to customize the export of video to specific requirements, such as the need for a particular frame rate or another characteristic, rather than choosing a preset value.

Timeline

Probably the most familiar part of the Final Cut Pro interface to a new user coming from iMovie is the Timeline, which appears much like the iMovie Timeline (see Figure 24.4). In some ways, you get the form of Final Cut Pro when you're working in iMovie; for example, the iMovie Timeline has a solid bar stretching across to indicate a video clip. In iMovie, you can choose to go to a particular spot in the video, but that's about it.

The Final Cut Pro interface has evolved to meet the demands of people who need a good, reliable way to achieve complex, flawless edits. This type of editing might very well occur in an environment in which an accountant sits on one side, keeping track of every billable minute, and a chain-smoking client sits on the other side, changing his mind every second. The 30-second commercial must run in major markets, and the drop-dead deadline is a taxicab ride to the FedEx drop-off point to the airport, and everyone is waiting.

And a tool like Final Cut Pro can deliver.

24

FIGURE 24.4

The Timeline in Final Cut Pro.

Transitions and Effects

It's possible that some of the most common reasons for people to be inspired to get into Final Cut Pro are that they run out of transitions in iMovie and hit the extent of what can be done in the program. There are people who might argue that a good digital video maker should be able to craft an excellent film based on making cuts alone, simply going from scene to scene, with no special effects of any kind. And this can work well when the right artistry is employed.

It might be that if you're making videos for yourself, you might never need any of the advanced capabilities of Final Cut Pro. But if your interests include the idea of creating/editing video for potential clientele, you'll inevitably want a repertoire of possibilities to enable you to satisfy the needs of the person who's writing the check (see Figure 24.5).

Effects and transitions then, in all their many varieties, represent an area of digital video where simply having the *ability* to achieve a certain thing can get you a paying gig. Or, if you're simply out to have some fun, becoming familiar with a wide range of possibilities can open up new lines of thought and creativity. The transition from iMovie to Final Cut Pro can be smooth in this area—you basically end up getting a whole lot more to play with!

FIGURE 24.5

Effects, the next generation. Just don't overuse them. Perhaps it's good to learn through minimalism, and let your clients be the ones to drag you into judicious or gratuitous use of something like a star wipe.

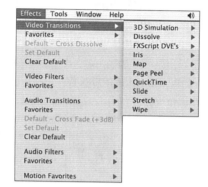

Rendering

Ah, rendering. It seems the capability of programs to eat up processing power tends to catch up with and exceed the development of faster processors. Basic digital video, such as in iMovie, in which you deal with a single layer of video and more or less simple changes that are made to that layer (such as the Brightness/Contrast effect or perhaps a fade in or fade out), doesn't really push the computer that hard. You might almost take it for granted that working with video is like any other application: Changes you request are implemented immediately, and you get to see the results at once (see Figure 24.6).

FIGURE 24.6

Rendering is the mother of investment in more RAM, a faster hard drive, and whatever the latest processor is, waiting invitingly for you within the pages of MacMall. Such goodies tantalize you into finding clients who'll pay you to have fun, driving you onward from iMovie into the realm of Final Cut Pro.

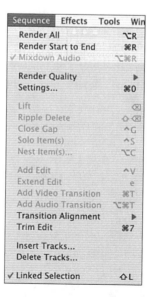

Welcome to the world of high quality video. With great power comes great responsibility, and unless you have terabytes of RAM sitting around, you'll occasionally need to make plans to take a walk or a vacation while waiting for the computer to render.

In terms of human experience in rendering, it's almost a step backward to work with video in Final Cut Pro. You have the ability to create any number of effects and layers and adjustments, but you actually have to wait for them?

Luckily, Final Cut Pro includes some fascinating capabilities to deal with higher-bandwidth video. The video that comes from a typical camcorder looks okay, and it's okay for most people. But it's compressed video, and therefore doesn't meet the needs of many professional situations. Many circumstances require an editor to work with what is known as *uncompressed* video, which takes up an incredible amount of hard drive space and processing time. But there are ways around this, and one of the great things about Final Cut Pro is that even if you need to work with the best quality video, you don't have to necessarily edit the raw video itself. You can edit offline and render later.

Let's say you're working on an hours-long video, which takes up a kajillion gigabytes of storage space as uncompressed video. You want to get home and watch TechTV, but you have to stay because all the equipment you need to work with uncompressed video simply will not work on your PowerBook.

Enter Offline RT, which is a fancy way of saying *temporary file*. With Final Cut Pro and Offline RT, you can do many of the things you'd like to do, such as see previews and effects without having to wait for nearly as long, all on a computer that doesn't have to be specially equipped with high-capacity or high-speed hard drives. Then after a night of TechTV and old *Tom and Jerry* episodes, you can go in the next day and use the temporary file you generated to finish your project. The temporary file serves as a kind of script, directing whatever computer you have that's connected to your original uncompressed video files that take up the cubicle next to you and generate enough heat to keep you warm during the winter.

An Approach to Learning Digital Video—Fun, Profit, Nonprofit

Exploring iMovie is a great way to get started in digital video—it enables you to have fun without getting too complex. On a Mac, there are simply fewer hassles, fewer configuration issues, and fewer problems in general. Apple hasn't achieved perfection yet, but iMovie comes close to it as being a way to get excited about digital video. Making your own movies is *fun*!

But what do you do if you want to make a profit, or even just a wage, but are having trouble getting started? Not-for-profit organizations represent the perfect opportunity. You don't necessarily need to have all of your skills completely developed to be helpful to a nonprofit organization, which might not have the budget to pay corporate rates for video editing anyway. It's almost a certainty that if you look a little bit, you can find some group or organization—local, national, or otherwise—that would welcome the opportunity to take advantage of a video editor's willingness to help out in return for a project that can then be a portfolio item.

In the process of working with a nonprofit group, you might gain a sense of satisfaction and become more confident with your tools in an environment where there isn't as much pressure, and you might come full circle to having fun—the iMovie caterpillar becomes the Final Cut Pro butterfly.

Introduction to DVD Studio Pro

DVD Studio Pro is a fully customizable DVD authoring environment. It enables you to go wherever DVD can go, and gives you the flexibility to make a project as simple or involved as you want.

Figure 24.7 shows the Graphical View of DVD Studio Pro 1.5, which has areas for working with project elements as icons, a Property Inspector for making adjustments to settings, and additional windows for keeping track of graphics, audio, and video files that are used in a project.

FIGURE 24.7

The Graphical View.

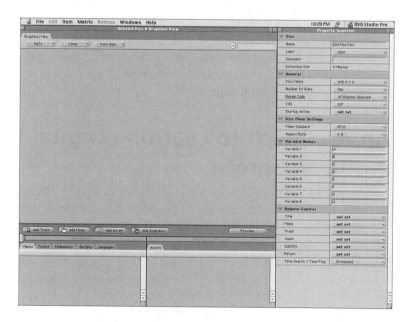

When you create a DVD project and have the freedom of doing anything that DVD can do, there's potential for a fair amount of underlying complexity. But the great thing about DVD Studio Pro is that it serves as a professional, capable tool, yet provides a familiar way to accomplish professional-quality projects.

A person who has used iDVD will know he's in a different place, but the place will have a sense of home to it, with graphic icons to represent different parts of a DVD project (as shown in Figure 24.8), and easy-to-learn buttons and menus that can be used to turn out a family memory disc or a cutting-edge Hollywood production.

FIGURE 24.8
Tiles in the Graphical View, with lines indicating connections between project elements.

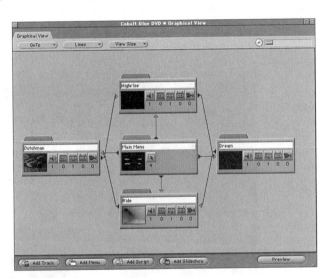

24

Differences Between iDVD and DVD Studio Pro

One of the most common reasons why a person might want to eventually get DVD Studio Pro is to have additional flexibility in making decisions about how a DVD will come out. That could include everything from having the ability to put whatever you want on a DVD menu to being able to make subtitles and include surround sound on a DVD project.

Advanced DVD Features

An interesting characteristic of DVD authoring is that it's often a real team effort between a variety of programs. For example, DVD Studio Pro has the unique capability to incorporate image files from the popular Adobe Photoshop image editing program.

You might have heard of Photoshop—it's probably the most common way that digital images are edited and adjusted on computers around the world. Photoshop is similar to DVD Studio Pro in that it has features that can be used by the beginner, yet has the capability to satisfy the most demanding professional applications.

Creating Photoshop files that serve as the basis for DVD menus is one of the most enjoyable things about putting together a DVD Studio Pro project. You create separate, adjustable layers in a file that includes digital images and text. Those layers are imported into DVD Studio Pro, and provide a visual path for your audience to experience the DVD through the interface that you make in DVD Studio Pro. The end result is a series of DVD menus that people click through to choose a video that you have on the DVD (see Figure 24.9).

FIGURE 24.9

Making a DVD menu design in Photoshop. You can also use Photoshop Elements, a less costly yet fully functional cousin to the full Photoshop (www.adobe.com).

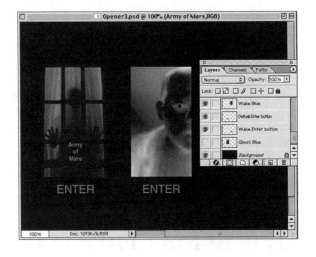

DVD Studio Pro also includes advanced features such as subtitles, which make for an easy way to develop DVDs for multiple languages. You can also use subtitles to simulate closed captioning, to put lyrics on the screen, or for any other purpose you can imagine. The subtitles can be turned on and off at any time by the audience unless, of course, you block the remote control (see Figure 24.10).

Perhaps one of the most exciting features of DVD Studio Pro (for musicians at least) is the ability to encode for Dolby Digital. That means if you have sound files that have been properly mixed for surround sound (5.1 channels = front left and right, rear left and right, center, and low frequency/bass effects), you can use DVD Studio Pro to encode the sound and include on your DVD project! For perspective, consider that not too long ago, before Apple acquired it, the included surround encoder program seen in Figure 24.11 cost several thousand dollars.

FIGURE 24.10
The Subtitle Editor.

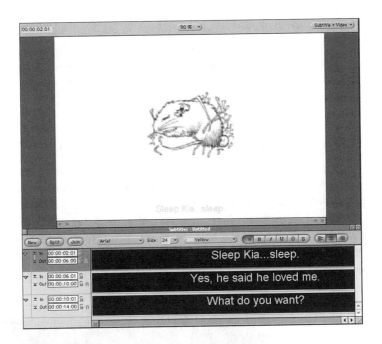

24

FIGURE 24.11
The A.Pack encoder.

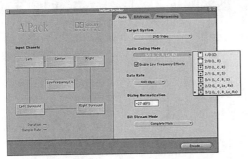

Adjustable Video Encoding (MPEG-2)

The foundation of DVD is video, and the method that engineers came up with to fit the video on the DVD disc is called MPEG-2, so all video must be encoded for it to get on a DVD. iDVD does it automatically with limitations, whereas DVD Studio Pro gives you the ability to either use presets or make your own choices.

DVD Studio Pro allows you to encode video into the MPEG-2 format, and allows you to choose how much to squeeze (compress/encode) the video when putting it on DVD.

IDVD's preset encoding makes things simple, but limits the amount of video you can put on a DVD disc (60 minutes high quality/90 minutes good quality). DVD Studio Pro, on the other hand, enables you to simply open video files and choose the settings you like for encoding. You can tweak the settings according to your needs—for example, if you want to fit more video on a DVD disc.

Putting Together a DVD in DVD Studio Pro

Although you can develop anything from a simple DVD with no menu and just video to a full-blown extensive training disc with hundreds of menus and animated motion backgrounds, there are some common things that go into a DVD. And the most popular programs used to create the ingredients of a DVD include Photoshop for menu graphics, Final Cut Pro for advanced video preparation, Adobe After Effects for developing motion menu video, and even programs such as Flash MX, a tool that's increasingly used to generate video (see Figure 24.12).

FIGURE 24.12
All digital roads can lead to DVD Studio Pro.

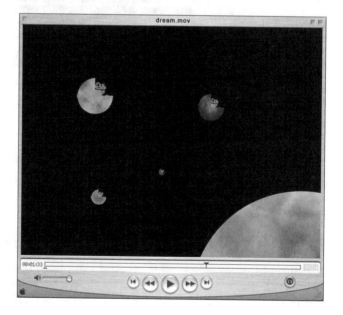

Macromedia's Flash MX is increasingly used as a tool to make animations with a project file that can be used to simultaneously develop animation for both the Web and broadcast-quality video. See *Flash MX Design for TV and Video*, the first book to seriously address this emerging field.

Creating a DVD project in DVD Studio Pro is similar to doing so iDVD in that you import files. But because you're creating your own graphics and so on in DVD Studio Pro, there's a wider range of file types, including MPEG-2 video, Photoshop files, and audio files (see Figure 24.13).

FIGURE 24.13

The files that make up a music video DVD.

The files are then imported into DVD Studio Pro. Figure 24.14 shows a main menu tile that uses the Photoshop file shown earlier, connected to a track tile, which incorporates a video and audio file. This sample is the basis of the DVD. The menu enables an audience member to select the video, and when the video is done, to go back to the menu.

FIGURE 24.14

The menu tile is connected to the track tile.

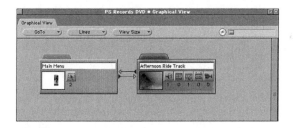

And what fully featured DVD-authoring program would be complete without a Property Inspector? DVD Studio Pro enables you to fine-tune a host of adjustments or simply go with the presets (see Figure 24.15).

Throughout the process, the user is given convenient pop-up menus that provide easy access to parts of a project. For example, in Figure 24.16, the `cbdvdmotionmenu.m2v` file, an MPEG-2 video file, is being selected to serve as a background video for a motion menu. (A *motion menu* is simply a DVD menu that has something moving in the background.)

FIGURE 24.15

The Property
Inspector.

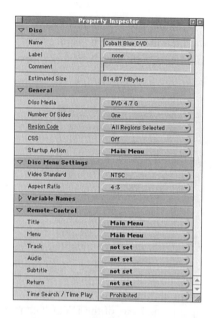

FIGURE 24.16

Selecting a file for the
video menu.

When you have your media files in place and are ready to make the project interactive, you'll use the Menu Editor, which enables you to create buttons for a user to click on to view your DVD. In Figure 24.17, you see a motion menu with video animation in the background and selection indicators on menu choices that DVD Studio Pro uses to enable you to determine where the buttons lead (that is, which music video a user sees when she makes a selection).

In the end, DVD Studio Pro plays the role of helping you to combine the digital media files into a format that a DVD player will understand. Essentially, a DVD author chooses how a DVD will work, and DVD Studio Pro acts on these choices to produce a DVD disc that you can put in a DVD player.

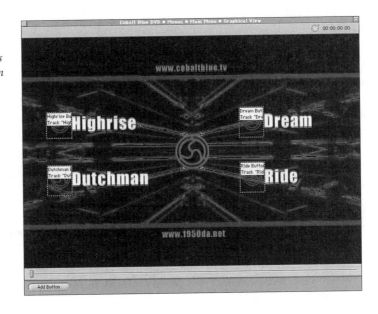

Summary

In this hour, your learned about Final Cut Pro and DVD Studio Pro, two professional-level programs from Apple that expand upon the features that you've learned for iMovie and iDVD, respectively. An exploration of iMovie and iDVD can lead very naturally into the wide world of video editing and DVD design, whether it ends up being a hobby, a profession, or both.

In the next hour, we'll take a look at the idea of getting some sleep. It's been a long 24 hours, but it's been nice spending time with you. Treat your friends well, look at the sky once in a while (to catch the stars or sun), and remember to have your camcorder with you at all times... with a charged battery. You never know when a sasquatch might come running out of the forest and give you a big hug. Maybe the sasquatch is a metaphor for creative inspiration, or perhaps it is a real sasquatch—who knows?

Workshop

The Workshop consists of quiz questions and answers to help you to develop a better grasp of the capabilities offered by Final Cut Pro and DVD Studio Pro. First, try to answer the questions *before* checking the answers. Then read the explanations, even if you get the answers right—the explanations will contribute to your overall understanding of digital video and DVD.

Q&A

Q Can I open my iMovie projects in Final Cut Pro?

A Yes, if you have a project you've created in iMovie you can open it up and work with it in Final Cut Pro.

Q Can I open up iDVD files in DVD Studio Pro?

A Nope, not in the current version, yet one can always join the author in hoping that such dreams come true. But you can take the same video you used in your iDVD project and import it into DVD Studio Pro. DVD Studio Pro doesn't make graphics of any kind for you, but it will gladly accept your donations.

Q Why are you so silly sometimes?

A When I was writing the *DVD Studio Pro Bible* with my friend Chad Fahs, sometimes I just had to try and break things up a little bit because the technical territory that we covered was vast and the journey long. And some of this sort of stayed with me; I've been behaving fairly well with this book, but as you might have noticed, I slipped in a few things once in a while. This book has been a lot of fun to write.

Quiz

1. Which typically takes a longer time to render: a project in iMovie that makes use of most of its features or a project in Final Cut Pro?

    A. iMovie will probably take longer because it isn't as advanced.

    B. Final Cut Pro will probably take a longer time to render because you can use a lot more layers.

    C. iMovie will take less time to render because it's more streamlined and less complicated.

    D. B and C

2. What's MPEG-2 encoding?

    A. The process of preparing graphics for menus

    B. The process of preparing video for CD burning

    C. The process of preparing video for use on DVD

3. How do you get more than 90 minutes of video on a DVD in DVD Studio Pro?

    A. You can't; it's just like iDVD

    B. By setting the video length to 120 minutes

    C. By adjusting the MPEG-2 encoding

4. How many editors does it take to screw in a light bulb?

   A. 4

   B. 3

   C. Editors don't bother with replacing light bulbs—they are too busy watching their *Lord of the Rings* DVDs over and over again. And over.

   D. None of the above

Quiz Answers

1. **D.** The moral of the story is that although Final Cut Pro is great, its very capability can lead to a lot of rendering.

2. **C.** MPEG-2 encoding is the foundation of DVD.

3. **C.** Technically speaking, to affect the video, you adjust the bit rate, which is measured in megabits per second, or Mbps. You typically try to balance the amount of video you want to fit on the disc with the level of quality you want to achieve. It's a good idea to leave open the option of removing material as early as the video editing stage of a DVD, so that you can go for a higher quality of video because you have less video to deal with. The higher the bit rate, the higher the quality; the more space the video takes up, the less video you can fit on a DVD.

   For inquiring minds who want to know more, dive into Jim Taylor's DVD FAQ at `www.dvddemystified.com`, or simply purchase his book. It's great and well worth it for curious people who really want to know what's going on. The book is a definitive source of DVD information, includes a helpful DVD that has relevant examples of video, and can also be used for weightlifting. (Sorry, Jim. I couldn't resist.)

4. **D.** Editors don't actually even use light bulbs—they burn the candle at both ends. They are the unsung heroes of the book publishing process.

24

PART V
Appendixes

Hour

Appendix A

Getting Good Digital Video

(adapted with permission from Mary Cagney)

Lighting

Lighting contributes greatly to the quality of your video or iMovie. To get a sense of the difference between footage under less-than-ideal lighting conditions compared to a well-lit situation, you have only to compare the Alunniland video of cats in Hour 23 with the Mena video (a Sugar glider) in the first half of Hour 8. You'll realize that the latter was shot with much better lighting conditions than the Alunniland video.

Although lighting is important, the current technology in digital camcorders has limits as to the amount of light that can be absorbed—a smaller amount than traditional film cameras.

Film has a broader dynamic range than video, meaning that it can pick up more nuances of light and shadow. For more information, see http://www.kodak.com/US/en/motion/news/wallis.shtml.

Consider some of these basic guidelines to help you to make iMovies that shine!

- Don't shoot people or objects with a bright light (natural or artificial) behind them.
- Having the sun behind the item that you're taping can produce flares in the video. (*Flares* are tiny patches of light that appear in movies.)
- Shiny surfaces can reflect light directly into the camera, so avoid them.
- Use the backlight feature on your digital camcorder, if available, when you shoot subjects in bright light. Without it, your object will turn into a dark shadow.
- Use the Nightshot setting on your camera, if one's available, for shooting video at nighttime.
- Some camcorders have a *shoe*, a clip-on light connector, that provides more light than a backlight. Use the shoe light attachment if one is available.

Exposure

Exposure is the amount of illumination that your camera picks up. It determines how light or dark the video that you shoot will be. The more light that strikes the camera, the lighter your video will be. All digital cameras have an auto-exposure setting that sets the exposure settings automatically for you. Some cameras have different exposure settings for different indoor and outdoor environments such as a sports event, snow, and sunset.

In bright light such as a snowy landscape, the auto-exposure setting reduces the amount of light admitted to the camera. In low light, the auto-exposure setting increases the amount of light admitted to the camera. In general, auto-exposure works reasonably well, but if you aren't satisfied with the results, playing with the manual settings will help you to understand what is possible.

Image Stabilization

If you've seen *The Blair Witch Project*, you'll have noticed that there's a lot of jerky movement with the cameras. The directors claimed that this was intentional. Or, maybe they were fooling everyone—perhaps the real reason was because the movie was made with small handheld digital camcorders without the image stabilization feature turned on.

Image stabilization is a great feature—it minimizes the effect of small movements associated with handheld filming, and it can help to reduce or eliminate the problem of the jitters and jiggles. It's also much easier to use than a tripod. A *tripod* is simply a stand with legs that you can put your camcorder on. (But getting in the habit of using a tripod when you can will yield a stable picture.)

Video Vocabulary—Framing Shots

Video producers have their own language to describe different types of video shots. It helps them to communicate effectively with each other. There are basically three types of shots: wide, medium, and close.

- Wide shots are used to establish the context or environment of a video scene. For example, a scene showing a landscape is a wide shot.
- Medium shots are the most widely used shots and eliminate many of the background distractions in a movie. For example, a scene of two people talking is a medium shot.
- Close shots are used for emphasis, reaction, and detail. For example, a scene of one person's face is a close shot.

Focus

Like exposure, focus is an issue that's normally handled automatically by camcorders.

Zooming

Although most camcorders have a zoom-in/out feature, most professional video makers rarely zoom. When going from a wide establishing shot to a medium or close shot, it's best to pause your recording and then zoom. Editing zoomed video can be problematic. It's easier to cut between a wide shot and other shots.

A

APPENDIX B

Getting a DVD Manufactured

Apple made history in January 2001 when it introduced a new line of G4 Power Macs that included built-in DVD burners because the combined price of the G4 and the burner ($4,000 U.S.) was the same as a standalone DVD burner at the time. To go with the hardware, Apple brought iDVD and DVD Studio Pro to the world.

If you have a SuperDrive in your Mac, or if you buy an external FireWire DVD burner (see Figure B.1), you can burn your own discs. As long as it's a DVD-R or DVD-RW drive and not a DVD +RW drive, your DVDs will play in about 90% of the players out there. Note that iDVD doesn't work with external drives, although other DVD applications, such as DVD Studio Pro, do.

iDVD works only with a SuperDrive, not with third-party DVD burners.

FIGURE B.1

External DVD drives are available for use with some applications for burning DVDs.

Manufacturing Discs

More and more local video production-type companies are offering the service of duplicating DVDs, which basically means they can make copies of your DVD, put labels on, and probably even have some options for packaging. This is basically another way of burning your own DVDs. It's just that someone else is burning them to the same discs you would and is probably saving you a lot of time.

There's still the question of less than 100% compatibility for discs burned in iDVD, but the only real way to ensure that your project will play in all players is to send it off to be manufactured. DVD manufacturers are increasingly accepting DVD-R discs as masters. If you have the need, you can send in a DVD you burned on your Mac and have small or large quantities produced.

To get a DVD manufactured, do the following:

1. Go online and investigate your options. Call a manufacturer or two and ask questions. One to try is e-Media Vision, Inc., online at www.emvusa.com (see Figure B.2).

   Be sure to get enough information that you understand what you need to provide in terms of files and so forth, and so that you can get a sense of the options and prices.

2. As your project is developing, think about the art that will appear on the disc. If you aren't a designer, you might want to hire someone to make a nice-looking design. Templates are usually available for download, such as the one shown in Figure B.3, which is for a small, 3" (80 mm) DVD that companies such as e-Media Vision are capable of making.

FIGURE B.2

e-Media Vision, Inc. is an example of a DVD manufacturer that you can visit online and then work with to get a project done.

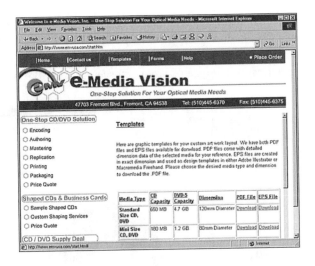

 3" DVDs can play in anything except slot-loading drives found on some iMacs and PowerBooks, and they can hold a little over 1GB. These small discs are great attention-getters because they aren't that well-known yet.

FIGURE B.3

The digital art that will be imprinted on a fully manufactured DVD, as seen under development in Adobe Illustrator.

B

3. A DVD manufacturer might be able to provide you with a *proof* of your art—an electronic file that looks like the final product. You'll sometimes have to use a special printed reference known as a PANTONE color guide to match the exact color. But in other cases, the type of proof you see in Figure B.4 will suffice.

FIGURE B.4

The same disc art we saw in Figure B.3, sent back by the DVD manufacturer as a final proof of how the colors will appear on the disc.

4. After you've made the production arrangements and sent in your master disc, be patient as your DVD is being put together, and prepare for the pleasure of receiving the finished product (see Figure B.5).

FIGURE B.5

A finished DVD with disc artwork and case.

Additional Possibilities

When you make your own DVDs, whether you record all of them yourself or send them off for manufacturing, you can also make printed inserts for the DVD cover case. Figure B.6 shows an example of a graphics file designed for use in Adobe Illustrator. Illustrator has guidelines that a manufacturer uses to generate a final printed piece, which can also be used to help plan a self-printed cover.

FIGURE B.6

Additional DVD-related art: a template in Adobe Illustrator format for the outside cover of a standard DVD case.

APPENDIX C

Links and Resources

- **Official Book Sites**

  Sams Publishing Book site: www.samspublishing.com

  Enter this book's ISBN (0672324849) in the search box and click Search. Click the book's link on the resulting page to be directed to helpful information, links, and downloadable files.

- **DVD Information**

  www.apple.com/imovie—Official info on iMovie

  www.apple.com/idvd—Official info on iDVD

  discussions.info.apple.com/—Apple's official discussions page with a special forums for iMovie and iDVD

  www.danslagle.com/mac/iMovie/iMovieFAQ.html—The "unofficial" iMovie FAQ, hosted by Dan Slagle

  www.dvddemystified.com—General DVD info

  www.dvdspa.com—Official site for *MacWorld DVD Studio Pro Bible*

  www.2-pop.com—Good discussion board

- **DVD Manufacturing**

  www.emvusa.com—Full-service, competitively priced CD/DVD manufacturing, shaped discs, 3" discs, and so on

  http://www.sanyolaserproducts.com—Full-service DVD manufacturing

- **DVD Authoring**

  www.1950da.net—Specializes in music video DVDs

- **Author Web Sites/Favorite Links**

  www.cftw.net—Not-for-profit/cultural awareness

  www.minivids.com—Flash-based music videos

  www.cftw.net/glf—Headquarters of Gerbil Liberation Front

  www.cobaltblue.tv—Production company

- **Guest Star Web Sites**

  www.wendydebias.com—Wendy is another very cool performer.

  www.detholz.com—Rock. Very Good Rock. Enough said.

  www.cftw.net/glf—Very, very silly, but actually has received some airplay on radio and television around the country and tends to make people laugh when they see the video. The GLF needs Conan O'Brien or someone like that to give it exposure. If one of you is actually reading this book, I'll gladly teach you iMovie in return for an interview for the GLF.

- **Additional Resources**

  www.all4dvd.com—Great source of DVD training in California and New York. Makers of excellent external FireWire hard drives and such. These guys really know digital video and DVD, and their drives have been approved by Apple—a special discount at All4DVD is available for readers of this book through www.all4dvd.com/imovie. (If you talk to Adrian or Henry, tell them to send me some Swiss chocolate.)

- **Retail**

  Support your local Apple retailers. The value they provide is the kind of expertise that you probably won't find at a mail order company or mass superstore.

  My local retailer is MacSpecialist, a great group of people who'll probably be taking over the Midwest. They've got all kinds of expertise and training and serve the Chicagoland area with a smile… usually.

  That's Dan Occhipinti on the left in Figure C.1, and there's a big tall sasquatch on the right who just picked up a copy of Thinkfree Office on his way home to go work on some iMovie book. (Thinkfree Office is a nice low-cost alternative to Microsoft Office: www.thinkfree.com.)

FIGURE C.1

MacSpecialist: A fine example of your local Apple retailer.

GLOSSARY

16:9   An aspect ratio that corresponds to a standard movie screen or wide screen TV; the screen is sixteen units long by nine units tall.

4:3   An aspect ratio that corresponds to a standard television or computer monitor.

8mm ("8 millimeter")   A standard format for early camcorders; the tape is 8mm wide. Standard 8mm videotapes are "analog" tapes—they are non-digital.

Analog   Non-digital. VCRs that use standard VHS tapes represent typical analog video.

Analog Source   A non-digital source with an analog ("non-digital") signal, which in some cases needs to be converted into digital format.

Analog-to-Digital   The process of taking material in analog form and converting it to digital. Example: taking an older 8mm tape and converting it to digital video by capturing it into the computer.

Aspect Ratio   The relation between horizontal and vertical screen measurements for video or film. (For example, see the glossary entries for 16:9 and 4:3.)

Capture/Capturing The process of hooking up a video device such as a camcorder or VCR and inputting the video into the computer. The typical scenario is connecting a digital camcorder through a FireWire cable, and inputting the video onto a computer's hard drive.

Chapter Marker An invisible marking point added to a movie that allows viewers to go directly to a specific scene by bypassing what came before it. Marked chapters are listed on a menu screen so viewers can select them. iMovie can be used to create chapter markers in projects, which can then be exported to iDVD for the addition of menus.

Clip Shelf ("Shelf") The area in the main iMovie window where individual video clips not yet used in the project are represented.

Clip View The alternative to the Timeline view in iMovie. In the Clip view, you see icons that represent video clips that have been added to the project, appearing the same as they do in the Clip Shelf except that they're in order as they will appear in the movie. *See also* Timeline View.

Compositing The process of combining several video clips into one image, typically done in a program such as Adobe After Effects.

Digital 8 A common tape format for digital camcorders, pioneered by Sony. The quality is not quite as good as Mini DV, but the tapes are cheaper, and a Digital 8 camcorder can read older 8mm tapes.

Digital Source A video signal that is already digital and does not need to be converted in order to be used on a computer. Example: a digital camcorder generates a digital source signal that can go through FireWire into a computer.

Digital-to-Analog A process where a digital signal is displayed or recorded onto analog (non-digital) media. Example: When you output an iMovie to a VHS tape, you are making a digital-to-analog conversion.

Download The process of taking a file from the Internet and putting it on your computer.

Drop Zone An area in some iDVD themes into which movies or photographs can be dragged for instant customization. (Themes containing drop zones have a labeled space into which video or image files are to be added.) Drop zones differ from video buttons, which can also be customized, because they don't represent a selectable menu item.

DV-NTSC A format for digital video that is used in countries that have an NTSC television system. The U.S. uses NTSC; England uses PAL.

DV-PAL   A format for digital video that is used in countries that have an PAL television system. England uses PAL; the U.S. uses NTSC.

DVD   Digital Versatile Disc.

DVD-R ("minus R")   The kind of blank DVD disc that you use in your SuperDrive. The DVD-R format is the most compatible with DVD players.

DVD-ROM Content   Computer files added to a DVD that can be accessed from a computer with a DVD-ROM drive. Such files are different from the content that will play in a DVD player.

DVD-RW ("minus RW")   A rewritable disc; a DVD-RW disc won't play in as many players as a DVD-R disc, but it has the advantage of being able to be erased and reused.

DVD+R ("plus R")   A newer format that is like DVD-R but is not as compatible with as many DVD players.

DVD+RW ("plus RW")   A competing format that is like DVD-RW but is not as compatible with as many DVD players.

Effects   An effect in video is when you make the video look different by having the computer process it in a certain way. Example: Changing the color of the video is an effect.

Export   When you take a video clip and turn it into a file that you can use for a particular purpose. Example: To use an iMovie on the Web, you would export the iMovie in a Web format.

FireWire   Apple's trademarked name for the Emmy Award–winning data transfer standard it developed. FireWire utilizes a unique method of transferring/capturing video from a camcorder into the computer, which can also be used to connect external hard drives and other devices that benefit from high-speed data transfer. In non-Apple devices, this standard might be referred to as IEEE 1394 or i.Link.

Frame Rate   The speed of a video clip or film. Example: A video clip that displays on NTSC (U.S.) televisions would have a frame rate of about 30 frames per second, so there are 30 images that flash by each second to give the effect of motion.

Gigabyte ("GB")   About 1,000 megabytes. Example: A new PowerBook Titanium at the time of writing can include up to 60 gigabytes of hard drive space, which would be equivalent to about 45,000 floppy disks. (A floppy disk holds about 1.4 megabytes.)

Hard Drive   The permanent storage in a computer. When you download or save a file on the computer, you save it on your hard drive.

Hi-8   An older, analog videotape format. Hi-8 tapes can be captured into digital format by putting them in a Digital 8 camcorder.

iMedia Browsers   The name by which Apple documentation refers to the Photos, Movies, and Audio tabs in iDVD is *iMedia Browsers* because those tabs were designed to link to content related to iPhoto, iMovie, and iTunes, respectively.

Kilobyte ("K", "KB")   About 1,000 bytes (technically, 1,024 bytes). Example: All the images on a typical Web page may come to about 100K.

Megabyte ("MB")   1,024K. A floppy disk is about 1.4 megabytes.

Menu   A DVD screen that presents viewing options that can be selected. *See also* Submenu.

Mini DV   One of the most popular tape formats for digital camcorders.

Motion Menu   Any DVD menu screen in which there are video or video buttons.

Multiplexing ("Muxing")   A technical name for the process a computer goes through when preparing a DVD. Multiplexing combines and encodes the various files that go into a DVD, into a format a DVD player understands.

NTSC   National Television Standards Committee; the television standard used in the U.S. and other countries. It specifies a refresh rate of 30 interlaced frames per second, with each frame containing 525 lines and up to 16 million colors.

PAL   Phase Alternating Line; the television system used in Europe and other countries.

Pixel   An individual dot on the computer screen.

Rendering   The process of processing a video clip when you have made a change to it.

Shelf ("Clip Shelf")   The area in the main iMovie window where individual video clips not yet used in the project are represented.

Sound Track   The audio portion of a video project that's separate from the track containing video clips. In iMovie, there are two sound tracks available. (Video clips may also contain audio, but separate audio elements are added in sound tracks.)

Streaming   Streaming media is video or sound that begins to display on your computer before it's completely downloaded; the file is played *while* it downloads instead of *after*.

Submenu   A menu other than the top-level menu on a DVD. A submenu screen contains options that can be selected and also leads back to a previous menu.

Text Button   A button on a DVD menu that contains only a text label for the linked content. The alternative to a text button is a video button.

Theme A theme in iDVD is a look, or template, you can choose for a screen of your DVD project.

Timeline View The alternative to the clip view in iMovie. In the timeline view, video clips and sound track elements that have been added to a project are displayed to represent the amount of time they last and when they will occur in the overall project. *See also* Clip View.

Title A portion of an iMovie that contains text added apart from the video. Titles can appear over a blank screen, or over top of video.

Transition Video effects added at the point where one video clip ends or begins or where two video clips come together. iMovie offers several transition options for gracefully opening, closing, or blending video clips.

Upload The process of transferring a file to the Internet.

VHS-C An older analog tape format for camcorders. To capture video from VHS-C, you would need to purchase something like a Dazzle DV Bridge, which has RCA-style connectors like the kind on your camcorder or VCR, and also has FireWire, so that you can capture into your computer.

Video Button A button on a DVD menu that contains a thumbnail representation of the linked content. The alternative to a video button is a text button.

Widescreen A video signal or television that is much wider than usual, designed to simulate what you see in a movie theater. When applied to video, the term *widescreen* encompasses a broad range of aspect ratios, including 16:9, that require cropping in order to fit the 4:3 aspect ratio of standard television and computer screens.

INDEX

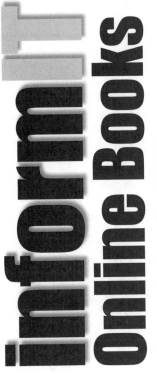

Your Guide to Computer Technology

www.informit.com